THE WOMAN'S GUIDE TO STARTING A BUSINESS

REVISED EDITION

By the same authors

Supergirls: The Autobiography of an Outrageous Business

THE WOMAN'S GUIDE TO STARTING A BUSINESS

REVISED EDITION

BY CLAUDIA JESSUP
AND GENIE CHIPPS

An Owl Book

Holt, Rinehart and Winston
New York

First published in January 1980 by
Holt, Rinehart and Winston,
383 Madison Avenue,
New York, New York 10017.

Published simultaneously in Canada
by Holt, Rinehart and Winston of
Canada, Limited.

Library of Congress Cataloging in
Publication Data.

Jessup, Claudia.
The woman's guide to starting a business.

Bibliography: p.
Includes index.
1. New business enterprises—United States.
2. Women in business—United States. I. Chipps, Genie,
joint author. II. Title.
HD69.N3J47 1979   658.1'1'024042   79-1932
ISBN Hardbound: 0-03-047131-1
ISBN Paperback: 0-03-047126-5

Designers: Karin Batten & Elliot Kreloff

Printed in the United States of America
10 9 8 7 6 5 4

ISBN 0-03-047131-1 HARDBOUND
ISBN 0-03-047126-5 PAPERBACK

CONTENTS

PART THREE: BUSINESS READING AND INFORMATIONAL SOURCES

ACKNOWLEDGMENTS

We give our special thanks to our friends and new acquaintances for their help and continuing interest. And our appreciation to all the women who let us interrupt their busy days to be interviewed.

PREFACE

The crucial point is to recognize that, in this era, the opportunities for living the American dream are open to the American woman as well as the man. If you want to grab the challenge, go ahead.

Sylvia Porter

So much has happened along the frontiers of women-owned business since this book was first published in 1976 that we were delighted when our editor, Jennifer Josephy, wanted to know if there was enough new information to warrant an updated edition. This resulting book, expanded considerably from the original, is a tribute to the incredible rise in interest in female entrepreneurship as both an economically viable and a rewarding career alternative for women today.

"This is not a trend; it's a phenomenon," says Ava Stern, founder of *Enterprising Women,* the first national periodical for women business owners and independent professionals. Stern reached some 22,000 women entrepreneurs around the country between 1975 and 1978, through the publication and the New York Association of Women Business Owners, which she founded in 1976.

According to the Census Bureau, in 1972 there were just over 400,000 women-owned businesses in the U.S., a mere 3.1 percent of the total businesses then operating. A recent survey by a Chicago firm, Esmark, Inc., estimates that today there are closer to a million women-owned businesses. "Not only have the numbers doubled," Stern reports, "the quality and growth orientation has notably increased. The last conference *Enterprising Women* co-sponsored in Dallas drew women from around the country who spent upwards of $300 apiece to attend. And all of them left with more contacts and deals underway than they had expected. I am convinced that women's progress as entrepreneurs is beyond that of women in corporate management."

Many things have contributed to the phenomenon. The sources for information and access to money have considerably opened up in the past few years. The Federal Equal Credit Opportunity Act was passed in 1975. There have been antidiscriminatory rulings in the field of insurance. Women's banks are springing up in major cities around the country. So are women business owners' associations, both independent organizations and, in Washington, D.C., the National Association of Women Business Owners, which, thus far, has given birth to chapters in eleven cities. Banks, colleges, and other organizations are sponsoring seminars and workshops on business entrepreneurship for women. There is a surge of female enrollment in graduate business schools. Independent companies, such as the American Women's Economic Development Corporation (launched in New York City, with plans for nationwide expansion), are being established with funding to develop training programs for women going into business for themselves.

The Small Business Administration has initiated a "National Women's Business Campaign," comprised of nationwide seminars for women, dealing with all aspects of setting up and running a successful business. "In addition," says Patricia M. Cloherty, first female deputy administrator of the SBA, "the campaign will offer a combination of management and financial assistance, and aid in securing government contracts." Since 1977 the SBA has targeted $100 million quarterly for guaranteed loans for women entrepreneurs. The agency is also establishing special representatives for women in every regional and district office.

More help may be coming from the government. An interagency Task Force on Women Business Owners was initiated by President Carter in 1977 and supervised by Secretary of Commerce Juanita Kreps. The final report of recommendations, presented in June 1978, enumerated the obstacles faced by, and the need for expanded statistics on, women-owned businesses.* It outlines problems which have never before been documented in a single volume. Women entrepreneurs are still awaiting action on the recommendations, but the

---

* Limited copies of the full Task Force report are available through the Office of the Ombudsman, Department of Commerce, Washington, D.C. 20230. For a summary and analysis of the report, see *Enterprising Women*, vol. III, Issue II (July/August 1978). (See bibliography.)

report has served to heighten the awareness of the general public and government. The nation is beginning to realize that women business owners are a valuable and tangible force in the American economy.

So the facts are in, and the action is escalating. Women entrepreneurs are gathering momentum. They are no longer alone in their fight for economic independence, isolated from one another and from access to knowledge, money, and power. There's still a lot of territory to cover and more barriers to be broken down, but as the situation stands now, the future for women entrepreneurs looks better than ever.

Claudia Jessup and Genie Chipps
New York City, April 1979

PART ONE

THE BUSINESS OF WOMEN

FORBIDDEN FRUIT

The first step is believing in ourselves, understanding that we are indeed smart, even if we aren't rich. And the second is giving up the myths of power....

Gloria Steinem

Back in the days of the Garden of Eden, it was Eve who bit the apple first. But that wasn't where she went wrong.

Her big mistake was in giving Adam a taste of that forbidden fruit from the tree of knowledge and power. Adam liked it so much that he wouldn't give it back, and men have been chomping away on it ever since.

The myths of power have grown up out of a world where men hold the reins. They serve the purpose of maintaining power in the hands that hold it. There is no more substance to the myth that business ownership is a man's world than there was to the bogeyman scares that kept you in line as a kid. When you got old enough, you realized there was no bogeyman to be scared of. The same goes for the myths of power.

As Denise Cavanaugh, first president of the National Association of Women Business Owners, reports: "Owning your own business means being willing to take responsibility and not feeling that it's an extraordinary step to take."

3

Anybody starting a business runs into problems. A woman starting her own business runs into more problems. But the biggest obstacle of all to overcome is driving out that bogeyman, sweeping aside those power myths that have collected around you all your life. One reason there are comparatively few women running their own businesses is that it simply never occurs to many women to try.

There are special problems that women face, and serious ones—establishing credit, securing loans and financing, and more. Getting money is difficult because many women don't have track records as business owners, and they lack the network of business connections that most men enjoy. There is also the special starting handicap of too little business training: many women come to business ownership through very indirect routes. But if it's occurred to you to start your own business, and if you've got the confidence, the determination, and the patience to go about setting it up thoroughly and properly, those problems aren't going to stop you.

The essence of successful business is good ideas, and women who start businesses tend to be strong on ideas and enthusiasm. Not that the ideas have to be groundbreaking. Filling a community need is the basis for most successes.

Entrepreneurs are apt to be highly motivated people. The very act of starting a business is a creative innovation, but a woman is more likely to carry that creativity and innovation into the way she runs things.

Few businesses make money right away. If you are your own sole source of income, you'll have to be willing to modify your lifestyle. For until you can take a steady draw, you'll be living off the fraction of your savings you haven't invested in the business.

If you don't have to worry about supporting yourself with your own income, so much the better. There are enough factors of the system working against the aspiring female business owner; don't feel awkward if a few work in your favor. If you have a husband who brings home a paycheck large enough to pay the rent and keep life running smoothly, use that peace of mind to build your confidence for getting things off the ground.

You'll need confidence, and you'll need a lot more than that. The mortality rate of small businesses is discouragingly high:

over 50 percent fail. There are no statistics available as to whether women-owned businesses fall above or below that median. In fact, until very recently there have been no statistics on women-owned businesses at all. But things are changing.*

Jeanne Wertz, testifying before the Joint Economic Committee of the Ninety-third Congress, reported, "In my survey I found that the business of women going into business is booming. Women are in and are entering business ownership in significant numbers; at all ages; in all types of business; in every geographic area.

"By far most of these new entries are women setting up shop by themselves or with other women. One can speculate that this phenomenon is a fallout from the women's movement, the result of new options, new freedoms, new lifestyles. . . .

"The factors that determine the difference between success . . . and failure are in this order: money, motivation, determination, expertise in a particular field, access to expert advice, and time—which brings one back to money. It takes money to buy that time."

And it takes careful, meticulous planning and management to make effective use of what money and time you manage to put together. You have to learn everything about the kind of business you're interested in owning and all about business itself. After all, there's a whole lot more to it than just selling a product, providing a service, or flipping a switch to activate the machinery.

The first part of this book is a blueprint for planning and management, presenting a general guide to starting and succeeding in your own business—retail, service, manufacturing, or whatever. Some sections will apply more to one type of business than another, but most of the information is valid across the board. It points up some kinds of discrimination you're apt to run up against because you're a woman, and it

---

* In 1976 the first nationwide statistical portrait of women-owned businesses was published by the U.S. Department of Commerce, Bureau of the Census, Office of Minority Business Enterprise: *Women-Owned Businesses in 1972.* Available for $4.40 from the Government Printing Office, Washington, D.C. 20402.

maps out procedures that are basic for anyone who is serious about starting a business, or buying one, and making it work. Don't make the mistake of confusing discrimination with poor planning; nothing is more self-destructive than crying "male chauvinism!" over a failure that was caused by your own ineffective preparation, presentation, or management.

Susan Davis, writing in *Ms.* Magazine (June 1973), summed it up by saying, "Although many women are intrigued with the idea of being self-supporting through business ownership, few know how to start.... Women who are interested in business tend to be heavy on creative ideas and light on financial plans."

The second part of this book presents the experiences of a number of women who have managed a workable balance between those two ingredients. They have also demonstrated an ability to think on their feet and the flexibility to cope with all kinds of situations as they arise. A number of them freely admit, too, that they have been lucky—a nice extra when it happens, but not something to write an insurance policy on.

They are people who have not been afraid of the risks because they are involved in a learning, growing experience. They are propelled by their own self-esteem, not by the expectations of others. They believe that the experience they have gained is priceless, and they find what they do exhilarating. They are finding dignity and fulfillment beyond home and family, which in turn enrich their personal relationships and their own sense of worth.

Maybe their example will give you the impetus you need to go ahead if you've been turning a business idea around in your mind. Do it! That way, at least you'll know what happened; you won't be left with years of might-have-beens. And if you do it right, there's no reason why it shouldn't work. No matter what the outcome, you'll wind up gaining more than you lose.

Business writer Nancy Borman notes: "We must break through the male fortress if we are to succeed in business. Overcome fears of larger sums. Study banking. Share this lore with one another. Learn about bankruptcy. Find out what would really happen if you could not meet a payment on a loan. And get successful men to give away some of their 'secrets.'"*

---

* 1974, *Majority Report*, 74 Grove Street, New York, New York 10014.

Back in the sixth century B.C., Lao-tzu wrote, "The journey of a thousand miles must begin with a single step." That first step, as Gloria Steinem says, "is believing in ourselves."

This book will try to help you the rest of the way along the thousand miles.

ALL THINGS CONSIDERED: AN OVERALL CHECKLIST FOR GOING INTO BUSINESS

What we plan we build.
Phoebe Cary

So you want to start a business. At least you think you do. Before you begin fantasizing about how you'll spend your first million, let your brain consider more realistic immediacies. You'll never again have as much time as you do now to spend on the tangibles and intangibles of your potential enterprise. The more you plan before you open your doors for business, the better off your business will be.

It takes time to get a business on its feet, and many women defeat themselves by taking the plunge too quickly, with too little money. Some businesses can be organized in a month or so, but most will take approximately six months of advance groundwork. Many advisors feel that a potential entrepreneur needs a full year's preparation before she's off and running.

A good business plan is the key to your future success. Even if you intend to start a small business with only yourself to answer to, a written blueprint will enable you to anticipate, and solve problem areas in organization, staffing, marketing, and financing.

Once your doors are open to the public, you will be racing to keep step with your brainchild. Besides actually doing business with paying customers, you will have to choreograph the background goings-on of your office, factory, or store. That means taking care of all the nitty-gritty details: keeping books and records up to date, handling payroll, paying bills, supervising your staff, constantly reevaluating goals, and mapping out new strategies. A business can't tread water; it must grow to stay healthy. And as its owner you are going to be very busy. (That's not a prediction; it's a fact.)

Before risking valuable time, energy, and money, you need to know if your business idea will work, and how. You need to know how much profit you stand to make and exactly what procedures must be followed in order to manipulate the strings of success.

Besides steering you in the right direction, your written business plan will form the basis for proposals to banks and other potential investors. It will provide instant information to your accountant, banker, lawyer, and partners, should you choose to take any on. A detailed business blueprint can help persuade suppliers to grant you credit and might even convince future customers to place advance orders. In addition, it will become a constant source of reference—something by which you can measure your growth. A good written plan will also guide your decision making.

The rest of this book will unravel the mysteries of each specific area of business with which an entrepreneur must deal. But first, you must picture the whole forest. Below is a series of questions to be answered before you do another thing. Get out your pen and paper, and, clearly and concisely, analyze yourself, your potential business, and your goals.

YOUR BUSINESS PLAN

The Concept

What will your business do? Outline, as specifically as possible, your idea, product, or service. Include: a physical description of the product, how and where it will be manufactured; a description of the services you will offer and how they will be administered; or, a description of your store, how it will look, what it will sell. What will you name the business?

Who is the potential user of your product or service? Describe your desired customers and the market in which they exist. (List the sources of information used to make your projections.) Is there a need for your business, and why? If your idea is innovative, explain why it will appeal to your market.

Who is your competition? Assess these businesses, and explain how your product or service represents variations and improvements over existing ones.

Marketing Your Business Idea

How will you reach your market? Explain how your product or service will be sold: sales force, distributors, advertising and publicity, location, image and graphics, promotion, etc.

How do you propose to enter the market? What will constitute your selling tools? How will you organize a sales campaign? Discuss these factors in detail. For example, if location is key, provide details of proposed ideal locations. If advertising will be your prime motivator, tell where you plan to advertise, how often, and why? How much will your ad campaign cost? What will your ads say? Who will write and design your ads?

What is the image you wish your business to project? Will you have a logo and other graphic identification (slick brochures, etc.) Interior design? Sales force? Location? The aura with which you surround your business, and make it attractive to the buying public, will help clear a niche in the marketplace for you.

The People

Who are you? Why are you equipped to make this particular enterprise a success? As owner you will be your company's most important asset. Describe your background, strengths, and weaknesses— what talents do you bring to the business; in what areas do you lack experience? Include your previous work and life experience, your skills and know-how, and your analysis of what the job of running your company will entail.

Provide work biographies of your partner(s) and other people who will be involved with the vital operation of the business. How many employees will you need at the onset? Indicate which areas of responsibility and authority within the business each person will cover.

Outline the outside businesses or services which will be key to your company's smooth operation, e.g., wholesalers, suppliers, agencies, postal services, customs, business contacts, neighboring businesses, independent contractors, and so forth.

List the names of your lawyer, accountant, banker, insurance agent, and marketing or management consultant. What services do you expect to receive from them?

Financial Estimates

How much capital will you need to launch your business? Estimate all your costs, including rent, utilities, decoration and fixtures, deposits and credit payments, supplies, inventory, printing costs for stationery and brochures, advertising, grand opening, promotion, consultation fees, travel, insurance, and unexpected expenses. Be generous with your estimates because everything costs more than you think it will.

How much capital will you need to operate your business for the first eighteen months? Include all of the above, plus estimates for salaries, taxes, and allowance for growth.

Show cash flow projections based on three growth potentials—low, expected, and better-than-average. With your accountant, figure your break-even points within each category. You must estimate a profit within a reasonable amount of time if your market analysis has been accurate.

List sources for capital and terms of financing: personal savings, debt financing (money which is repaid, with interest), equity financing (money obtained through the sale of stock in the company).

Long-range Planning

What are your motivations for going into business, and what do you expect to gain? It is important to analyze your reasons for wanting to launch this particular business and where you want it to go. Ask yourself where you would like to be in five years and whether you are willing to make a long-term commitment to your enterprise.

Will your business be a primary income, or supplementary? How much money must you realize from your time and financial investment in order for the business to be a personal success?

List desired standards and growth for the business. What new products or expanded services do you envision?

How will you handle personal and family obligations while running a business full time?

Envision all the things which could possibly go wrong and affect your business (poor economy, loss of major suppliers or partners, etc.), and figure out alternative solutions to every problem.

Write out your answers to all these questions. Once on paper, try testing your idea out on family, friends, and business associates. Their reactions can send you either back to the drawing board or marching ahead toward fame, fortune, and independence.

Be realistic, but don't let anyone discourage you in this preliminary stage. Too often, innovative ideas disintegrate under stolid scrutiny—too much logic can ground your starship before it's even launched. At this stage, let your creativity reign—just channel it in the right direction.

You may have trouble answering some of the above questions in detail because you lack expertise in a particular area. However, each element is covered in the upcoming chapters. After you have finished the book, return to your business plan and answer the questions again. You may be surprised to find that some of your perceptions may have changed between now and then.

If the business you envision doesn't seem to have enough financial potential, you will have to revise your idea. Or come up with another business that *will* work.

WHY BUSINESSES FAIL

Remember, six out of ten new businesses fail within the first five years. The primary reasons for failure are inexperience, incompetence, mismanagement, and undercapitalization. Your business plan will help you stay on top of potential problems and setbacks.

Some of the more specific reasons for business failure are listed below. Read and beware:

> Entrepreneur's lack of experience (and inability to keep on top of things)
> Inaccurate record keeping (and records not kept up to date)
> Poor management of money
> Lack of advance planning
> Misuse of time (not tackling duties in order of priority; not delegating responsibility)
> Problems with employees
> Weak marketing plan
> Owner's inability to grow with the company (to keep reevaluating progress and setting new goals)

ARE YOU READY TO BECOME AN ENTREPRENEUR?

Before you take the entrepreneurial plunge, you must have a realistic view of your strengths and weaknesses. If you haven't already analyzed your administrative adequacy, stop right where you are and take an objective appraisal of yourself.

(Just like those fictional women who look in the mirror and *really see* themselves for the first time.)

The owner of a business has to be in total control, a Jill who masters all trades (or at least oversees them), able to dazzle clients, fix typewriters, and interpret profit-loss statements, all in the course of a day's activities.

Can *you* do it? Evaluate all your pluses and minuses, no matter how trivial. What do you have to offer, and what do you lack?* Owning and running a successful business, no matter how small, takes a number of ingredients. Some things that help:

> The imagination to come up with a good idea for a successful venture
>
> The energy to maintain physical and mental health
>
> The enthusiasm to believe in your plan and to *enjoy* what you do
>
> The drive or the will to work harder for yourself than you have ever worked for anyone else
>
> The time, since there are numerous occasions when you will have to work overtime to meet deadlines, balance the books, etc.
>
> The determination that your plan *will* work
>
> The discipline to *make* it work
>
> The individuality, flair, and creativity to set you apart from the competition
>
> The ability to evaluate facts and make decisions, quickly and effectively
>
> The poise to keep your head under pressure
>
> The strength to endure the inevitable crises and fluctuations in the economy that will affect your business
>
> The sense of humor that will make the dark days bearable and the good ones even better
>
> The understanding for *and* from others around you. If

---

* Send for the excellent questionnaire "Opening Your Own Business: A Personal Appraisal," published by *Small Business Reporter*, Bank of America, Dept. 3120, Post Office Box 37000, San Francisco, California 94137, vol. 7, no. 7, one dollar. This will help you extensively evaluate your entrepreneurial qualifications.

you have a family, they must be behind you 100 percent—or you may be forced to choose between them and your business.

The experience necessary to succeed. Education and practical training in the field itself and know-how in dealing with the public. (If you are *not* qualified, start working *now* toward gaining the experience you will need to start a business sometime in the future. While obtaining educational and on-the-job training, be formulating your plans so that you will be prepared and will make as few mistakes as possible. Take courses—at night if necessary—on business and money management—finance, bookkeeping, business law, management, marketing and promotion, etc.)

You must be able to risk the possibility of falling on your nose and be undaunted by it. No one should embark on a project of this scope without knowing how much of herself she is willing to put behind it, both physically and psychologically.

In other words, the more you know about yourself and your business before you start, the better. (When you set out to borrow capital, the noneylenders will look at you, the owner, to gauge your business' potential for success.) And talk to other women entrepreneurs. Learn firsthand about the sorts of obstacles you will be up against.

Then—if you are still convinced you have a viable business idea—go out there and show them you can do it.

3

THE BIRTH OF A NOTION

The vitality of thought is in adventure. Ideas won't keep. Something must be done about them.

Alfred North Whitehead

Of all the plateaus in the business canyons, the idea stage is the most exhilarating. Beyond that the climb gets tough; opening your business and keeping it going, especially the first crucial year, can be a lot of work. At the beginning, however, you can luxuriate in the *concept*. What is it? Where do you find it?

GETTING THE IDEA

When you think up business ideas, it's best to stay in an area where you have contacts who consider you a credible professional. But there are exceptions.

For example, sometimes an idea *happens*. You're lolling in a hammock one sunny Sunday and presto! you conjure up the vision of a homemade-ice-cream parlor. In your mind's eye, you've bought equipment, devised recipes for Very Vanilla and Cinnaminty Chocolate, rented a shop near the high school, and you're proffering parfaits for profits.

Other people start with the desire to strike out on their own and scout around for a demand to supply. Still others, after a steady climb of education and on-the-job training, answer the call to solo with their special talent.

No matter how you arrive at your decision to go into business for yourself, you have to translate your idea into a practical step-by-step plan. Assuming the basic premise is sound, a company's success hinges on the solid foundation upon which it grows.

Analyze Your Community

For a start, take a look around you. Consider your area's economic base. Is it thriving; are new businesses moving in? Are large companies closing down or moving out? Does your business concept depend on good times when people become free spenders, or will you offer a basic product or service that your community *needs*? Your business doesn't stand a chance if your community cannot support it.

Defining the Idea

Define your idea—on paper. It has to make complete sense to you before other people can be convinced. Are you *supplying* a demand? (Your neighborhood needs a day-care center; an art supply store; auto repair clinic; or a hot-dog stand.) Or, are you *creating* one? (An exotic food delicatessen featuring 101 cheeses, knishes, and stuffed grape leaves; a nifty children's boutique with a play-yard in back; a game called "Widgie," destined to replace backgammon; an art gallery for local artists.)

Advance Preparation

After making your decision to go into business, don't rush it. You won't be able to foresee all the obstacles that will invariably dart across your path, but find out everything you can about your proposed business—its requirements, problems, rewards—*before* you start.

Talk to other women who are doing or have done the same thing. Learn from their successes and failures. Know what sorts of pitfalls are hidden in the shadows, and learn how to avoid them and to deal with others that crop up unexpectedly.

And remember Murphy's law: what *can* go wrong *will* go wrong. If you can unflinchingly face up to that in advance and *still* want to burst forth as an entrepreneur, you stand a good chance of succeeding.

NAMING THE BUSINESS

The name has to be *memorable*. Picture it up on a sign—it should look good and convey an idea of what you do or make or sell. The name should also establish the image you want to project. Avoid trendy names; they may be initially catchy, but inevitably they become passé and you are stuck with a name you loathe.

After you come up with a name, live with it awhile (and try it out on friends) before making your final decision. If it wears well and gets positive reactions, then stick with it.

If you use a made-up name (The Naughty Nite-lites Company) instead of your own (Gayle Halligan's Hardware & Haberdashery), you must file a *fictitious name statement*, also called *dba* (doing business as). This must be filed with your local county clerk, within thirty days after the start of the business. The registration fee is generally around ten dollars (In some states the dba must be filed with the state's department of taxation.)

Sometimes, the business is required to publish the statement for four consecutive weeks in a local or legal newspaper. Check with the clerk about this, and obtain the name of the cheapest recognized publication in which to run the statement.

This does not apply to corporations. Incorporating a business carries its own spools of red tape, which will be unraveled later.

TAKING ON A PARTNER

It is difficult, to say the least, to keep a business going on either creative or managerial skills alone (although you stand a better chance with the latter). If you aren't batting close to .300 in both of these areas, then reevaluate your situation. Realize your limitations in the beginning, before you start, and consider joining forces with an expert who will complement your capabilities.

You can *hire* someone to manage your business while you're out charming customers, or vice-versa. But experience of that magnitude generally cannot be budgeted into new businesses with limited capital. So the logical solution is to find a partner to co-own the business with you—someone willing to invest the money, experience, and dedication to make it succeed; a woman who will provide yin to your yang, balancing the scales where you alone might tip them.

Finding a Partner

How do you locate this superwoman, your business mate? Many women go into business with close friends. This is not altogether a good solution, since friendships have been known to run off-course with so much at stake. Some women link up with former business associates. A logical solution, but feasible only if that person enhances your total business picture. Some women choose male partners, and like all partnerships, some work out and some don't, depending on the professional compatibility of the people involved.

If you don't have anyone in mind, go to your business colleagues, banker, lawyer, or accountant. One of these sources may come up with the perfect person, based on their evaluation of your needs.

Check out your competition. Not that you're out to ruffle feathers, but there are many experienced women anxious to step from behind the scenes, yet lacking the courage to go it alone.

No matter how or where you find your partner, don't make a snap decision. This is a person with whom you will share a large chunk of your life, through ups and downs, year after year (if all goes well). It is a lot like marriage, and you both have to work out the problems as they arise, before they become insurmountable. Keep in tune with each other all the time.

Husband-Wife Partnerships

"Mom and Pop" businesses are going stronger than ever, but they've come a long way from the sweet couple who ran the corner candy store. There are no statistics available on how many of America's eight million small businesses are co-owned by couples, but there seems to be a definite new trend to this old idea.

In the past many husbands really ran the show while their wives worked not so much *with* them as *for* them. Things have changed. Today a husband and wife can work successfully side by side as equal partners, as long as each has something to contribute to the business at hand. Certainly husband-wife business partnerships are economically advantageous.

On the personal level, however, there are the potential pitfalls of any partnership. Each partner must have well-defined duties and areas of expertise in order to keep the partnership equal and the business stable.

It's difficult for any entrepreneur to keep business problems from spilling over into leisure time. Couples in business together must work even harder to maintain a harmonious balance between their home and professional lives. Before becoming partners, a husband and wife should analyze their personal relationship as well as their professional goals. Remember, both marriage and business have high mortality rates. If you are considering taking on your spouse as a business partner, each of you should know exactly what you're getting into and put it down in writing.

The Partnership Agreement

In the beginning, you and your partner(s) should write up an agreement, stating your intentions, delegating responsibility, and including buy and sell arrangements should one of you wish to withdraw at a later date. The law does not require this to be written—a smile and a handshake will do. But to avoid any misunderstandings, which could lead to future difficulties, get it in writing.

In addition, agree upon an impartial person, outside the business, who can serve as a mediator should any problems arise. This person can also act as a sounding board for new ideas or as a consultant, but she should be unbiased and have no vested interest in the business.

OBTAINING PROFESSIONAL ADVICE

Although many women say the "experts" discourage them, professional guidance is essential for a budding entrepreneur. Just remember, consultants can only *recommend* courses of action. You, as the owner, have to evaluate—objectively and intuitively—what is right for your business. After all, it is *yours*, and no one will care about it as much as you do.

Selecting Consultants

Choose people who are knowledgeable about small businesses in general, and your *type* of business in particular. Seek advisors who speak your language and will take an interest in you. Beware of people with large egos; they won't admit it when they don't know something. Beware, also, of consultants who have overextended themselves and are too busy to tend successfully to the needs of their smaller clients. If you don't get the results you want, when you want them, then do not hesitate to find someone else to assist and advise you.

Once you have established a working relationship with your advisors, keep in touch with them. Follow-up is essential. Make sure you both do what you say. It's a good idea to send a written memo or letter after each meeting, reviewing the topics discussed and which of you is handling each item.

Don't overuse professionals. Often you can deal with small crises yourself. If you use your lawyer or accountant for these, you're wasting money. Consult them only when necessary, after you have done some initial legwork.

HIRING FRIENDS AS ADVISORS

Be businesslike, *especially* with friends. To avoid later feuds, draw up a written agreement, outlining the specifics (services and charges) of what they will do for you, and you for them.

Establish all costs at the onset especially for budgeting professional experience. Get a minimum fee, and estimate it from there. Fees left in the air tend to plummet you back to earth when it's time to pay up. Discuss money for consultants' services first off Don't be afraid to shop around for professional services, and select the best person, at the best price, for your needs Look for quality, not bargain rates.

Finding Counseling Services

Shop around for professional consultants, including lawyers, accountants, insurance agents, bankers, etc. Check out all recommendations from business associates and friends before making any decisions.

If you cannot afford to hire anyone in the beginning, there are a number of free or inexpensive counseling sources.

The Small Business Administration (SBA) has several programs of management assistance and sponsors SCORE (Service Corps of Retired Executives) as well as ACE (Active Corps of Executives). Both these groups consult with new businesses on all facets of business management. The SBA also publishes free and for-sale booklets on every conceivable subject of interest to small-business persons. Contact your nearest SBA district office for information; there are more than a hundred offices located around the country.

In addition, the SBA now holds seminars and intensive workshops all over the country for women who are already in business or thinking about launching an enterprise. The SBA's Call Contact Program provides management and technical assistance to economically and socially disadvantaged small businesses. The expertise comes from professional consulting firms under contract with the SBA. The Small Business Institute (SBI) Program provides senior and graduate students of the nation's leading business schools as volunteers for on-site management counseling to small business owners. Also, SBA-sponsored University Business Development Centers across the country give counseling, training, research and development, and technical aid to small firms.

In 1977 the SBA launched its National Women's Business Ownership Campaign, an outreach effort to help more women run successful businesses. In a pilot program (currently available in New York City, but expanding into other areas), in conjunction with the American Women's Economic Development Corporation (AWED), this counseling program assists women entrepreneurs in solving their business problems.* It includes seminars on various phases of managing a business, regular consultation, advice, and specialized assistance.

The Economic Development Administration (EDA) of the U.S. Department of Commerce has research and development centers in twelve cities throughout the country, to provide management and technical assistance to small-business owners. They also help in finding capital and in developing loan packages. The EDA works with universities to provide free assistance in setting up businesses. For information, write the EDA office nearest you, or call (202) 967-5113.

OMBE (Office of Minority Business Enterprise, U.S. Department of Commerce, Washington, D.C. 20230) has regional offices providing management, training, and technical services and occasionally holds regional conferences on women in business.

The NAA (National Association of Accountants, 919 Third Avenue, New York, New York 10022) has 326 nationwide chapters which offer free assistance to anyone who is starting a business. The NAA works with the SBA on some of its programs as well.

There is also the National Association of Women Business Owners (2000 P Street, N.W., Washington, D.C. 20036).† It has individual members as well as affiliated chapters throughout

---

* For additional information, contact Beatrice Fitzpatrick, Executive Director, American Women's Economic Development Corporation, 1270 Avenue of the Americas, New York, New York 10019.

† There are currently eleven chapters affiliated with NAWBO, located in Baltimore, Boston, Chicago, Houston, Los Angeles, North Carolina (Raleigh/ Durham), Miami, Minneapolis, Pittsburgh, Washington, D.C., and Seattle. Write NAWBO for addresses and an update of cities.

In addition, several major cities and many smaller ones have local associations of women entrepreneurs, which are *not* affiliated with NAWBO (e.g., New York City, San Francisco). See the appendix for a list of addresses, and check with your local Chamber of Commerce.

the country, in every state, in every conceivable type of business. The association publishes a monthly magazine, free to members, by subscription to nonmembers.* In addition, Equitable Life Assurance Society has funded NAWBO to compile a national directory of women business owners.† The association is actively lobbying in Washington, D.C., for anything and everything that will help the woman entrepreneur, and it has been successful in seeking lucrative government contracts for women business owners.‡ Local chapters sponsor monthly workshops and seminars which are geared to the needs of their members. NAWBO's aim is to link together a continuing network of women business owners across the country, so that women will be able to enter the mainstream of our economic society.

Some large cities, or states, offer local programs, like New York City's Executive Volunteer Corps, sponsored by the city's department of commerce and industry. Check your area for similar services. Contact state and local Chambers of Commerce for other sources.

Trade associations, especially those composed of small companies, offer assistance programs, as do some large corporations, as a public relations gesture.§

Universities are a good source of advice and free help, and many offer lecture series and courses geared to women who want to start businesses. In addition, the National Home Study Council (1601 Eighteenth Street, N.W., Washington, D.C. 20009) provides a brochure, on request, of all accredited home-study schools. The National University Extension Asso-

---

* See the appendix for membership and subscription information.

† The 1979 directory will include women-owned businesses in Washington/Baltimore, Boston, and Chicago. (See bibliography.) Future editions will expand the national coverage.

‡ In 1978, NAWBO supplied the Department of Transportation with more than thirty thousand names of women-owned businesses capable of contracting with the railroads, resulting in six million dollars' worth of government contracts for women.

§ To find trade journals and newsletters in your field, see *The Encyclopedia of Associations* (Gale Research Company), available at your library. For specialized information pertaining to business periodicals for particular industries, write: National Business Publications, 1913 I Street, N.W., Washington, D.C. 20006.

ciation (Suite 360, 1 Dupont Circle, N.W., Washington, D.C. 20036) also provides a booklet (costing fifty cents) which lists accredited colleges and universities with home-study courses.

Banks, too, have begun holding workshops and seminars for women entrepreneurs. The Bank of America publishes the *Small Business Reporter* (Department 3120, Post Office Box 37000, San Francisco, California 94137). Write for a listing of back issues (available at a dollar per copy) on their series of business profiles, business operations, and business management.

Suppliers of your business equipment, inventory, or raw materials are key sources of useful information. As a goodwill gesture, they will become your grapevine of news on your competitors (their prices, new products, expansion plans) and can tell you of new businesses coming to town, national ad campaigns, etc. Wholesale suppliers can advise you about inventory (how much you need, the breakdown of sizes, colors, and styles) for your shop. But let the buyer beware. The salesperson selling you equipment for your shop or office or restaurant may try to oversell. On the other hand, she is out to win you as a repeat customer. She is knowledgeable about styles and types of fixtures, what kind of work load certain equipment will take, what's selling in New York and growing moss in Minneapolis. *Ask and listen.* Get several opinions before settling on a supplier.

Sometimes, groups of small-business owners gather for informal meetings and the exchange of advice. Talk to other women business owners, and organize such a group in your community if none exists.

Still another source of advice would be entrepreneurs in another town who are in the same business as you. You can pay them a fee (say, a hundred dollars) to spend time with them studying their methods, routines, and time-saving devices. Or, arrange an exchange program with a female business owner in another area—have her come to observe you for a day and give advice, and vice-versa.

Finally, refer to the bibliography for a listing of books, services, and women's business groups. And check your local library for all available reading matter on your type of business. There are books and magazine articles on all facets of going into business as well as how to start all types of businesses.

PREPRODUCTION: TYING YOUR SHOESTRINGS

A bad beginning makes a bad ending.
Euripides

It takes money to start a business, even on a shoestring. Some businesses require a greater initial outlay (for equipment and inventory) than others. Before you withdraw your savings or borrow money, know exactly how much you need, and why.

ESTIMATING YOUR COSTS

After you've defined precisely what your business is going to do and before you consult with anyone else, figure out what it's going to cost to get your plan on its feet. This involves a healthy amount of homework. First, estimate your *fixed* expenses—rent, telephone and utilities, licenses, insurance, taxes, and office expenses. Then, the *variable* costs—supplies, equipment, furnishings, inventory, personnel and payroll taxes, advertising, the services of an accountant and lawyer, repairs and maintenance, cleaning service, and so forth.

Be diligent about obtaining current prices so that your estimate will be accurate. Determine all your expenses for the entire first year. No business can expect to make a profit right away, and you have to begin with enough money to be able to ride out the dry periods without being thrown.

Starting on a Shoestring

Many small businesses can begin on a shoestring budget by keeping overhead and operating expenses down to the bone. This involves working from home or renting an inexpensive space; buying secondhand furnishings and supplies; avoiding regular employees by hiring temporary people only when needed or by taking on partners.

Other small businesses, like retail stores or restaurants, require substantial financing. They must pay higher rent for a prime location. There are usually high initial costs for remodeling (building partitions, installing additional plumbing and electrical outlets). Expensive equipment and fixtures are basic requirements: air-conditioning, refrigeration units, adequate lighting, display cases, to mention a few. The furnishings and decor must provide an attractive ambience. In addition, there are heavier costs for inventory or supplies, insurance, advertising, and help.

Stores and small manufacturers also require additional capital to help them over seasonal slumps. If you anticipate all of these varying costs in the beginning, you won't be forced to shut down six months later because of undercapitalization.

Working from Home

If you work free-lance or deal in a craft or service where direct customer contact is minimal, you might consider working out of your home. As business grows, you will expand, and then, especially if clients begin coming to *you*, you may want to move to a more prestigious or convenient locale. But so long as you designate a specific business space, one that won't have to be set up and dismantled every day, starting off at home is often an economical and practical solution.

Most people are attracted to working at home because they will be saving money on the high cost of commercial rent. For women with families a home office is also an ideal situation. They can close the office doors to family interruptions, yet still be available when needed.

However, if you work at home, you have to like *being* at home. Many people feel claustrophobic when working and living in the same quarters.

Aside from personal considerations, there are certain businesses where a level of professionalism must be maintained. Working from home may be wrong for your business image or the type of client you want to attract. If your home office is in the suburbs, expect to find some clients who may not want to travel far for consultations or don't particularly like wading through a kitchen or family room to your desk.

As far as the legalities of working from home, check into your local zoning laws to make sure you are situated in an area where you can operate a business from home and where you will be allowed to display a sign. Consult your local city and county authorities regarding licences or permits required for your particular enterprise—for example, the board of health for food-related businesses. Talk to your insurance agent about any special coverage that you may need for fire, theft, and such.

The primary concerns in setting up a home office are privacy and adequate work and storage space. Dusting the breakfast crumbs off the dining-room table and then hauling out the typewriter is a bad idea—from both an organizational and a financial point of view.

Current federal tax law stipulates that in order to qualify for a home office deduction, "the portion of your home that you have allocated for business purposes must be used exclusively and regularly for your business or employment."*

---

* For additional information, send thirty-five cents to the Superintendent of Documents, U.S. Government Printing Office, Washington, D.C. 20402, requesting Internal Revenue Publication No. 587, *Business Use of Your Home.*

Selecting a Profitable Location for an Office or Storefront

Opening a store or other business where image and convenience are prerequisites for success requires planning. Look around. Don't grab the first space you see because the landlord says three other people are panting to sign the lease. The most charming nook overlooking a flowered courtyard might as well be in Italy if no one can find it. Don't depend on word-of-mouth advertising. Unless you're selling gold bullion at a 50 percent discount, you are not going to attract a steady flow of traffic by being chicly inaccessible. Aim to find the best space you can afford, smack-dab in the center of the business action.

Your *type* of business also influences your choice of location. If you deal with other businesses or depend on a heavy lunch hour trade, then the downtown business district is your target. A friendly little neighborhood bakery should be in the middle of a friendly little neighborhood, a college bookstore near the college. Or maybe you need the hubbub and clientele of a shopping center to sell your wares. Match your location to the customers you want to attract, making sure you are near public transportation and adequate parking facilities. If you will be open at night, check for good street lighting.

High-traffic areas mean higher rents, but they bring in more money, too. It's generally penny-wise and pound-foolish to choose a second-rate location. Talk to your banker and other business colleagues who know about profitable locations before making your final decision.

If you are renting a storefront, obtain the occupancy history of the location. Find out why stores have failed there in the past. Was the failure linked to the location or due to other circumstances? Talk to adjoining or nearby business owners.

After you have considered your locational requirements, explore all the available rentals to satisfy your spatial requirements. You obviously want the most square feet for your money, but the layout is just as important. It must be a workable space with room to accommodate all your needs, whether they be desks and file cabinets or dressing rooms and display cases. Moving around is expensive, so try to find a space that will last you a good long time. If you plan to make additions or repairs, get your landlord's approval, and then get checked out by the appropriate authorities (building inspectors, fire department, board of health) before you lift a hammer.

Study your lease before signing it, and have your lawyer check through the provisions. Points to be considered are:*

> Who owns and pays for any changes made to the property, both during the lease and at its termination?
>
> How long is the lease, and what are the provisions for renewal? (Try to negotiate for a short-term lease, with an option to renew for a long period of time.)
>
> Are there any restrictions in the lease (or the zone) that may apply to your business? (In some parts of the country you can get a protection clause in which the landlord agrees not to lease next door to an identical business.)
>
> What compensation do you have in case of fire or property condemnation?
>
> What insurance coverage does the landlord provide, and at what amounts?
>
> What are the provisions for subletting or assigning the space? (Try to negotiate a cancellation option in case you need to vacate the premises before the lease expires.)
>
> Who pays for heat, air-conditioning, electricity, repairs?

Try to plan your opening date so that you're not paying rent without an opportunity to recover the expense. Landlords sometimes take a "hold" deposit on space, with rental starting on a specific date.

Sharing Office Space

Another low-cost possibility is to share an office suite in a prestigious location with other small-business owners. In that way, you can share a secretary or receptionist, telephones, reception area, and conference room with other professionals. If your business relies on the image of a posh location, this may be the most inexpensive way to go.

---

* For more details on negotiating a lease, see *Enterprising Women*, June 1978. (See bibliography.)

Buying a Building

Small businesses seldom get into buying buildings, but if you are considering this alternative, have a lawyer negotiate the deal. This includes examination and certification of the deed to make sure that you are really buying what you're paying for.

An Office Abroad

For twenty-five dollars a day, small and medium-sized businesses may set up an office in foreign cities around the world. The Department of Commerce has launched a program setting aside office space at government trade centers abroad. The fee covers office space with typewriters and telephones, access to telecommunications, and areas where marketing displays can be set up.

The program is called the Product Marketing Service. Users of the service must alert the government three months ahead of their intended visits. The department will also arrange for secretarial help and will provide interpreters for an additional fee. For details, contact your nearest Department of Commerce District Office.

Additional Considerations

If you are renting, you'll probably be required to put down the first month's rent in advance plus at least a month's rent as a security deposit, returnable to you when the lease expires (assuming you haven't left the place an irreparable shambles). Find out what services (garbage collection, janitorial, etc.) and what utilities, if any, are included in the rent. Utility companies also require an initial deposit, which accrues interest.

ANTICIPATING YOUR OPENING

Equipment and Furnishings

By now, you have estimated exactly what equipment you will need to start. Next, explore the possibilities of buying it versus leasing. For long-term use, it is more practical to own your equipment, but equipment that is leased is tax-deductible, which can be advantageous to new businesses. Sometimes you can evaluate brands of merchandise, like electric typewriters, by renting on a short-term basis before sinking your earnings into a permanent purchase.

When buying, consider secondhand equipment for saving money, or talk to suppliers about arranging payment terms. Remember, you can acquire additional paraphernalia as you go along, so don't go overboard before you discover what you really need. Take it a file cabinet at a time. The same advice applies to other office, restaurant, or store fixtures, not to mention decorative trappings like hanging ferns and wall-to-wall carpeting. Not that you have to resort to orange crates, but better that than blowing your capital on Eames chairs to sit on while you wait for the phone to ring. Ingenuity can do more for your image than going into debt for the sake of authentic elegance.

Before making major purchases, shop around for ideas as well as bargains. Consider buying equipment from places that are going out of business; check your newspaper for announcements and sales.

Telephones

Your type of business will dictate the number of telephone lines you'll need. Don't go berserk in the beginning with lighted hold buttons and multiple lines, but if you will be doing a lot of telephone business, have enough lines so that one will be free for incoming calls. Some phone companies, for only a minimal extra charge, can provide a nonlisted, separate number on which you can conduct all outgoing business, thus freeing your other line(s) for incoming calls. Many prospective clients are annoyed by busy signals and don't bother to call back.

Telephone companies offer a variety of extra services, clever devices, and sophisticated equipment, varying according to location. Talk to a telephone sales representative, and learn what is available before you place your installation order. Know your basic requirements, however, and don't be dazzled into ordering more than you'll need and increasing your monthly overhead.

Besides an initial deposit on which you collect interest, there is an equipment installation charge, so get everything you'll need installed at one time. Be sure to have the phones hooked up well ahead of opening day so that you will have your telephone number for your ads and stationery.

AN ANSWERING SERVICE

If you are free-lance or planning to work in and out of your office, you should invest in an answering service. There are several types: the automatic answering machine, the professional service which picks up on your line, and the service which provides you with an outside number for messages.

The automatic machine attaches to your telephone, plays your prerecorded message to callers, and allows them about thirty seconds in which to record their message. For an additional sum, you can purchase an attachment that allows you to call in and pick up your messages.

Professional answering services which hook up to your telephone vary widely in price and quality, according to the hours you use them. Most services that offer bargain rates are usually basement quality, providing rude personnel and scrambled messages. When you shop around for services, compare friendliness as well as prices. You usually pay more for charm and accuracy, but it can be worth it.

The cheapest type of service is one which provides its own number. People call that number directly to leave messages for you. It's very impersonal, but for some free-lancers or very small businesses it's a possibility.

Supplies

The amount and description of supplies you need will depend upon your business. (When feasible, buy supplies in quantity; this lowers the cost per item. Think three to six months ahead when placing your orders. The more storage shelves and cabinets you have, the better. Bulk orders save time.)

LOGO, STATIONERY, AND BUSINESS CARDS

The minute you have an address and phone number, have your stationery and business cards printed.* If you can't afford a free-lance artist, you can design your own letterhead, logo, and business cards. All you need is a steady hand, some art supplies, and press type.† Do a layout, and have it photostated‡ before having it printed. Or talk to your printer, who may be able to give you ideas by showing you samples of letterheads or styles of type you may wish to use.

You may wish to have a graphic designer create an individualized logo for you. Once you have adopted a logo, use it on everything you have printed—stationery, shopping bags, sales checks, order forms, labels, ads, etc. In the beginning, to save money, have a rubber stamp made with your logo to reduce printing costs.

In any case, before making any final decisions check several printers or lettershops (specialists in small jobs) for quality (which can vary considerably) and price estimates.

The least expensive type of printing is called one-color, which sends the paper through the printing press only once. A one-color printing doesn't have to be black and white; it can be brown ink on yellow paper, green ink on beige, maroon on blue, whatever combination appeals to you.

Two-color printing, considerably more expensive, means that two colors of ink are used, and the expense stems from

---

* Some people choose to have their first stationery printed up with a Post Office Box address if they haven't yet found an office or plan to work from home. But unless you continue using the box number, it's cheaper to have a rubber stamp made up and avoid having stationery printed until you have a permanent address.

† Press type is pressure-sensitive type which is transferred onto another surface. The type comes in predesigned letters, numbers, decorative borders, and line drawings. There are many brands, and any good artists' supply store carries myriad styles. Each brand publishes a catalog of styles.

‡ Photostating is an inexpensive photographic copying process. Your printer can print from your original layout, but it's generally smoother to print from a photostat. Many smaller cities, however, do not offer quality photostating, so before entrusting your original to the photostater, have a look at the quality of her work. Check for crystal clarity, and watch for thumbprints. A bad photostater, like a sloppy film developer, can mess up your original work and provide you with an unusable copy.

running the paper through the presses twice. The more colors you use for stationery or brochures, the higher the cost.

Line drawings are simple to reproduce. If you have a clever logo and plan to stick with it, then consider having a permanent plate made so that later supplies can easily be reordered by phone.

You might also consider having second-sheet stationery printed as well, using your name and address in small type (usually across the bottom of the page). Besides its use as a second page for business letters, it can be used for such things as business forms and price lists.

Paper comes in many weights, measured in pounds. For example, ten-pound paper weighs ten pounds per thousand sheets. The heavier the paper, the more expensive. Select paper that looks and feels substantial and still folds easily.

Envelopes are featured in many sizes, but the most practical is the standard business size. The envelope size should match your stationery. Have at least twice as many envelopes printed up as stationery because they can be used for sending checks and other enclosures besides letters.

The larger the quantity you have printed, the less expensive it is. One hundred business cards might cost you six dollars, and five hundred only ten dollars, because once the press is set up it doesn't cost proportionately more for a larger run. Order enough supplies to last for a reasonably long time, and reorder when the supply starts dwindling.

Additional Costs

The budgeting for additional start-up costs (for inventory, specialized manufacturing equipment and raw materials, restaurant supplies and fixtures, etc.) depends on the amount of your capitalization and the scope of your plans. Again, your future suppliers are usually willing and able to furnish good advice, based on their knowledge of, and dealings with, other small businesses in your field of operations. Take advantage of their assistance.

5

LEGALITIES: THE STRONG ARM OF THE LAW

If you can't give me your word of honor, will you give me your promise?
Samuel Goldwyn

The American business system is a minefield of laws, and trying to find your way without an expert is business suicide. *Get a lawyer*, the sooner the better. It will cost you some money now, but it will save you a lot more later on. And be professional about it; don't rely on a cocktail party briefing from a lawyer friend who hasn't evaluated your particular situation in detail. That sort of offhand advice could end up costing you more than legal fees. Business success or failure may hinge on your lawyer's knowledge, interest, and advice.

WHY DO YOU NEED A LAWYER?

The legal decisions start from the word *go*. First off, what kind of legal entity is your business going to be—a sole proprietorship? Partnership? Corporation? Your lawyer can advise you on the merits and drawbacks in your case and draw up the proper papers. Then there are taxes, contracts, leases, licenses, labor, and dozens of other potential headaches that aspirin won't cure.

Setting up a business haphazardly can be ruinous. In terms of time and money lost, hasty decisions are sometimes irrevocable. Suddenly discovering that there are taxes or licenses you weren't aware of, which you now owe, with penalties for neglect tacked on, can run you right out of your working capital. This is not meant to scare you off, just to alert you to potential problems.

Aim toward establishing a continuing relationship with your lawyer. She should be knowledgeable and interested in your business and on the lookout for changing laws and license requirements that can affect your business. All through your business life your lawyer will be a soothing presence in the background, available for both crises and routine legal matters.

Choosing a Lawyer

With so much at stake, you want to find the right person. A woman—if you can find one of the current 9.2 percent of today's lawyers—may be more in tune with your wavelength.* At any rate, look for someone interested in your project and knowledgeable about your type of business. And one who is not too expensive.

Shop around. Ask friends, business associates, suppliers, trade associations, other small-business owners, your accountant or banker, local women's business association, or your local chapter of NOW. Or contact the women's bar association in your state.† You might also consult professors at nearby law schools or librarians at law libraries.

Lawyers specialize in different fields: taxes, corporations,

---

* More than five times as many women are practicing law today as there were in 1950. There are more women today in law school than in any of the other professional schools.

† For further information in seeking women lawyers, contact: National Association of Women Lawyers, 1155 East Sixtieth Street, Chicago, Illinois 60637; National Association of Black Women Lawyers, 715 G Street, N.W., Washington, D.C. 20001; or, Association of American Law Schools, Women in the Legal Profession, Rutgers University School of Law, Newark, New Jersey 07104.

patents, criminal proceedings, and so on.* Find one who is well versed in the problems of small businesses. You'll have to decide what size law firm to deal with, too. There are large ones, with partners and junior partners and clerks in abundance, and homey two-person operations where they empty their own wastebaskets. The big setups may offer you a wider range of expertise; the small make you feel more comfortable. Choose someone who comes well recommended, someone you trust.

You won't have to put a lawyer on retainer, but you will have to pay for all the time she spends on you (lawyers keep time sheets), even for that initial session to discuss your business. Most lawyers have an hourly fee;† you should find out what it is, and what it includes, before setting up the first meeting, to avoid misunderstandings later. You may be able to negotiate on a flat fee to cover the initial counseling and the setting up of the legal structure for your business. Find out if you will be charged for phone calls, duplicating of documents, and so on.

Get as much information for your money as possible. Before seeing your prospective lawyer, have a basic idea of the type of business structure that is best for you. Define your business and your general goals clearly. Be as well informed as you can, and prepare a list of questions or points you want to cover during this initial session. That way you won't waste time and money floundering through basics you should already know. Also, this thorough preparation will help you evaluate the quality of the advice you're getting.

---

* For an introduction to patent matters, write for the booklet *General Information Concerning Patents*, published by the U.S. Department of Commerce Patent and Trademark Office. Available from the Superintendent of Documents, U.S. Government Printing Office, Washington, D.C. 20402, price seventy-five cents.

† In 1976 the American Bar Association revised its Code of Professional Responsibility to allow attorneys to publish brief biographical data and fees for initial consultations in several kinds of directories, including the Yellow Pages. Several states have now sanctioned print, radio, and television advertising for lawyers, but just for consultation fees and hourly rates. Some law firms even accept payment by credit card.

PATENTS

If you've invented a better mousetrap or a mechanism to facilitate travel into hyperspace, and you want to be protected from others stealing your idea and capitalizing on it, then you'd better get a patent. Not that it's easy. Obtaining a patent is expensive because the procedure is highly technical and time-consuming and nearly always requires the assistance of a patent attorney.*

A patent search of the nearly four million existing patents must be instituted. The patent application is complicated and almost impossible to prepare without legal help. All this is expensive and can cost anywhere from $400 to $1000. To top it off, the Patent Office can take up to three years to approve an application.

Obtaining a patent gives you the power to prevent others from using, manufacturing, or selling the patented product for a certain length of time. But receiving a patent does not necessarily stop others from challenging it. The term *patent pending* offers you no legal protection.

Many professionals advise an inventor to file her patent (for her protection) and then to find a financial backer to license it and pay royalties. The feasibility of this depends on how much you are willing to give up to see your invention get off the ground.

Your Legal Rights

Regulations concerning licensing and insurance are loosening. Use your lawyer, but also do your own homework. Keep up with the changing laws through your local government agencies (Small Business Administration, Department of Com-

---

* A list of registered patent attorneys (booklet no. C21.9/2:974) is available for $3.70 from the Superintendent of Documents, Government Printing Office, Washington, D.C. 20402. In addition, contact the Office of Invention and Innovation, Technology Building, National Bureau of Standards, Washington, D.C. 20234. This new government office is set up to give assistance to anyone who has an idea for a product or gadget which will "improve the quality of public life."

merce), your local Chamber of Commerce, women business owners' association, and trade journals in your particular field. The more information you can gather on your own, the lower your legal fees.

STRUCTURE OF THE BUSINESS

There are three legal forms that a small business can take: individual proprietorship, partnership, or corporation.* Each has different applications regarding taxes, management, liability of the owner, and distribution of profits.

Often, a small business will begin as a proprietorship or partnership and then, after a year or so, when the business has gotten off the ground, file for incorporation. The following is an explanation of the three business structures, to give you a preliminary glance at the pros and cons of each.

Individual Proprietorship

This means that you are the high lama and lay down your own rules, at least for day-to-day managerial decisions. A sole proprietorship is the easiest business structure to start and least complicated to dissolve. It is the oldest form of business, so that the laws regarding it are firmly established. A freelancer is considered a sole proprietor since the same legalities and taxes apply.

LEGALITY

The structure is very flexible. You don't need government approval, but you must check with local authorities to determine whether a license for your particular business is required

There is no legal time limit for a proprietorship. The business automatically ends when you stop doing it.

---

* Other specialized forms of legal structures (but not considered necessary for small businesses) are joint stock companies, syndicates, pools, and Massachusetts trusts.

LIABILITY

As sole owner you are personally liable for all business debts, to the extent of *your entire personal holdings.* In addition, you do not have the full tax benefits of the tax-deductible plans (including pension and profit-sharing) that are available to a corporation.

ADMINISTRATION

All policy and day-to-day operations rest with you, as owner-manager. You're in full charge, in complete control of organization and profits.

PITFALLS

Many single ownerships fail because the person at the helm should *not* be steering alone and may sink from inexperience, inept management, or undercapitalization.

TAXES

The business profits will be taxed as personal income. In addition, many states levy a state income tax on profits from an unincorporated business. (Check with your local tax bureau or your accountant.) Individual proprietors have to pay federal social security tax, although you will not need Worker's Compensation and Disability insurance (because single proprietors are owners, not workers). (See Chapter 14.)

RAISING MONEY

A single owner can raise money to begin or expand her business by borrowing, purchasing on credit, or investing her own money into the business.

Since you are solely responsible for your business debts, potential moneylenders will evaluate your personal wealth to provide collateral for the loan.

If you are considering a business which, by its very nature, will require a large investment in equipment or inventory to operate successfully, then you should probably not consider sole ownership.

General Partnership

The next structure to consider is dual ownership, or general partnership. Actually, a partnership may consist of two *or more* owners. As a legal structure, a partnership is easy to begin and to terminate. At the onset, the partners should sign an agreement stipulating intentions and buy-sell arrangements should one partner wish to withdraw at a later date.

LEGALITY

There is the same operating flexibility as in a proprietorship. There are no federal requirements for starting, although you must check with your city and state to see if a business license is needed. A partnership ends by dissolution by the partners or the withdrawal of any one of the partners.

Some states require that partners file a Certificate of Conducting Business as Partners, which identifies all partners by name. This must be filed with either the local county clerk or the state. If the partnership is working under a fictitious name, then a dba (doing business as) form is required by some states.

LIABILITY

The partners are responsible, and personally liable, for all business debts, the same as a sole proprietor. In a partnership each member can bind the other so that one partner can cause the other to be personally liable. Also, there are not the tax advantages of benefit plans, such as pension and profit-sharing, that are available to corporations.

ADMINISTRATION

Each partner has an equal responsibility, with the various operating functions divvied up. The combined abilities and experience of two or more owners give the business a stronger chance of succeeding. New concepts and business policies need only an oral agreement by the partners before going into effect.

The disadvantages are obvious. Many partnerships have dissolved over disagreements on basic business policies. And, barring dissolution, the bad blood caused by these conflicts can make daily operations intolerable. For this business structure to work, the partners must be compatible and confident that they are working toward a mutual goal.

TAXES

The partners are taxed separately on their individual returns. Each partner is fully responsible, and liable, for all debts and taxes incurred by the business, regardless of the amount of her investment in the business (with the exception of *limited partnerships*, covered below). Some states require a tax on unincorporated businesses, so the profits from the business are taxed; check with your accountant.

RAISING MONEY

It is easier for two people to raise money for their business than just one. There is more money to begin with, if each partner chips in, and the combined resources of the partners can make up the collateral when they apply for a loan or look for investors. Because of their liability for business debts, a partnership may be granted better borrowing terms than some small corporations. This full liability often makes outsiders more willing to extend credit.

Limited Partnerships

A limited partnership allows you to limit the liability of one or more of the partners, to the extent of the amount of *money they have invested* in the business. (Limited partners are required to invest either cash or tangible property; they cannot contribute services as an investment.) Besides the limited partners, at least one general partner must be designated to oversee the daily operations of the business.

Limited partnerships are more complicated to set up, since a legal written contract must be filed with the state. This lessens the degree of flexibility as the partnership must adhere strictly to the laws of the state in which it is organized.

Some states require you to file a Certificate of Limited Partnership, as well as a dba form if your business uses a fictitious name. This agreement is technical and must be drafted by your lawyer, then filed with the state according to your state's tax regulations. Some states charge a filing fee.

ADMINISTRATION

The limited partners are not permitted to advise in the active administration of the business. If they do, they become general partners and are thus fully liable for all business debts. Limited partners are, of course, allowed complete access to information on the daily goings-on of the business, including the books and financial statements.

RAISING MONEY

The same rules apply as those for a general partnership if additional capital is needed. The limited partners, though, are responsible only to the extent of their personal investment. Many times, general partners will take on limited partners in order to raise money for their business.

Corporations

A corporation is a complete legal entity unto itself. In effect, it is an artificial human being, society's civilized monster. It can sue, buy property, and exercise many other privileges of living people. It cannot marry, but it can merge; it cannot vote, but it can influence votes; it cannot hold public office, but it can control those who do. You don't have to be a mini-conglomerate to incorporate. There are many small-business corporations.

LEGALITY

A corporation must adhere formally to state laws. The scope of the company's activity, as well as its name, is restricted by a charter and is, therefore, more complex to establish than the other business structures. It must be set up according to the legal procedures of the particular state in which it is formed.*

In most states, it is legal to incorporate without the services of an attorney, which can mean a savings of several hundred dollars or more.† However, there is a great deal of work involved, and unless you have confidence in your abilities along these lines, it is advisable to hire a lawyer.

To incorporate, three or more people (depending on the state) must organize and become officials in the new corporation. (In the case of a sole proprietor who decides to incorporate, the other two people do not have to be equal partners or major shareholders. For example, a lawyer or accountant could be designated.) Next, they file their "articles of incorporation" with the state's commissioner of corporations. Afterward, there is a filing fee and an initial franchise tax to be paid.‡ Next, there must be an official meeting, conducted with recorded minutes, to deal with the specific organizational and operational details.

---

* In general, it is necessary to incorporate in the state in which you plan to do the majority of your business. For example, because of the advantageous Delaware corporate laws, many corporations are formed in Delaware, although the owners often never set foot there. They hire, for an initial fee plus a minimum annual fee, another corporation to act as a registered agent. This agent files all necessary corporate documents.

If a Delaware corporation is not based in Delaware, then it must register in the state in which it does most of its activity as a "foreign" corporation and pay an initial fee, varying from state to state. For more specific information on Delaware corporations and a list of filing fees of other states, the reader is referred to Ted Nicholas, *How to Form Your Own Corporation for Under $50.00*. (See Bibliography.)

† See Nicholas, *How to Form Your Own Corporation for Under $50.00*.

‡ The filing fee is based on the value of the corporated stock and, therefore, quite reasonable for most small businesses.

The exact amount of franchise tax varies vastly from state to state. As of this writing, the fee is five dollars in Wyoming and two hundred in California. The franchise tax is based on net income, attorney's fees, and other expenses.

LIABILITY

The major advantage that corporations have over the other business structures is limited liability. The company is responsible for its debts only to the limit of its assets. Therefore, you, as owner, are not liable for any of your company's debts, although you may lose what money you personally invested.

TERMINATION

Since a corporation has a life of its own, the retirement, illness, or death of any of its officials does not automatically end it. The certificates of stock, representing ownership or investments made in the business, may be transferred from one party to another without interfering with the company's operations. A corporation can be sold (through stock transfers), go bankrupt, or simply fade into the sunset (although it takes at least three years for a corporation to die a natural death.)

Because of the complexities involved in each method of dissolution, both your lawyer and accountant should be consulted so that it may be put to rest as painlessly as possible.

FREEDOM OF ACTION

No other state is legally required to recognize a corporation except the state in which it is formed. However, every state permits out-of-state or "foreign" companies (with the possible exception of utilities and common carriers) to do business within their borders so long as they comply with the rules and regulations of the state. This often involves filing legal documents with proper state authorities and paying specified fees and taxes. A corporation appoints (hires, actually, for a minimum fee) a representative, called a registered agent, in that state to take care of the legal red tape. To find a registered agent in the state in which you wish to do business, consult a lawyer or that state's department of commerce and industry.

Sale and exchange of corporate stock is governed by state 'blue sky laws," which protect the potential investor. (The phrase was coined by a legislator who remarked that many companies sought to "capitalize the blue skies.")

The selling price of the stock relies on the current worth

(assets) of the corporation. The amount of stock a person owns depends on how much money she is willing to invest in the business, according to its growth needs. The more money you invest in a new corporation, the more control you will have.

ADMINISTRATION

If a proprietor becomes a corporation, she does not necessarily have to lose control of her business. In many small corporations the sole proprietor can retain ownership by buying the majority of stock in the new corporation. The same applies to a partnership that becomes a corporation; the partners can divide the majority of stock.

Stockholders may participate in the policies and day-to-day operations of the company, but not necessarily. A corporation is not liable for the actions of its stockholders just because they have invested in it.

PITFALLS

There is a great deal of time-consuming paperwork in running a corporation, such as keeping the corporate records and filing additional tax returns. Also, if a corporation is run by people who own only a small percentage of the stock, there is the risk of ineffective management because those in control have very little personally at stake in the company's success or failure.

TAXES

Corporations pay taxes at rates different from individuals. The business is taxed separately and liable—rather than the owners—for all its debts, one of the most favorable aspects of incorporating. But corporations pay heavy taxes. Income tax rates on corporate net income are: 17 percent on the first $25,000, 20 percent on the next $25,000, 30 percent on the next $25,000, 40 percent on the next $25,000, and 46 percent on income over the excess of $100,000. The income can also be taxed doubly, first as earnings and again when distributed as dividends to shareholders. (See the section, "Subchapter S Corporations," below.) Have your accountant or lawyer provide you with a calendar outlining all the responsibilities of the corporation, including the filing dates for all taxes.

A corporation is generally in the most advantageous position to raise capital. It can borrow by putting up corporate assets as collateral. A large corporation may "go public"—that is, sell stock shares, and attract a wide range of investors. Money obtained from selling stock or a percentage of the company is called *equity capital.* There is no financial risk for a stockholder beyond her investment.*

However, if a corporation takes out a loan to finance its debts, the lender may require a personal guarantee from the owners. This eliminates the limited liability to the extent of the loan.

Subchapter S Corporations

The Internal Revenue code permits small-business corporations to be taxed at individual rates. Thus, a closely held corporation (with fifteen shareholders or less) can avoid heavy corporate taxation by allowing each owner-shareholder to report her share of the company's profits (or losses, for deduction) on her personal income tax return, as is done in a partnership.

This is definitely the ideal corporate structure for new or low-income businesses. Have a lawyer give you the specific details as they apply to you and your business.

Corporation Filing Requirements

Many states require domestic corporations to file an annual statement identifying the company's officers and their addresses, as well as giving the corporate office address. This filing fee runs around five dollars.

Cooperatives

A variation of the three standard business forms is the cooperative, a legal structure which can be set up as either a partner-

---

* Any gain on a stockholder's investment will be taxed at preferential capital gain rates. If the corporation elects to issue Section 1244 Small Business Corporation Stock, any loss a stockholder realizes from her investment may be deducted as an ordinary loss, to the extent of $50,000 in any tax year.

ship or a corporation. Cooperatives are generally associated with agriculture, housing, child care, and crafts designers and artisans.*

A cooperative is created by any group of people having common economic or physical needs. The cooperative does not make money for itself. Net profit is shared among its members, according to a predetermined method of allocation. Cooperatives are managed by the members, board of directors, and, often, hired management. The cooperative is controlled democratically, usually with each member representing one vote.

A cooperative group may choose to be incorporated, or not. Some states have laws covering the incorporation of co-ops.† When incorporated, the cooperative members are not personally liable for any debts the cooperative incurs, and the taxes on profits are paid by the corporation.

If the group is not incorporated, it is viewed as a partnership. All members are liable for business debts, and the profits are taxed as individual income. If your group is considering the cooperative alternative of business structure, be sure to contact an attorney.

Federal, State, and Local Licensing and Regulations

FEDERAL

Certain types of businesses engaging in interstate commerce are subject to federal regulations, licenses, and permits. Check with your lawyer or accountant, although generally these regulations do not apply to small businesses.

STATE

Contact your state's department of consumer affairs to see if your specific business must obtain a license. Licenses are issued for a specific time period, generally a year or two.

---

* For further explanation, see Program Aid Booklet no. 1001, *The Cooperative Approach to Crafts*, by Gerald Ely, published by the USDA Economic Statistics and Cooperative Service.

† Some cooperatives incorporate under the District of Columbia Cooperative Law and then incorporate in their own states as out-of-state corporations.

Most small businesses are regulated at the local level. Check with your city *and* county to learn if you need any sort of license to do business. Sometimes both require one.

Find out about local zoning laws to make sure you conform. (Some city or county zones will not allow signs in front of a business. You should check out zoning restrictions in any case, but especially if you do business out of your home or apartment.)

Should you ever remodel or add onto a building, you will have to meet building code standards, as well as fire or police standards.

If you deal in food (making or selling it), you must meet the standards of your local board of health.

Bankruptcy

There is no terrible stigma attached to bankruptcy. Bankruptcy is the only sensible way to go when you want to get out of a financially unsuccessful business, yet the creditors are creeping around your doors. It's not so bad. Bankruptcy laws are federal laws. The proceedings are conducted in an orderly way, enabling the people involved to make the best out of a sad situation.

Individuals and unincorporated partnerships can file for bankruptcy without the services of a lawyer. The filing fee is fifty dollars, which may be paid in installments by obtaining permission from the officiating judge.

Corporations must be represented by an attorney for bankruptcy cases. The legal fees are reviewed by the court, and a projected method of payment is set down. Sole owners and partners can be liable to the extent of their entire personal holdings. Owners of corporations are liable for their debts only to the limit of the corporation's assets.

There are two types of bankruptcy which pertain to small businesses. *Chapter Four* is straight bankruptcy, when there is no possible way for the business to be reorganized in order to become profitable. *Chapter Eleven* is partial bankruptcy and can be filed when the condition of the business is not completely hopeless. The business is then given another chance to become profitable, but you must be able to show how and why you think you can turn things around.*

Among the forms to be filed, you must itemize a summary of all the debts you owe and property or assets you own. Certain items (such as alimony and child support) are exempt from bankruptcy action. Get a list of exemptions from your state, to be used as a guide to filling out the forms. As the proceedings get underway, you will be expected to appear in court as well as to meet with your creditors.

Because of all the complexities involved, business bankruptcy should be handled by a lawyer, regardless of whether the business is incorporated.† But let's hope you will never need to use this information.

LICENSES—WHERE TO GET THEM

For your convenience, here is a listing of legalities which must be dealt with (depending on the sort of business you wish to start):

License to do business	Local office of state tax department
Dba form (fictitious name statement)	Local county clerk or state tax office
Certificate of partnership	County clerk's office or state tax bureau
Zoning regulations	County clerk's office
Seller's permit (sales tax resale number for retailers)	Local board of equalization
License for food sale or service	Local and state health departments
Health/safety requirements and labor information	U.S. Department of Labor

---

* Chapters Four and Eleven bankruptcy can be filed for with forms provided in a kit, published by Julius Blumberg, Inc., available at legal stationers across the country. Each kit contains complete filing instructions and costs under five dollars.

† Costs vary from state to state. In New York, fees range from $300 upward, depending on the case. Legal Aid can seldom assist in business bankruptcy.

Information on federal taxes; Employer Identification number; social security and unemployment	Local office of Internal Revenue Service
Worker's Compensation	State insurance fund, or state worker's compensation board
Disability Insurance	State department of human resources development or state disability office

Choose a lawyer you trust, and then trust your lawyer. You're going to be in business for a long time. Over the years she will advise you, handle your contracts and agreements, represent you in front of licensing boards, courts, and regulatory bodies. She'll counsel you on equity financing, purchasing inventory, choosing the best fiscal period for your taxes, interpreting new laws and regulations, working out credit assistance, negotiating leases, and selling or terminating the business.

Listen to your lawyer; she knows the law. But listen to yourself, too; it's your business. Ultimately, *you* will have to make the decisions.

6

ACCOUNTING: BLACK AND WHITE AND (NEVER) RED ALL OVER

Heaven knows how to put a proper price upon its goods . . .
Thomas Paine

Great ideas must translate into financial language and percentages, and profits must be transformed into everyday patois. Accountants interpret, bookkeepers record; but it is the Certified Public Accountant who reads the numbers and turns them into facts and predictions. CPAs are the seers of the business world. You can show them what you have, and they'll tell you if it works.

Every business owner is faced with a barrage of decisions as the company moves from day to quarter to year. A new entrepreneur learns quickly that an accountant's assistance is invaluable.

Besides depending on your accountant, take time to educate yourself. Enroll in a good course in bookkeeping, accounting, and finance. Dun & Bradstreet, the business information and credit-rating service, reports that most business owners say that if they had it to do all over again, they would have started out armed with this knowledge. It will help you relate better to your accountant and to the world of numbers and ledgers.

FINDING THE RIGHT ACCOUNTANT

Get firsthand recommendations from business associates or other small-business owners in your field, people who have actually worked with the accountant and can vouch for her expertise and trustworthiness.* If you receive recommendations for several accountants, talk to them all. You will work closely with an accountant on a continuing basis, so select someone who is knowledgeable and experienced in *your type of business*; whose advice, ideas, and judgment you respect; and with whom you will enjoy working.

When you interview a prospective accountant, find out which services are included in her basic fee, and which are extra.† Fees are generally quoted on an hourly basis, with an estimate given of the time involved. Assume (but ask to make sure) that for a quarterly or yearly fee she will take care of your quarterly reports, sales and other taxes, and trial balance sheets. She should also do up a profit-loss statement at the year's end. Find out whether your accountant will represent you in case of a tax audit.

A verbal fee quotation is okay, but don't hire anyone without agreeing on the price ahead of time (and this applies to every other area of your business as well). Never accept a vague "Don't worry ... I'll give you a fair price." It may turn out to be fair, but if it's more than you intended to pay, resentment builds and all the initial goodwill collapses. Remember, everything always costs more than you expect it to.

In short, when choosing an accountant, compare costs, and compare experience in the field and in your type of business. Choose the professional who is best qualified to handle your needs. At the outset, ask for an engagement letter, reviewing the services provided, and how much the fees will be.

---

* For additional help in locating an accountant, write: American Women's Society of Certified Public Accountants, Thompson, Hine & Flory, 1100 National Bank Building, Cleveland, Ohio 44114; or, American Society of Women Accountants, 327 South LaSalle Street, Chicago, Illinois 60604.

† Tax returns for the single proprietor are usually extra since she pays business taxes on her individual tax return.

THE ACCOUNTANT'S SERVICES

An accountant is truly a multifaceted person.* She will:

> Compute initial costs, based on your estimates
> Figure out your profit potential
> Establish your break-even point
> Help you set fees and prices
> Set up your bookkeeping system
> Draw up (and teach you how to read) financial statements
> Advise you on the tax advantages of the three major business structures as they apply to your own situation
> Introduce you to a banker
> Help with loans (by preparing financial projections and vouching for you)

On your first meeting, be prepared to provide your accountant-to-be with an outline of your business. (This can be done orally.) Besides the concept itself, include any marketing surveys (no matter how informal) that you have conducted. Indicate your business' potential—your community's need for it and its distinction from existing competition. Include the estimated expenditures you have already itemized for overhead, supplies, and equipment.

The accountant will check your estimates for accuracy and suggest realistic costs where your initial estimates are low (and they probably will be). Then she will work out your profit potential—that is, how much money you must make to meet expenses and how much more to realize a profit.

She will help you establish fees by setting standards that are based on competitive prices plus your operational costs. If you are dealing in an unusual service, where there is no standard fee structure, she will set a pricing formula for you. Knowing what to charge for services is a major stumbling

---

* The National Association of Accountants (919 Third Avenue, New York, New York 10022) offers free assistance to anyone starting a business. It has 326 nationwide chapters.

block for inexperienced entrepreneurs. Making five hundred dollars on one job is not necessarily something to gloat over unless you know that it is sufficient to cover the costs directly related to the job—including labor and billing time.

SETTING PRICES FOR YOUR BUSINESS

The Break-even Point

Setting accurate prices for your product or service cannot be done until you have established your break-even point: tally up your overhead (fixed expenses and variable costs), and then hone down this figure to a time basis. For example, if your fixed monthly overhead is $1,000, then the weekly figure is $250. Based on a five-day week, you will have to earn $50 per day just to *break even*. Anything over that, less additional expenses, is profit.

The Basic Formula

The next step is to find out what similar businesses are charging for their products or services. With this in mind, you can set your prices competitively, based on Labor + Expenses-Materials + Overhead + Profit = Price. The actual percentage you will tack on for profit fluctuates, according to the type of business you're in—service, retail, or wholesale manufacturing.

In figuring any prices—for products or services—you have to cover the time spent for selling (advertising), buying supplies, and bookkeeping. You can figure that 50 percent of your costs will be for specifics (e.g., labor, direct expenses like raw materials), 20 percent for nonspecific costs (e.g., general equipment, overhead, miscellaneous supplies, gas for your car), and 10 percent for selling costs. The remaining 20 percent will go for profit.

You must constantly reevaluate your use of time, cost of materials, etc., and what you charge. If you don't charge enough, your work will be undervalued. Keep up to date with your competition and their prices.

Estimates

For large-scale jobs or special orders, you must be prepared to provide the client with a price estimate, based on labor costs and expenses. Before pricing a job, however, try to determine the client's budget. (Often, clients keep this information top-secret, hoping you will quote them a lower price.)

Estimates are difficult to assess accurately until you have accumulated experience in similar jobs. Since unexpected obstacles often arise, tack on an additional 25 percent to your estimate to cover these hidden costs. The fastest way to lose clients is to end up charging a significant amount over the original estimate. (In mid-job, should you discover that your estimate was too low, inform the client right away and negotiate a new cost estimate.)

Advance Deposits

Sometimes the smaller the price, the harder it is to get paid. Anytime you take on a new client, obtain a deposit for the service or product. Waive it later on for regular clients, unless you need partial advance payment to cover your own outlay of expenses connected with the job. In general, the amount of the deposit should be half of the total bill.

Consideration of Intangibles

For certain creative businesses, the higher your fees, the more apt you are to convince people that you are worth that much. You must base the price of your service or product on its value to the *client*, an intangible which overrides your basic costs.

In setting fees, always balance psychological buying practices with economical ones.

PRICING FOR SERVICE BUSINESSES

Since expenses are usually negligible in service businesses, they must calculate their costs in labor. This time cost is generally doubled to cover overhead and general expenses. Then the total of these two categories is doubled, in order to make a profit—2 + 2 = 4 + 4 = 8 (total cost including profit).

Services are highly competitive, but if you engage in a unique project for which there is no basic fee structure, then divide the hours you expect to work by the income you need to cover expenses and make a profit.

In computing labor costs, don't neglect indirect expenses. For example, time spent in cleaning a typewriter must be considered in pricing a job involving the use of a typewriter (e.g., typing letters, bills, etc.). Don't forget to charge for transportation if the job involves numerous meetings at your client's office. Keep receipts for every expense involved with every job. Unless you do, hidden costs can drain your profit.

Miscellaneous Creative Services

Examples of such services include landscape design, shopping services, creative agencies, party planners, etc. Many services establish their fees based on a percentage of the total job, including expenses. This percentage varies according to the exclusivity, individuality, or competition of the service, but it generally ranges from 10 percent to 20 percent. Discuss what your percentage should be with your accountant.

Also, be sure to establish a reciprocal discount (usually 10 percent) with other stores, suppliers, or specialized talent that you use on a regular basis in executing jobs for your clients. It is up to you to decide whether you pass this discount along or hold on to it.

RETAIL PRICES

The standard retail price is a 100 percent markup *per item* over the wholesale price. If, however, you specialize in unusual crafts, artwork, antiques, groceries, or imported items, then your prices will be geared to the current market value of those items. According to the SBA, most retail profit doesn't begin to accrue until the second year, often longer.*

Another essential part of retail pricing is seasonal mark downs. Unsold merchandise must regularly be marked down in order to reduce inventory and free both your cash and your shelves for new purchases. Monitor your markdowns so that you can spot a pattern in your unprofitable buying. Remember, the more skillful your buying in the first place, the fewer markdowns you will have.

CONSIGNMENT PRICING

If you are a craftsperson and want to sell your work on consignment, you have to set your price—what it will sell for retail. The store will take a consignment percentage (usually 30, 40, or 50 percent), and when the item is sold, you get the remaining percentage. If it doesn't sell, then you must reclaim the item.

Always sign a preliminary agreement with the store, stipulating the number of items you leave with it, the date, and percentage rate. Have the store send you a monthly check along with a list of items sold and any requests for more. Stay in touch with the store, and keep records of what has sold and the money taken in.

From the store owner's point of view, it's attractive to offer merchandise without having to purchase it. However, many retail stores shy away from accepting items on consignment because of the hassle of the extra paperwork and bookkeeping involved.

WHOLESALE PRICING

You have, to know accurate up-to-date costs in order to set prices. The formula is generally Time (labor) + Expenses

---

* The SBA offers a free pamphlet, no. 193, *What Is the Best Selling Price?*, which gives guidelines for pricing a product. Available from your nearest SBA office.

For additional information on retail costing, see: *How to Open Your Own Shop or Gallery*, by Leta W. Clark, St. Martin's Press, New York; and, *Financial Manual of Retail Stores*, Fairchild Publications, 7 East Twelfth Street, New York. New York 10003.

(including overhead, selling, equipment, and raw materials) + Profit (the amount you wish to make, usually 20 percent) = Wholesale Price. In other words, you must be able to make a profit by selling your product at 50 percent of the retail price.

Every item a manufacturer designs, reproduces, and sells must be costed separately. The original costing must be revised whenever any changes are made in the design or when labor, raw materials, equipment, or overhead costs escalate.

How much profit you can make per wholesale item is based on your own research (in stores and catalogs) of the potential market: how much you estimate the item can sell for at retail (which is, generally, double the wholesale price). If you cost out an item and decide that it cannot be produced to sell at a fair and competitive price, then you must revise your estimates. You must either consider less expensive raw materials or try to cut down on overhead costs.

CHANGING PRICES

Once you have set a price, you are not stuck with it. Although you don't want a reputation for fluctuating fees, you have to adjust them to match the seesawing costs of labor and materials. In addition, keep in step with your competition—lower or raise your prices accordingly. Read trade magazines in your field to keep up to date with price trends.

BARTERING

Bartering is a time-honored practice, and many individuals and business owners still engage in it. There are times when it's beneficial for you to exchange your product or services for someone else's. If you're a lawyer and one of your clients is a cabinetmaker, why not give free counsel for a wall of badly needed bookshelves?

The key is to make sure that the items or services to be bartered are of equal value to the recipients. And while bartering serves a purpose, your accountant will advise you that it never quite takes the place of money in the bank.

JOBS FOR PUBLICITY'S SAKE

Small-business owners are sometimes talked into taking un-profitable jobs in exchange for "good publicity." Women's subliminal volunteering instincts often make them prey to this kind of pitch. But no matter how much you enjoy what you do, you are still in business to make money. If you don't, you won't *stay* in business.

Occasionally, however, there are times when it doesn't hurt to do a good deed—just so long as you don't lose money on the project. You will have to weigh the advantages before you take the job. Will it allow you to explore new areas you've been dying to tackle? Then the experience gained is worth it. Or maybe you want to attract publicity by having a celebrity on your client roster? (Stars usually want discounts for gracing your business with their superstatus.)

More publicity can be gleaned by volunteering your service or product for charity benefits or community celebrations. "Paying your civic dues" creates goodwill, and your participation makes you feel good, too. Or you might decide to do a job at cost, as a favor to an advisor or friend, to repay a kindness.

But what about *turning down* a job? The ability to make these discriminations comes with experience, and you will certainly make mistakes before you've developed the right mix of hard heart and soft touch. There are jobs that you can't afford to do and must refuse, in order to free up time to attract more lucrative accounts.

KEEPING BUSINESS RECORDS

Many innovative entrepreneurs are brought to their knees with fear of The Books. But if "you gotta have a gimmick" is the first order of business, "you gotta have a plan" is the next. Write everything down, and your books will tell you how your business is doing. You may think that you can carry every-thing in your head at first since it's a small business and yours. But it isn't that easy.

After you get going, a lot of facts and figures start vying for a choice location between your ears. Your daily, monthly, and yearly records turn into a memorandum of past events as well as a forecast of future trends. They help you accentuate the positives, eliminate weaknesses, and prevent costly mistakes in tax return preparation.

Bookkeeping has been referred to as "organizational common sense." Really, that's all it is . . . a place for everything with everything kept up to date.

The Bookkeeping System

Most small businesses can get by with reasonably uncomplicated record-keeping systems.* Have your accountant set up the *simplest* system for your needs, based on the following records:

> Cash receipts—money taken in
> Cash disbursements—expenditures paid out
> Sales—to be recorded daily and summarized monthly
> Payroll—the record of wages and withholding deductions
> Equipment—assets in equipment, office furnishings, etc.
> Inventory—a record of the company's investment in merchandise or raw materials
> Accounts receivable—a record of balances owed to the company
> Accounts payable—a record of what the business owes its creditors and suppliers

And who runs this system, day to day? *You*, that's who. At least in the beginning, learn by doing it yourself. Don't allow your accountant to burden you with a time-consuming system of keeping records. Be sure you understand how it is done. So long as you keep track of what's coming in and going out,

---

* To supplement your accountant's record-keeping explanations, the following Small Business Administration books are helpful: Small Business Management Series no. 15, *A Handbook of Small Business Finance*; Management Series no. 32, *Financial Recordkeeping for Small Stores*; and Harvey C. Krentzman, *Managing for Profits*. Also see Mary Lee Dyer, *Practical Bookkeeping for the Small Business* (Chicago: Henry Regnery Co.).

along with costs for labor and expenses, you'll be just fine. When money starts pouring in and things get more complicated, then you can hire a bookkeeper.

While you alone are shouldering the burden, don't neglect it. It's just a matter of setting aside a couple of hours regularly every week. It becomes a habit, like brushing your teeth. If you do it while the transactions are still fresh in your mind and the receipts within easy reach, it won't take long.

Bookkeeping Methods

All the data of daily business transactions must be recorded as each item occurs for later transfer onto a permanent ledger as a debit or a credit. These records are compiled monthly or quarterly into a financial statement: a balance sheet of assets and liabilities and owner's capital on a specific date; and a profit-loss statement of income and expenses covering a specific time period.

THE SINGLE-ENTRY SYSTEM

This system is a simple chronicle of the money going out and coming in. Your record of every dollar spent—the date, amount, and purpose—and every dollar earned—the date, amount, and description of the item or client's name. Save all bills and receipts for everything, no matter how minuscule the amount.

Enter this information into a ledger page daily or once a week. On a monthly basis, total the columns of cash received and disbursed. If the money taken in is more than that going out, you've made a profit. If the opposite occurs, you'd better work twice as hard next month. If you have outstanding accounts receivable at the end of the month, then this profit-loss sheet doesn't tell the whole story.

THE DOUBLE-ENTRY SYSTEM

In this system, you record everything twice—once under debits and once under credits. Every transaction is a balance of the two: if you spend $200 on a typewriter, you have depleted your cash, but you have increased your assets.

Stationery and office suppliers have various ready-made systems for keeping business records, and most small businesses can use standard account books. Have your accountant recommend the best one for your needs.

Always record transactions in pen, not pencil. If you make mistakes, cross them out, don't erase.

If you use a simplified double-entry system, then you'll need the following books: a sales-cash receipts journal; a cash disbursements-purchases-expense journal; a general ledger (to record assets, liabilities, and capital); an accounts receivable ledger; an employees' compensation record; and, of course, a business checkbook.*

The Profit-Loss Statement and Balance Sheet

There are two systems of recording income and expenses: cash and accrual. Whichever method you elect, you must use it consistently.

The *cash method* shows only the receipt of income (cash) and the actual cash disbursements (expenses). Many businesses rely heavily on credit accounts, so that the cash method of recording transactions is not a reliable reflection of profits and losses during a specified time period.

The *accrual system* reports all transactions which take place during a specified period, whether or not the payments have yet been made. In other words, you deduct expenses as they occur and add income as it is earned, even if you haven't been paid by the client.

A profit-loss statement based on the accrual method is the more accurate account of cash and credit transactions

---

* Business checks may be purchased from office suppliers instead of banks. There are one-write check systems which provide, along with your checks, an automatic accounting system. You write a check and carry it forward, and it takes the place of a cash-disbursements journal. These one-write systems are terrific for poorly disciplined people.

For additional information on all bookkeeping methods, see *Portfolio of Accounting Systems for the Small and Medium-Sized Business*, 2 vols. (Englewood Cliffs, New Jersey: Prentice-Hall).

during a specific period, thus making business analysis easier.

To establish the realistic condition of your business, tally up the gross profit (money taken in); then subtract all your overhead costs and expenses. The resulting figure is your net, or actual, profit.

The balance sheet shows the ratio of inventory to sales (credits to debits), to indicate whether inventory is too high and sales too few. In a service business, it compares sales to profits to detect whether the profits are high enough to make a satisfactory profit.

Being busy from nine to five isn't enough. The productivity of your time must be measured in profits. Balance sheets and profit-loss statements are thermometers of your success or failure.

Profit Mix

There are additional ways of analyzing your financial statements. Even if you are showing a profit, are there services or products that are losing money? You have to reexamine continually all areas of your business and sweep the dust out the door (not under the rug).

In some cases, however, a loss area may be part of your company's image or prestige. Figure out why, and how much, it is losing, and decide whether its overall contribution warrants your continuing it.

Profit Trend

This is the overall picture of your profit. Is the profit increasing in proportion to your total business volume? Or is it simply holding its own or declining? The fact that you show a profit is not necessarily an indication that your business is growing.

Annual and Quarterly Expenses

Don't overestimate your monthly profits. Allow monthly allotments toward periodic or annual expenses like taxes, insurance premiums, licenses, equipment rental, maintenance expenses, and the like.

CASH FLOW

Cash flow is the play between income and expenses—the amount of actual cash that is flowing in and out of your business at any given moment. It provides the money with which to work between billing and payment (order and delivery) and covers out-of-pocket expenses. Your creditors (moneylenders, suppliers, landlord, etc.) demand that you pay your bills promptly, yet your customers often take several months to pay you. You have money, on paper, but the cupboard is bare in regards to cash on hand.

In order to *know* how much cash you can expect to have—cash to work with between billing and payment (order and delivery)—do a cash flow analysis, either monthly or quarterly. (Have your accountant help you in the beginning; you can take over from there.)

A cash flow statement covers three areas:

> *Source of cash*—whatever brings money into the business, i.e., sale of products or services, payments by charge customers, capital from loans, and money earned on interest, etc.
>
> *Cash going out*—whatever you must spend to keep the business operating, i.e., overhead, inventory or supplies, repayment of loans, etc.
>
> *Cash schedule*—the comparison between this and other months (or quarters), i.e., a business barometer which shows whether you are generating more or less cash than in previous months. This will enable you to see where you need to cut back on expenses (and growth spending) in the coming months.

Knowing exactly how much cash you have on hand to spend will force you to develop alternative sales methods. In this way, you can balance your cash flow and compensate for slack periods and seasonal buying.

If you are owed money (and can prove it), yet need to meet impending bills, you can take out a short-term bank loan to cover expenses, as long as your credit is in good standing. But if you keep up with your cash flow, you should be able to avoid this kind of bind.

Financial Projections

Your accountant can assemble all pertinent information on your company's financial position for potential lenders and investors. This presentation will include a profit-loss statement and balance sheet, or projections if you haven't started in business yet.

Rely on financial projections. Putting them together entails identifying every potential cost, which is then entered on spread sheets for analysis. All costs are recorded in relation to specific time periods so that the cash flow can be computed. Your accountant's cash flow projections will help predict what amount of capitalization you will need to carry you along the inevitable rocky road down which every new business must travel.

STORING BUSINESS RECORDS

Metal file cabinets are not fireproof. Certain records must be stored in safety in case of fires, flooding, etc. The ones to be tucked away safely (in a fireproof safe, bank safety deposit box, or on other premises) are the ones that will provide the most information—current profit-loss statements, balance sheets, and tax returns—if disaster strikes.

Store any records that will help you collect insurance, report losses for tax deductions, and borrow money. Reestablishing a business also requires lists of customers, suppliers, inventory, equipment, production information, so these items should also be kept in a safe place. Review your storage records periodically, and bring them up to date.

Small-business owners can suffocate under the amount of paper that must be saved. Since business records must be accessible, the most space-saving method is to store them in indexed, numbered, corrugated containers on metal bookshelves.

Microfilming your records saves storage space but is time-consuming and costly. Also, microfilm must be kept in special humidity-controlled safes.

How Long Must Records Be Saved?

You can decide how long to hold onto routine records and correspondence, and your accountant can inform you of your state's statute of limitations for specific documents like canceled checks, vouchers, and receipts.* The table below is a general guide to the length of time one is required to retain records of certain business transactions:

Indefinitely	A copyright, trademark registration, letter of patent (even though they have a definite expiration date)
	Corporate by-laws, minutes of stockholders' meetings, annual reports
	Equipment maintenance records and warranties (for the life of the equipment)
	Certain correspondence, insurance policies, and contracts
	Annual operating records and the general ledger (balance sheets, profit-loss statements)
	Deeds
	Copies of ads, brochures, publicity, and business memorabilia
Six Years	Contracts and leases (unless renewed periodically)
	Records of lawsuits (these must be kept from six to ten years)
	Cash receipts and disbursements records
	State and federal income tax returns (and records corroborating them)
	Major-purchase receipts
Four Years	Payroll records (including wage payments and withholding deductions for income tax and social security)
	Accounts receivable and paid invoice records

* The statute of limitations ranges from three to twenty years according to state but averages six years.

Three Years	State and local sales and use tax records
	Routine purchase records
Two Years	Employee time sheets
	Petty cash vouchers
	Monthly bookkeeping records
One Year	(until annual audit of the books is completed)
	All production records and receipts
	Accounting records and supporting documentation

Poor record keeping kills more businesses than bad craftsmanship or marketing. Hire a bookkeeper as soon as you can realistically afford one. Nevertheless, at the beginning it's important to follow a system that can be maintained by you or someone with minimal experience or training in bookkeeping.

Once you've found your accountant, keep her up to date on new developments. Rely on her advice, because she can see you from the other end of the telescope and focus on your potential problems before they explode.

INSURANCE: RESTING ASSURED

Oh, dry the starting tear, for they were heavily insured.
William S. Gilbert

Yes, insurance is yet another expense, but one which should be thoroughly considered since small businesses are least likely to withstand losses of any kind. Insurance premiums are fixed costs that become security blankets covering against fire, theft, and other losses that could not be absorbed by a small company. Insurance also provides additional financial stability, often making it easier to obtain credit. Later on, increased coverage, such as group health or life insurance plans, make it easier to attract and keep good staff members.

Before buying any insurance, figure out what you have to lose, whether you can afford to lose it, and how much it will cost to cover the risk. Then decide if you can cover the loss yourself, out of your company's general operating costs. For example, if the only item in your office worth stealing is a twenty-year-old electric typewriter, then it's cheaper to replace it outright than lay out money to insure it. On the other hand, if you stand to lose an entire inventory of antique birdcages, insurance premiums are negligible compared to your potential debacle. Insurance replaces a *possible* large loss with a small but continuing cost—the premium.

Talk to your agent, and then buy what insurance you can afford. And then keep reevaluating your needs. What you do today may not be valid or meet the needs of your business in five years. There may be an increase in the value of your business, or a reduction, and your insurance coverage should be altered accordingly.

Discriminatory practices in underwriting, by the way, have been eliminated by law. A good agent will keep your interests in mind and help you keep premium costs at a minimum. She will keep you abreast of changing regulations and laws (which vary between states) involving business insurance requirements and benefits.

FINDING THE RIGHT INSURANCE PERSON

The insurance person you choose should be flexible enough to whip up a policy tailored to your specific needs. Currently, only a small percentage of all insurance brokers are women, but if you can find one of them, chances are that she will take a more personal interest in the success of your business.* In locating the best person it is advisable, as always, to look for personal recommendations.

Even if you don't sign up right away, it's a good idea to consult with an insurance person before your start-up, so that you can budget the cost for later on. Invite prospective agents to see your working premises for the initial interview. This way, the person can see for herself the extent of the coverage needed.

Try to get quotes from at least two different people. Even though rates are similar among companies, there is sometimes a disparity among benefits. *Guard against overinsurance.* There are ambitious brokers around who will try to sell you more insurance than you need. Listen to their suggestions,

---

* In general, insurance *brokers* insure property, and insurance agencies insure people. It is important to be insured with a company that is financially stable. If you are dealing with a small company, check it out in *Best's Insurance Reports* (in your reference library), which publishes the financial rating and analysis of insurance companies. To locate women brokers in your area, write the National Association of Insurance Women, 1847 East Fifteenth Street, Tulsa, Oklahoma 74104.

talk to other small-business owners, and decide for yourself what your real needs are.

The Independent Agent

This person usually specializes in property or liability insurance and works on commission from several insurance companies. She can, therefore, put together all of your insurance requirements, and since you are her client, not the insurer's, you will receive better, more personalized service should you have a claim. Because she deals in different types of coverage, she has a greater knowledge of the various types of insurance. Just make sure she has extensive contact with several insurers who can supply all the coverage you will need, at reasonable prices.

The Direct Writer

The direct writer works directly for a specific company and is not an independent businessperson. The advantage of dealing directly is that because you are going to a specific insurer for a specific type of coverage, the cost is lower. Many insurance companies specialize in certain areas and can offer a great deal of experience in that type of coverage. Lloyd's of London, for example, specializes in unusual kinds of risks that no other company will handle—from marine research to Marlene Dietrich's legs.

INSURANCE COVERAGE

Basic insurance needs to be considered fall into the categories of casualty, accident, health, and life.

Casualty Insurance: Liability

Liability, which includes both general and automobile, is about the most necessary type of coverage for a small business. General liability insurance covers you in case accidents are incurred by employees or clients on your premises. This includes both personal injury and damage to personal property. Unintentional negligence on your part (frayed rugs, unpacked boxes blocking an aisle) is no defense. One lawsuit, if you are found guilty, could wipe out the total assets of your company and force you out of business.

Liability insurance should include product liability (if applicable) and auto insurance (if not separately covered). Car liability insurance should be carried on any staff member who uses her own car for company business (if your state has not passed a "No-Fault" automobile insurance law).

Casualty Insurance: Property

FIRE INSURANCE

If you are renting an office or storefront, check with your landlord to determine the extent of her coverage that is applicable to you. (Generally, landlords' policies will not cover your equipment and inventory.) Then you may want fire insurance, which covers losses caused by fire and lightning. You have to purchase additional coverage for protection against explosion, windstorm, hail, smoke damage, car damage, riots, and so forth.

CRIME INSURANCE

This covers crimes committed by people outside the business. If your bookkeeper is pocketing company funds, for example, her pilfering constitutes an "inside job" and is not covered in this type of policy.

Robbery insurance covers the taking of property from a person by force or threat of violence.

Burglary insurance protects inventoried merchandise and safes, but there must be visible marks of forced entry—no sneak thieves.

Storekeeper's burglary and robbery policy is designed for small businesses and covers up to $250 worth of loss. Larger businesses need more complete crime coverage, at much higher premium rates—especially in high-risk locations.

All-risk insurance is designed for retailers and wholesalers; it covers their entire stock of goods from all perils except those specifically excluded by name on the policy.

Transportation insurance covers shipments of goods during transport.

Business interruption insurance protects a business if it is forced to shut down, either totally or partially, after loss from an "insured peril" (fire and such).

Glass insurance protects your plate glass windows, glass signs, glass doors, showcases, or countertops.

Power plant insurance covers against losses from explosions of furnaces, electrical equipment, engines, steam boilers, etc.

Rent insurance protects against damage from sprinkler leakage, etc., in rented buildings.

Accident and Health Insurance

DISABILITY AND WORKER'S COMPENSATION

If you have any full-time staff members, you are required by law to pay Disability and Worker's Compensation.* This can be purchased from a state insurance fund or private insurer. Premium rates are determined by the employee's salary and the type of work involved, varying from 1 percent of salary in a low-risk job to 10 percent or more. It is tax-deductible for corporations only.

In a corporation, the owners are considered employees, and they have the option to insure themselves, but not the obligation.†

A sole proprietor is not considered an employee of her business and is therefore not required to have Disability or

---

* Check your state's requirement, as the application for Worker's Compensation varies widely, and some workers are exempt. In some states, you are exempt if you have fewer than four employees.

† The Worker's Compensation Law requires the same treatment for executive officers as "employees." Failure of a corporation to provide insurance for executive officers would subject it to legal penalties.

Worker's Compensation (or unemployment, although she must have social security). Partners also are not considered employees, unless the partnership is incorporated. In general, Disability insurance for you, the owner, is a good idea. There are several types of policies available, including *Disability income insurance* and *business overhead insurance*. These will keep you and your business going (by paying part or all of your fixed overhead expenses) while you are temporarily laid up.

MEDICAL AND HOSPITALIZATION INSURANCE

This is not required by law, but with the cost of doctors and hospitals nowadays, it is risky not to have it. It is also a "fringe benefit" most employees look for these days. There are many plans available, and group health is less costly than taking out an individual policy. A "group," by the way, can consist of as few as two people. Medical premiums are tax-deductible only for corporations.

Life Insurance

Small businesses can use life insurance to add to their financial stability since it qualifies as collateral for a loan. Individual life insurance policies are available to sole owners and partners. For single proprietors, it can furnish cash for heirs who must continue or dispose of the business.

For partnerships and corporations, life insurance may provide the necessary cash for funding buy-sell agreements in the event of a partner's or stockholder's death, and it can also be used to pay estate taxes.* In a partnership, it protects the business since the partnership is legally terminated with death. Group life insurance policies are tax-deductible only for corporations.

Any personal expense (such as medical or life insurance) that your corporation can pay for represents a tax savings. For example, a corporation can "give" up to $50,000 of group life insurance to an employee income tax–free.

---

* In the event of the death of a partner (or major shareholder in a corporation) the buy-sell agreement forces the estate of the deceased to sell and you, the remaining partner, to buy their share of the business. The money for this transaction comes from the proceeds of the insurance.

TERM AND PERMANENT LIFE INSURANCE

There are two basic kinds of life insurance and hundreds of variations.

Term life insurance means you are paying to cover the event of death; the company pays if you die, but it has no value as long as you stay alive. It's renewable every few years.

Permanent life insurance generates a cash value and it can be collected in twenty years, when you are sixty-five, or at whatever time the policy stipulates. You can hold on to the policy or surrender it for cash value. You can also borrow against the cash value at a low interest rate because you are actually borrowing your own money.

KEY PERSON INSURANCE AND BUSINESS OWNERS' INSURANCE

Key person insurance insures any person whose death could mean a substantial loss to your company. For example, if you manufacture the clothes of a specific designer, the loss of the designer could be disastrous to your business.

Business owners' policies can protect an owner against losses from disability or medical expenses or her dependents against losses from her premature death.

RETIREMENT/PENSION PLANS

The Individual Retirement Annuity Plan

This plan (IRA) covers individuals who are not usually covered by an employer's plan. Basically, it is a voluntary contribution by an employee of her own money before taxes are applied. It can be frozen if you change jobs or become part of a profit-sharing plan. It enables you to pay taxes on less money and is similar to the Keogh Plan in its applications. For more information, visit your local bank or savings association.*

---

* To understand all the pluses and pitfalls of the IRA, see Avery Comarow, "Getting the Ire Out of IRAs," *Money* Magazine (November 1978). (See bibliography.)

Qualified Pension Plan (Profit-Sharing)

This plan is set up by a corporation for its employees and is tax-deductible. It is not obligatory but is often a drawing card to attract qualified people to your company.

A new simplified pension plan now permits employers to provide retirement benefits for their employees by making contributions to the employee's Individual Retirement Annuity Plan (IRA), instead of establishing and maintaining a qualified plan. Under the new rule, each employee sets up and maintains her own individual IRA, to be governed by all the regular IRA rules regarding distributions, withdrawals, and such. The employer's contributions to her employee's IRA are deductible by the employee on up to $7,500 or 15 percent of her earned income, whichever is less.

Keogh Plan

The Keogh Plan is a pension/retirement plan for people who are self-employed (free-lancers, sole proprietors, or partners).* You may contribute annually up to 15 percent of your net taxable earned income. This money is tax-deductible (with a ceiling of $7,500 generally), but it must remain in this fund. There is also a mini-Keogh plan where you can put away as little as $750 per year, tax-deductible.

The interest and dividends the money accrues each year are tax-free, too. When you retire, you pay regular taxes on the money as you withdraw it from the fund, but by then you are likely to be in a lower tax bracket. You cannot withdraw your money before you reach the age of fifty-nine and a half (if you do, you will have to pay a penalty).

The Keogh Plan is not mandatory for self-employed people.

---

* The Internal Revenue Service's Publication no. 560 gives further information regarding requirements for the Keogh Plan; savings banks can explain it also.

BONDING

For a fee, a business can secure bonding, which shifts the financial responsibility for a *specific job or employee* to a licensed bonding company or insurance firm.

Fidelity Bonds

These protect the business owner against employee theft and embezzlement. The employee (the "principal") is bonded by either a licensed bonding company or insurance company. There are three types of fidelity bonds: *Individual bonds* name a specific person; *schedule bonds* list all names or positions to be covered; and *blanket bonds* cover all employees but do not identify them by name or title, so that hirings and firings can take place without affecting it.

Bonds stay in effect until their cancellation. The limit of liability is always included, indicating the maximum sum to be paid.

Surety Bonds

These guarantee that the employee will carry out the specific job she was hired to do. If she is inept or quits, you can collect on the bond. (These are often used in the construction business, enabling bonded small contractors to compete against larger companies in bidding for jobs.)

Keep in contact with your insurance agent. There are complicated rules and regulations regarding insurance, and laws constantly change from state to state. Premium rates fluctuate, business needs grow, and you must be on top of them in order to keep your prices in line with your overhead.

BANKS:
WHERE CREDIT IS DUE

Women, like princes, find few real friends.
George, Lord Lyttelton

Banks are in the service business. In return for your money, via checking and savings accounts, it is their business to serve *you*. There is a growing effort nowadays (still a forced one in some banks) to make a woman feel at ease and her business sought. Women are encouraged to open checking and savings accounts, but when it comes to applying for a loan—especially a business loan—banks still treat women the way Dracula treats daylight. True, a large percentage of the nation's wealth is in women's names; most of it, as we all know, is in name only. But the situation is changing. Women are now protected by law against credit discrimination.*

---

* The 1975 Federal Equal Credit Opportunity Act (ECOA) prohibits credit discrimination on the basis of sex or marital status in mortgage lending. Credit worthiness is now based on the ability to pay one's bills without being bound to the credit rating of a spouse or ex-spouse. In March 1977, however, the Federal Reserve Board determined that the ECOA could *not* be applied to women for business credit purposes. But since women can get personal credit through the ECOA, and after getting personal credit they can then establish business credit, the ECOA does help women establish business credit.

In order to use money effectively, women must understand it thoroughly. Instead of avoiding the subject, once the genteel thing to do, it is time to realize that the economy in general, and one's own economy in particular, are areas one can scarcely afford to neglect. Remember, a lot of U.S. Treasurers have been women.

To erase the fear of numbers—diminishing, multiplying, running our lives—we have to learn to live with them. And if you're going into business for yourself, then your future success relies to a great extent on your ability to control the dollars with sense. No matter how fantastic your accountant and banker may be, it is you who must conduct the orchestra.

ENTER ... THE BANKER

When you start your business, even if you're working free-lance, open a business checking account. It is both professional and practical to keep business accounts separate from personal ones, even if they are with the same bank.

Have your accountant or lawyer introduce you to a banker at the outset of your business if you haven't already lined up someone you respect. (Practically speaking, a recommendation will present your business in a sounder light than will your coming in cold off the street.) As with all other people with whom you will work closely, your goal is to establish both a banking relationship and a friendship with your banker. Listen to professional advice while you shop around, but make your own decision as to the banker and bank you feel will help you the most.

Rapport with banking people cannot be underestimated. Many male bankers are willing to help women, but they are often paternalistic. More and more women are becoming bank officers these days,* and a woman is apt to be more sympathetic to your project. Remember, however, that she is still a banker and cannot waive banking standards because you are her sister.

---

* And opening banks, too. The First Women's Bank opened in New York City in 1975 after three years of planning. In Maryland, the State National Bank has turned the management of its Bethesda branch over to women. The Women's National Bank, in Washington, D.C., the first federally chartered women's bank in this country, opened in 1978, as did the First Women's Bank

No matter how small a business you start, laying the basic groundwork (for later expansion loans, etc.) is imperative. At the first appointment with your prospective banker, be prepared to explain your business, your professional background, what you plan to do, and where you aim to go. After you've settled on your banker, keep her up to date on your progress. Call her every few weeks. It is not a waste of her time; she wants to know how you're doing, to participate in your growth whenever she can.

Besides the sympathetic banker, the bank itself must be considered. Banks are competitive businesses. They offer numerous services besides cashing checks and issuing loans. Some large banks are set up to help small businesses with payroll management and tax paying, thus saving you the expense of a bookkeeper. But in general, small businesses are best nourished by small banks, where there is close contact with the officers, easy access to the president, and the tellers know you by name. Most large banks simply cannot grant you the same personal attention.

BANK SERVICES

After your business is set up, you may want to look to your bank for a number of additional services. Large banks may offer a more varied selection of services in order to attract new customers, but all banks are set up to help you in ways you probably haven't required before. Banks, depending on their size, can provide some or all of the following services (and it is up to you to ferret out what your bank can do for you):

> Provide personal service plans to help reconcile your monthly statement
> Transfer funds anywhere, by wire or cable, saving the days it usually takes for a check to clear

---

of Maryland. There is the Connecticut Women's Bank, as well as women's banks in San Francisco, Los Angeles, San Diego, and Richmond, Virginia, with others planned for Boston, Chicago, Denver, Miami, and Seattle. There are also two women's savings and loan associations in the country. Look for similar developments in your area.

In addition to full banking services, these banks sponsor seminars for women business owners, and many have libraries available to their customers, with books and periodicals on credit and finance.

Set up and keep records for employees' benefits, like profit-sharing and retirement

Establish Keogh (federal tax-favored retirement) plans for sole proprietors or partnerships

Provide a lock box system to pick up and process checks for faster payment if you do a lot of business in other cities

Run credit checks for you on any new client or supplier, both in the United States and overseas

Offer payroll management services, including taxes

Issue you a letter of credit, outlining terms of payment, for a supplier

Introduce you to affiliates in other areas of the country, or abroad, if you plan to expand

Act as your register and transfer agent should you (if incorporated) decide to go public

Help you find another business with which to merge, or a buyer if you want to sell

Sell tax-exempt bonds and notes

Become trustees of your estate

Guarantee a cash reserve up to $5,000 (for special accounts)

Issue charge cards, such as Master Charge or Visa

Offer (for a fee) an investment management service

Rent safety deposit boxes for your important records

Stop payments on checks. (Don't reissue a check that has been lost until you have stopped payment on the original.)

Certify checks (which some businesses require until you have established credit)

Issue check-cashing convenience cards for branches

Find out what your bank will be able to offer you as you grow. Bank policies vary, but all work within the same basic framework.

OPENING A BUSINESS BANK ACCOUNT

Banks require a business or personal reference if you are not known to them or introduced via a respected businessperson in your community.

If you are doing business as a sole proprietor or under a fictitious name, you must submit a certificate of business (available from your county clerk for about ten dollars) to open an account. A business must also have a federal Employer Identification number in order to open a bank account. In order to get it, use your social security number if you are a sole proprietor, or file Form SS-4, available from the Internal Revenue Service. A partnership must also provide a list of partners and stipulate which ones are authorized to sign checks. If you are incorporated, you must hand over a copy of the corporate resolutions, a list of officers, and the names of those authorized to sign checks and negotiate loans. (This can change as the business grows.)

It is also possible to have a signature card on file for anyone else on your staff who goes to the bank for you. In this case, there is usually an agreed-upon limit for cashing checks.

It's an excellent idea to keep a separate bank account for tax monies, so that you won't inadvertently use tax money for day-to-day operating expenses. This is especially advantageous for retailers and services required to pay sales tax, so they won't be caught in a bind at tax time.*

Your Credit Rating

Business life is a cycle of "creditability." What's happening now is based on the past, and your future credit hinges on now. When a new business seeks to establish credit, the creditors look to the owner's personal credit, since the business itself is an untried entity.

A single, working woman gathers credit when she opens a bank account, takes a personal loan, or acquires charge cards. A married woman must maintain her own financial identity, separate from her husband. (If you open a joint account with your husband, credit institutions regard this as establishing *his* credit, not yours. However, under the provisions of the Equal Credit Opportunity Act, all you need to do is notify your bank and creditors that you want the credit history on your joint account reported in *your* name, as well as your hus-

---

* To obtain your resale tax number, apply to the board of equalization for a seller's permit. (See Chapter 13, under "Sales and Use Taxes.")

band's, and the change will be made.) Credit cards must be in her own name—married, maiden, or hyphenated. She should also keep her own personal checking account.

An excellent way to establish credit is to take out a bank loan and pay it back (with interest) on time. Banks, however, cannot grant loans just so you can establish credit; you must give a reason for taking it out—traveling, moving, etc. If you are just starting out on your own, someone may have to co-sign the loan with you (an accountant or a relative), but if you pay it back on time, the credit established is yours.

The key to financial independence is financial responsibility. Honor your loan payments, pay your credit card bills before interest accumulates, and never overdraw on your checking account, either on purpose or inadvertently. The same rules apply for your business—a company's history of debt-paying establishes its credit rating.*

The capitalist system revolves around credit references; if they're clean, the god of money smiles upon you. If not, you will be in for a lot of time-consuming hassles which sap your energy and your morale.

Under the Federal Equal Credit Opportunity Act, banks, retailers, and other lenders are prohibited from asking about your husband's credit standing. Creditors may not question women about childbearing plans (or birth-control practices)—matters which were formerly used by some creditors as a basis for granting or denying credit. Federal Reserve Board rulings prohibit a creditor's cutting off credit or requiring a reapplication upon divorce or separation. The 1971 Fair Credit Reporting Act guarantees your right to see your credit profile.†

---

* Business credit ratings are listed with Dun & Bradstreet. However, you are not required to furnish it with your company's financial information. If you choose, Dun & Bradstreet will list you, but not *rate* you.

† Your credit profile is generally on file with numerous credit reporting agencies in your area who have received credit reports about you in the past six months. If you've been denied credit, you can see your file for free, but if you're just curious, there is a fee, usually under five dollars. Look in the Yellow Pages for your local credit information corporations. After filling out the proper form you can obtain a printout of your credit file, either in person or by mail, not over the telephone.

Establishing Business Credit

If your business depends heavily on supplies—inventory, expensive equipment, raw materials, wholesale foods—then you have to establish credit. Even if you have more money than Scrooge, it is good business practice. Credit helps a business expand and cushions the blows in hard times.

Credit is simply others' belief that you can meet your bills. A creditor extends to you a certain amount of time (after delivery of the goods) before the payment comes due. This can vary from ten to ninety days (or up to two or three years for expensive equipment).

In retail or wholesale businesses, in which your suppliers associate with you on a continuing basis, the standard credit-establishing procedure is initially to pay in full for goods, at the time you order them. The total cost of initial inventory or stock has to be figured in your start-up budget. The next time around, you may pay half on ordering and the balance within thirty days, or in full upon delivery. By the third buying excursion, you should rate full credit.

From then on, it's fairly easy to have a credit line run on your business through one of the big credit firms. Dun & Bradstreet will research the list of suppliers with which you you deal and record the manner in which you organize your payments—in thirty days, sixty days, etc. It will check your bank references, audit figures of the business, and investigate your past credit relationships. This information is then condensed onto a computer card and is available to any subscriber who requests the information. Dun & Bradstreet makes no recommendation, either positive or negative—it's up to the supplier to decide whether you are a good or bad risk.

The apparel business, however, is a special case. Here, Dun & Bradstreet will advise suppliers as to the amount of credit you merit. Another important source of credit information is the Credit Exchange in New York City.* It is the magic word on Seventh Avenue; if you want a season's inventory and the time to pay for it, establish your business with the Credit Exchange.

---

* Credit Exchange Inc., 461 Eighth Avenue, New York, New York 10001; Dun & Bradstreet, Inc., 99 Church Street, New York, New York 10008.

But what if you don't have a credit rating?* No credit, no personal fortune—nothing but a bright idea and lots of drive. It's not a great position to deal from, but there are options. Probably your best bet is to draw up the solidest, soundest, most convincing presentation you can, outlining what your business will be and what it can do. Then use this to sell one supplier—the kitchen equipment dealer, say, for the restaurant you want to start. Make them see that they can't lose— the community is desperate for haute cuisine, and you're a Cordon Bleu chef of the first order. With your recipes and their stove and refrigerator, Chez Champignon is a surefire moneymaker. Then once the kitchen equipment people have come around, use your credit relationship with them as leverage to convince other suppliers. And—*voilà!*—you're on your way to a sound credit rating.

Most important: get to know your banker. She will help tailor her bank's services to your needs, no matter how large the bank or how small the business. Not all officers know everything, but they have access to any information you need. If you feel you are being shuffled to the bottom of the deck— because you're a woman or your business is too small to interest the bank with which you are dealing—then change banks.

Later on, it is easier to borrow working capital or get an expansion loan from a banker who has dealt with you over a period of time. Look around in the beginning before making a commitment. Usually, the bank that feels right to you will be right for you.

---

* To learn more about credit and establishing credit worthiness, write for the free booklet, *Women: To Your Credit*, published by Commercial Credit Corporation, Baltimore, Maryland 21202. Or call its toll-free number, 800-638-1900, or visit one of its eleven hundred offices around the country.

CAPITALIZATION:
A LOAN AT LAST

Business? It's quite simple. It's other people's money.
Alexandre Dumas, fils

Curtain up, light the lights ... your play is written and bud-geted, and now it's time to look for backers. In the theater they are called "angels," and for the woman seeking to start her own business, no word could be closer to the truth.

If a man and a woman both graduate (B.A., *summa cum laude*) from the same college in the same year, and both go to work at the same company, we all know which one will get into a higher tax bracket faster. And if they both decide to go into business for themselves, we also know who stands a better chance of raising the money to get it off the ground. Women *do* run businesses, so it's not impossible for them to get money. But it *is* harder.

One of the major reasons for business failure is under-capitalization. Women bankers state that women defeat them-selves by not having a clear-cut plan for how the money will be used. If a potential lender suspects that the money will be frittered away or discovers that the woman does not have a professional background to prove her stick-to-itiveness, then loans are not always possible.

You need to get money, but to get money, you have to prove you don't need it. Contradictory? Not really. When anyone borrows money, she is granted its use for a specific period of time, at which point it must be returned along with a fee for the privilege of using it (interest, dividends). Whether the source is a lender or an investor, a loan is a loan. No matter what the terms, a debt must be settled up, sooner or later.

Look at yourself and your business through the potential lender's eyes. Although confidence and enthusiasm score points, you must have a professional presentation to convince people to back your idea.

Also, the type of business that you plan to start and its potential for growth determine the amount of money that's available. The risk involved determines the interest rate you have to pay for a loan or the amount of your company's stock that you must give to an outside investor.

TYPES OF FINANCING: DEBT AND EQUITY

What is your ideal method of raising start-up capital (also called seed money and risk or venture capital)? There are two kinds of financing: debt and equity.

If you are going for *debt financing* (a loan), you have to outline explicitly how you intend to repay the money and what collateral will be used to assure repayment. Although interest is paid on a loan, it is tax-deductible as a valid business expense. With debt financing, an owner can retain complete control over her business.

For *equity financing* you must be able to predict for the potential investor whether the purchased stock will increase in value and to what extent.* There is no legal obligation, however, to return the investment or pay interest to the investor. By giving up equity, though, you are also releasing part of your control of the company. Never give up more than 49 percent or you'll end up back where you started . . . working for somebody else.

---

* See Chapter 5, p. 48 on equity financing.

HOW MUCH MONEY DO YOU NEED?

Use your accountant when raising money. Her professional evaluation of your idea will add credibility to your projections, in the eyes of the "money people." With your accountant's aid, you can estimate accurately how much money you need to blast off from the launching pad.

And how much money *do* you need? First, figure out your basic minimum expenses (rent and utilities, equipment and supplies, inventory or raw materials, and additional expenses such as advertising and staff, and salary for yourself).* Then double them. Expenses are always higher than your original estimate. Unplanned crises and disasters, which inevitably occur, must be anticipated.

Next, write down your break-even point (what your sales must be to meet expenses) and the volume of business you must have to make a profit (e.g., how much merchandise must be sold, or what services performed). Income must come in regularly to meet overhead and expenses as they come due.

So, you need enough money to cover your expenditures for the amount of time that it will take to get your business off the ground, with a flow of steady customers. Depending on the type of business, you should be cushioned for at least the first six months. (Prestige businesses, like art galleries, take a longer time to build a steady clientele than do stores, which are nestled right in the heart of the consumer mainstream.)

PLANNING YOUR PRESENTATION

Any potential lender must be presented with facts. And you must have these facts ready to present, in black and white, and indelibly stamped on your brain as well. Be prepared with the following information:

1. How much money you need. List separately what you require for rent, utilities, supplies, equip-

---

* If you are borrowing money, don't sketch in a higher salary for yourself than that of your former job. Money people aren't impressed. Besides, business owners frequently have to put money back into the business the first year or so. If you take too much money, your business doesn't stand a chance.

ment, inventory, advertising, qualified personnel, and/or working capital.

2. How you plan to use it. Give a complete breakdown of where the money will go. This financial projection should include a balance sheet indicating what shape your company will take *after* the money is obtained, i.e., projected gross earnings for the next several years.

3. How you are going to repay the loan. If you are going for debt financing, list what you can put up as collateral.

Then, define your scheme as to what your business will do; why there is a need for your business; who your competition is and how well they are doing and why; and how and why your company can successfully compete.

Outline this in depth—how you will go about it, how much money you estimate you can make. Point out any unique qualities that set you apart from the competition. Photographs and illustrations might round out such a presentation.

Indicate your potential market and your marketing plan—that is, how you are going to lure clients away from your competition and how you plan to advertise. If you have already lined up some advance orders or customers, so much the better.

Include financial projections for the first two years or so. Illustrate the success your business can attain, if all goes well and according to your course of action.

Next, the moneylenders will want to know about *you*, as owner (and your partners, if you have any):

1. Your business background. Include a résumé with special emphasis on experience and education in the field of the proposed business.

2. Financial and personal references.

3. Your personal financial statement—that is, your current personal worth and sources of income. (Include both savings and your outstanding bills and debts.)

In other words, do you have experience, and are you reliable?

You have to persuade your financial sources that you are a good risk. Bowl them over with your confidence, enthusiasm, and ability to see the forest *and* the trees. Emphasize your flexibility, including alternatives should problems arise, and your inclination to seize new opportunities.

MONEY! WHERE TO FIND IT

If a business has a track record—clients, accounts receivable, and encouraging balance sheets—it is easier to borrow money (for working capital or expansion), but in the beginning the old adage "You have to have money to get it" holds true. Raising money is a chunky stumbling block for novice entrepreneurs and, these days, even for seasoned ones. *Everyone* wants money for something.

And, unfortunately, women still have to field such real or implied questions as: What if you get married/pregnant? What if your husband gets transferred? You might as well be prepared for the inevitable and think positively.

Your written business presentation having been compiled, it's time to get the show on the road. The places to look for money are your own savings, your relatives, friends and close contacts, private investors, banks, small business investment companies, the Small Business Administration, and, if you're incorporated, a private stock offering. Keep in mind, however, that 75 percent of this nation's companies are very small. Only an estimated 5 percent of these have any potential for growth to any significant size. Therefore, small businesses must usually rely on self-financing, at least in the beginning.

Your Savings

Most potential moneylenders expect you to put more than your talent on the line. They want to see your own savings invested in your idea, figuring that the more you risk, the harder you'll work. This means you must invest every coin you can rub together. You may have more assets than you think. Consider borrowing against the cash value of your life insurance policy, cashing in your investments, or taking a second mortgage on your house. While you're getting your business off the ground, you could live off your spouse's salary or tighten your belt and scale down your standard of living. If you can raise at least 50 percent of the seed money from direct sources (you, plus family and/or friends), then you are in reasonably good shape.

Money from Relatives and Friends

People who are close to you—who believe in you and your ideas and energy—are often willing to invest money in your success. These people can (or cannot, depending on mutual agreement) become partners, limited partners, or shareholders in your business. For many female entrepreneurs, this is the only path open, especially if they lack the background and experience to impress professional moneylenders. The advantage of these loans is that they don't have to be repaid at a specific date. But don't take your friends to the cleaners. Borrow only from lenders who will be able to absorb the loss if your business fails. There must also be a thorough understanding of how long you'll need the money and how it will be used.

Ideally, you should be able to raise enough money from personal contacts to get started. Then, after your business has proved its earning power, go to banks or outside investors for expansion capital. They are a lot more open-minded when you have favorable financial statements to back up your enthusiasm. For everyone's protection, put the arrangements in writing—there's no such thing as a "friendly loan."

Private Investors

Your accountant, lawyer, banker, friends, and relatives may know local business people chomping at the bit to invest in new businesses. These people (doctors, dentists, attorneys, executives, etc.) are in high income tax brackets and can afford to take risks. Also, successful entrepreneurs have a soft spot in their hearts for people who want to be like them.

If you don't know of anyone personally, check the classified ads in local newspapers (usually listed under "Business Opportunities") for people with money to invest. Or run an ad yourself (including phrases like "ground floor opportunity" and "promising new business"). Besides local papers and business publications, a good place to advertise would be alumnae magazines, especially if you are an alumna in good standing.

Often, private investors are the best sources because they are interested in your success. They will talk your business up to their friends and associates. They can also act as advisors if you wish.

Not to look a gift horse in the mouth, but check out any potential private investors. Make sure they have the money they claim to have (ask around and run a credit check). If they have invested in other companies, talk to the owners and find out if the investor stuck with them, aided their success, etc.

Bank Loans

Unless you are a well-established businessperson, with a lint-free credit rating and a chubby checking/savings account, a bank will not lend you money to start a business. Banks seldom lend anyone start-up capital for a new business. If they do, they usually expect you to have raised at least 50 percent of the money you need (from your own savings and private investors, etc.).

As your business proves itself, you may want to take out a loan for working or expansion capital. If you've been keeping in contact with your banker, then you stand a better chance of getting the loan. Banks rely considerably on past and present account relationships. They will, generally, turn down a loan request if (1) you have been slow to repay past personal loans or have overdrawn your account with any regularity; or (2) you do not have an account with the bank and none is likely to evolve from the loan. Banks want interest from loans, but they also want your continuing business.

To grant a loan, a bank must be impressed with your character, integrity, and business credentials. They must be satisfied that you have marketable collateral although they are *not* looking to liquidate that collateral. They want the repayment of the loan with interest and must be confident in your ability to do so. Be sure to keep the loan officer informed of your progress, or lack of it, after the loan is issued. If you have already established a good relationship with your banker, even if she cannot grant a loan she may be able to recommend local private investors.

If your application for a loan is refused, ask why. Banks are required by law to tell you and you have a right to know.*

WOMEN'S BANKS

Women's banks are opening all over the country, but basically, they do not differ from any other commercial banks. Loans are granted on the basis of credit worthiness, without favoritism for women or discrimination against them. In other words, women's banks are not giving women an extra shake; they are giving them a fair shake. If you want a loan, you must be superprepared to show why you need it and how you intend to pay it back.

COLLATERAL

You are at the core of your banker's assessment of your company. The success of your business (and repayment of the loan) depends on you. If your business lacks adequate tangible assets (accounts receivable, equipment, inventory), then you, as owner, must guarantee the loan by putting up personal property.

---

* Banks differ in their policies regarding loans. If one bank turns you away, another may be more sympathetic, so keep trying. If you are turned down by two banks, you can then apply for a Small Business Administration loan.

In addition, the National Association of Women Business Owners (NAWBO) *Newsletter* reports: "In arriving at the decision to grant or deny credit, the commercial credit lender relies on commercial reporting services, such as Dun & Bradstreet and Equifax, Inc., in the collection and evaluation of information concerning credit-worthiness. Please notify the Senate Small Business Committee if you feel you have been unreasonably denied credit, or the business of suppliers, as a result of what you consider to be an unfair credit report compiled by a commercial reporting service. Write the Senate Small Business Committee, Minority Staff, 424 Russell Building, Washington, D.C. 20510."

In assessing your collateral, you must appraise your assets the way a banker would. A 1959 Chevy and Granny's hand-stitched crazy quilt won't open a banker's purse strings, even if these items are priceless to you. Collateral must be readily marketable—for example, business accounts receivable, inventory, real estate, stocks and bonds, life insurance policies, equipment, machinery, or any other tangible property with real value.

The collateral must be readily assignable, belonging to you outright with no hazy legal titles.* Real estate, life insurance, and so forth must be in your name.

Then, there must be a sufficient margin between the appraised value of your assets and the actual cash value (which can vary enormously, depending on the circumstances of the sale). Keep in mind the depreciation.†

Of course, all this is merely a formality, because if your banker suspects she will have to collect on it, you won't get the loan.

But what if you have no tangible assets to put up as security? Then you must have someone to co-sign the loan. This person can be a parent, sister, husband—any person closely connected with you who is willing to back you up by putting up the needed collateral that you and your business lack. They are not giving up money, but simply guaranteeing that they will stand beside you. If your business bombs out, then the co-signer remains responsible for the loan. If you wish, the co-signer can be designated as a silent, or limited, partner in your business.

It is not a positive experience to be informed that you alone are not a worthy investment, but nonetheless it happens and should be anticipated. To get a loan, you have to play your banker's game, or you lose out.

---

* Series E Savings Bonds, issued in your name, may not be transferred to anyone else.

† Margin guidelines vary, but a (high) general guide to figuring appraised/actual value would be considered as collateral: 75 percent of the value of stocks registered with the New York Stock Exchange or the American Stock Exchange, and 50 percent of the value of over-the-counter stocks; 80 percent of the value of corporate and municipal bonds, 90 percent for Treasury bonds and notes, and 95 percent of the value of cash items.

INTEREST

When a loan is granted, you must agree to pay a certain percentage of interest. Interest rates bob up and down like bubbles in the economy, and banks adjust their rates to compete. If money is in short supply, the rates go up; when things ease up, the percentage goes down. However, if your interest rate is 8 percent and your bank's rate goes above or below that percentage, you still pay the loan off at the agreed-upon 8 percent.

LOAN REPAYMENT

No banker on earth will approve a loan if she thinks the repayment will require too long a time or will come from collecting your collateral. If the projected cash flow of your business does not look healthy enough to guarantee repayment, then your loan will be turned down. A loan is never feasible if, in repaying it, your daily operating account runs bone dry.

Equity Financing—for Corporations

A small-business corporation, even if it's still in the idea stage, has a good chance of raising capital, but only if you have already established close contacts in the business community and have a solid background in the area of your proposed business. For equity financing, you should consult a lawyer, but a *private offering* of shares of stock (no more than twenty-five people may be approached to invest) need not be registered with the Securities and Exchange Commission (SEC).*

Venture capitalists are professional investors who give advice and money in return for stock in your company. However, your only hope of attracting this sort of investment is if you have a big business idea that may ultimately grow into a multimillion-dollar company.

---

* Dealing with the SEC is time-consuming and expensive in terms of legal and accounting fees. A *public offering* (not generally considered for small businesses), involving the offer of stock to more than twenty-five people, is required by law to be registered with the SEC.

You should continue to maintain controlling interest of your company if you take on financial partners and shareholders. If you don't, you will have given up your most important asset, the freedom to run your business as you see fit.

The Small Business Administration

The SBA has information (including management consulting services)—but not much money to offer women. As of this writing, about 14.3 percent of its loans go to women.* So far it does not consider women generally eligible for Economic Opportunity loans, available to people unable to acquire financing through other channels. Its money seems to favor one-man (yes, *man*) proprietorships and/or minority groups (a category in which it does not include women).

To qualify for an SBA loan, you must have been turned down by one bank (two in cities with a population over 200,000) and still feel that you deserve a loan. The SBA also sponsors "bank participation" loans in which it guarantees up to 90 percent of the bank loan up to $500,000.

The SBA is changing its policies toward women. It's still not easy to obtain financing from it, but if you have a marketable plan and patience, keep beating on its door, and don't let it beat you down. Be prepared for a lot of red tape and much back-and-forthing. SBA loans take time to come through (from six months to a year), and if approved, you will be subject to various restrictions. The SBA seldom provides venture capital.

Small Business Investment Companies

SBA-approved small-business investment companies (SBIC) and the Minority Enterprise Small Business Investment Com-

---

* This is a step in the right direction. For the first quarter of the 1979 fiscal year, the SBA has targeted $100 million for guaranteed business loans to women. Between October 1, 1976 and June 30, 1977, 14.3 percent of the SBA's business loans went to women, an increase of 3.3 percent over the previous year and nearly 7 times higher than 1972. In 1977, the SBA's New York office turned down half of the loan requests it received. Those denied loans lacked collateral, reassuring repayment prospects, or enough of their own capital (usually 15 to 40 percent of the total financing).

pany (MESBIC) are privately organized and managed. The lending policies vary considerably between the companies, but they provide both equity financing and long-term loans, as well as financial and management planning.*

To get anywhere with these companies, you must bombard them with cold, hard facts covering every aspect of your business. Special emphasis must be on its anticipated success, with accurate accounting of how you will spend the money—down to the last penny—along with financial forecasts.

For the most part, these and other venture capital companies are interested only in ideas that could turn into major national companies within their industry within five to seven years. To supervise the first stages of a business, it usually costs an active venture capitalist a hefty amount per year in salaries, office costs, and other expenses. In return, venture capitalists hope for at least 20 percent return per year to justify the risk they take and the time spent in nurturing a new business. Most fledgling enterprises simply cannot offer that rate of return.

Finance Companies

At commercial finance companies, the interest rates are exorbitant, but they make higher-risk loans. Consider this *only* if your business is in a position to repay, yet still looks too speculative to more conservative institutions.

Feminist Credit Unions

In the past few years, women around the country have begun organizing credit unions to make funds available to people who have trouble getting money from traditional lenders.†

---

* For more information and a list of local SBICs, write to the National Association of Small Business Investment Companies, 512 Washington Building, 1435 G Street, N.W., Washington, D.C. 20005.

† To locate credit unions in your area, consult Yellow Pages, your local NOW chapter or women business owners' association. Or contact the Feminist Economic Alliance, c/o Massachusetts Feminist Federal Credit Union, 186½ Hampshire Street, Cambridge, Massachusetts 02139.

However, in general there are only small amounts available, usually for individual borrowers, not businesses. Since feminist credit unions try to charge low interest rates and have little margin for bad loans, they must carefully evaluate a person's ability to repay.

Other Possible Money Sources

Other business people, such as suppliers of materials (wholesalers, retailers, or manufacturers) might be interested in considering your business as a mini-subsidiary.

Rounding up enough clients for your services who are willing to pay you in advance for their first job is another possibility. This would not provide you with much working capital, though, or anything to fall back on when you screech into your first slump.

EXPANSION FINANCING

Even after your business is underway and the profits are rolling in, there will come times when you need growth money (for newer equipment, larger space, increased inventory, new product development, etc.). Sometimes you just need working capital while you wait for customers to pay their bills. Don't panic. Second-round financing is easier to get since you've established your track record. The moneylenders can look at your business records and financial statements and see what's actually happening.

At this point, seek out your local banker. Invite the loan officer over to see your business. If you've been diligent and provided her with your financial statements right along, she'll know when you're ready to ask for help. Banks are much more willing to lend money for expansion since the risk involved is greatly reduced.

Anyone interested in founding a feminist credit union should write to the Feminist Economic Network (FEN), Post Office Box 20008, Detroit, Michigan 48220. The network also has training programs and consulting sessions for feminist enterprises, and publishes a newsletter, *The Bi-Monthly Regulator.*

Venture capitalists also provide growth money because the business is established. They will take less interest or stock than for a new enterprise.

The SBA also helps with expansion or assistance capital.

To find outside investors, it is important that you:

1. Plan your strategy and write out your presentation. Since your business has no history, you can predict a rosy future, so long as you have written projections to back it up.

2. Be willing to invest your own money, talent, and energy in your project. This is the best way to convince skeptics that you won't grow tired of the business.

3. Dress to look the way moneylenders would want you to look—successful. The more you look as if you don't need the money, the better your chances. Not that you have to Pucci and Gucci yourself up—just present yourself to your best advantage.

4. Look them in the eye. Be confident, enthusiastic, and optimistic, and honest in admitting any limitations or speculations about your plan.

Female entrepreneurs stand a better chance of raising start-up capital from their own savings, and friends, relatives, and close contacts who believe in their abilities. After a while, when the business gathers momentum, the conventional moneylenders will be more receptive.

Hang in there, and don't get discouraged. It may take time, but if you've got a super idea, then you'll find someone to gamble on you. In the meantime, keep focusing on your goals and regard red tape for what it is—a nuisance. The more hurdles you are forced to jump, the stronger you'll be at the end of the race.

10

ADVERTISING AND PUBLICITY: MUCH ADO ABOUT SOMETHING

There is only one thing in the world worse than being talked about, and that is not being talked about.

Oscar Wilde

THE MAKING OF AN AD

Advertising is an integral part of business. Like the neighborhood dowager who introduces newcomers to the community, an advertisement announces the arrival of your business. And advertising has a continuing function: to *introduce* a product or service; to *inform* the public of its features; to *persuade* people to try it; and, as time goes by, to *keep reminding* your public that you're still around and better than ever.

Advertising is only as successful as the product or service it is promoting. No amount of advertising will work if your shop is inaccessible, poorly stocked or staffed, or not open at convenient times. The point of advertising is to bring in new customers; you have to be equipped to handle them once they're there, or you'll lose them forever.

The Advertising Budget

The less you can afford an ad campaign, the more you probably need one. Without advertising, people won't know you're out there. Of course, many businesses can make a go of it from publicity and word of mouth, especially if they are situated in prime high-traffic locations. But sooner or later, business owners realize that they cannot drift. If they are to grow and to attract new clients continually, they must advertise.

Have your accountant help you plan a monthly advertising budget, projected at least six months in advance. There are no hard-and-fast rules for establishing an ad budget. Generally, it is anything from 2 to 10 percent of your estimated yearly gross. Keep at least 5 percent of that budget aside for special events (holiday celebrations, community activities, etc.). Spread the rest out in a consistent pattern (but don't spread yourself too thin). Steady advertising brings in customers. The more modest your budget, the more carefully you must chart your long-range campaign. Ads must be repetitive to be effective. Don't bother to advertise if you cannot afford a minimum of four ads a year.

Your advertising expenses will fall into two general categories: production and media. Production expenses include typesetting, photostating, art, copy, layout, and materials, when you are dealing with print. Broadcast production expenses run to things like studio time, equipment rental, tape, talent, and labor.

Media expenses are the cost of buying time or space in the medium that has been selected to present your message. Possibilities include television, radio, newspapers, magazines and periodicals, and others, which will be discussed in this chapter. In estimating your budget, make a list of the media available to you, and obtain rate sheets from them. Use these to determine the best places for *you* to advertise, and divide your monthly budget among them.

Make a chart, divided into months. Then list, in columns, the medium, cost of ad, size or length of ad, date ad must be submitted, and date ad will run. Later, include a description of the ad itself in order to keep track of what runs where.

Test your advertising ideas (and mock-ups of ads) on friends and business associates to get personal reactions as to which ads have the most impact.

Prepare several ads and rotate them, so that people won't tire of the same old thing. Budget for your peak season by allocating extra funds for heavier penetration at that time.

Cooperative Advertising

Ads jointly placed by more than one advertiser are cooperative ads. Often they are used by a store or service and its dealer/distributor, or supplier. Sometimes all the stores in a certain location will go in together on an ad. Many large manufacturers of brand-name merchandise often offer co-op advertising packages to shops that buy from them. Sometimes the manufacturer will pay the majority of the ad space cost in return for a featured store location for the merchandise. For a new business, this kind of advertising helps associate your name with already established operations and saves money into the bargain.

Advertising Strategy

To create an advertising strategy, start by answering questions about the nature of your business and your market.

First, determine just who *you* are. In what price range are your products or services? Is your emphasis on price, or on quality and service? What exactly are you selling? Is it one thing, or many? Are you easily accessible? What extras do you want to tell the public about?

Once you're sure who you are, decide who *they* are. What consumer group are you going after? When you've defined your potential market, then focus your attention on a prototype. Visualize this person, and direct your ads to her or him.

Ads are the ambassadors of your business. They must attract, inform, and establish the image that you want to project. Keep that prototypical client in mind while you're reveling in creative brainstorming; remember, what strikes you as devilishly sophisticated and snappy might not be right for your market.

Since many small-business owners handle their own advertising out of necessity, it's a good idea to take some evening courses in advertising and public relations. The more you know, the fewer costly mistakes you'll make.

The Copy

You have the choice of institutional or product advertising. The institutional ad is simply a general reminder to the public that your business exists, giving business name, address, business slogan (if you have one), and hours you are open. The product ad tells the reader about a specific service or piece of merchandise. In general, keep it simple. Those full-page ads chock-full of copy work only for certain very special cases. The quicker you can make your point, the better are your chances of getting it across. Go to the library, and check local ads for competitive businesses for the past year. Make note of how often they advertised, the size of the ads, how varied they were, etc. This will help you form your own campaign.

Your ad may vary depending on the medium you're running it in. Once you've picked the medium and decided on the size of your ad, look through the publication and see what ads catch your attention. Study them, learn from them. What makes them work? Many publications have media departments to help small advertisers create an ad, demonstrating what sort of message can be effective in the amount of space purchased.

A good format to follow is this:

> Headline. An eye-catching succinct phrase or question.
> Body. The sell. In as few words as possible, let the world know what you have and why they want it. Be believable and clear. Mention your product or company by name.
> Wrap-up. Price (if it's a selling point). List any extra incentives or other details. Tell how to buy or obtain more facts about the product or service.
> Finale. Mention any available catalog or brochure. Give company name, address, telephone number, and business hours. If you have a company logo, use it here.

For short-term ads (running in daily newspapers, weekly journals, local broadcast spots) you can tie in the weather, seasons, holidays, current events, or community activities with your copy. Keep tuned in to any special local or national happenings which are synergistic to your business. If you're writing broadcast copy to be delivered live by an announcer or disc jockey, keep her voice and style in mind.

In general, back up superlatives with facts, keep the name of your company up front, emphasize your advantages over the competition. Aim for impact and individuality in the copy and simplicity and consistency in the style.

The Art

In advertising terms, art is anything visual—drawing, painting, photography, even type style and layout. But a cluttered ad will defeat your message.

Art, like copy, should be kept simple. If you use an illustration, make sure it is persuasive and descriptive. Keep to simple line drawings, with no shading. Detailed sketches are harder to reproduce clearly. Check the quality of reproduction in the publication your ad will be running in. Photographs, for instance, do not often reproduce well in small-space newspaper ads. If you decide to use a photo (e.g., to advertise in the shop-by-mail sections in magazines), hire a professional photographer to take clear, well-lighted eight-by-ten-inch photos to accompany your ad. (The magazine will stat them down to correct proportions for your ad.) Omit illustrations unless they serve a purpose; otherwise, they'll just crowd the space and distract from the copy.

If you are having your copy typeset, choose a style that complements the message. Keep legibility in mind—you may be crazy about Old English lettering, but the public won't wade through a whole paragraph of it.

A publication's advertising or media department can advise you on typefaces and the use of borders. It will also inform you whether a cut (metal image) of your logo is necessary for its printer. If a cut is needed, you'll be charged a nominal fee for it.

Design your ads so that they stand out from the rest of the page. Study the competition; see what's being done, glean the best points, and understand what makes them good. Then use that background to do something even better and *different*.

Production

Who will do your ads? You will. In the beginning, while your budget is small, it probably won't make economic sense to go to an outside agency. And who knows better than you what you want to say?

If you really don't feel up to it, then hire someone to do it as inexpensively as possible. Check art and writing classes at local colleges, or look for a talented free-lancer. Talk to friends, and pick their brains for ideas.

Advertising departments of many newspapers and small magazines offer help in preparation of copy, artwork, and layout. Talk to them after you have written up a rough ad, and take advantage of their assistance.

For information on advertising in general and advertising ethics, contact your local Chamber of Commerce, Better Business Bureau, and trade associations.

If you're going to produce the ad yourself, start with the concept. Always stress the advantages of the product, never the product itself. For example, suppose you have invented a revolutionary little gadget. Don't say, "Introducing the Terrific Do-Everything Gadget . . . does fifty different things. Buy one today!" Vague claims don't leave a trail of afterimage. Present the facts: "Introducing the Terrific Do-Everything Gadget . . . it pops corn, cleans dentures, shreds cabbage, dyes Easter eggs, and makes peanut butter sandwiches *in ten seconds!*" People must be able to focus on a product in relation to their needs.

When you've got your copy, have it typeset or varityped. (Discuss the various methods with your printer, along with costs.) Or do it yourself with a good typewriter and press type. In some instances, hand lettering may even give the effect you're looking for.

If you are hiring an artist or photographer, look at her work first. Choose someone whose style complements your product and image. Make sure the fee is established in advance and fits your budget. Be clear as to whether there will be any additional charge for supplies and expenses. Young talent is usually the best for a small budget. Just be sure to explain exactly what you want, and keep an eye on the work in progress.

Do several rough layouts, to see what works the best. Experiment with different sizes for your headline; play around with ways of cropping and placing the artwork. Maybe you'll want to use a decorative border.

When you have done it the way you want it, assemble the ingredients on mat or illustration board. To work in different sizes, you can have your art and copy reduced or enlarged by photostat. Spread rubber cement on both surfaces, and let them dry before positioning.

For precision work, tear a piece of tracing paper or onion skin in half, and place the pieces slightly overlapping onto the mat board after the cement is dry. The tracing paper will not stick to the dried rubber cement, and it allows you to see through to your layout markings on the mat board, so that you can position things exactly where you want them. Then place the section of art or copy you're working with in position, and slip out one of the pieces of tracing paper from beneath it. When you've pressed that securely into place, slip out the other piece of tracing paper and smooth out the rest.

When the layout is complete, have it photostated to size. Then you can keep the original and give the "camera ready" copy to the publication. Don't have a printer make up permanent plates unless you plan to run the same ad all the time.

Advertising Agencies

Should the day come when you want and can afford an agency, gravitate to a small one. Small businesses are often treated like ugly stepchildren at the large successful agencies.

Before selecting an ad agency, talk to several. Describe your needs and your budget. Look at samples of their work, especially campaigns for businesses with budgets similar to yours. Follow the progression of ads for the same client, noting originality and continuity. Have them give you an idea of what they think they can do for you. Settle on an agency that will give you the most attention and best quality.

Ad agencies exist to inject professional creativity into your ads and to save you time and headaches. They conceive, execute, and supervise the ad from start to finish. All you have to do is nod with approval and pay the bills.

When an agency places your ad, the cost to you is the same as if you placed it yourself. The agency takes a 15 percent commission from the publication or station. This is where the agency makes its money, so the more you advertise, the more enthusiastic about your account the agency is likely to be.

You pay the agency for its expenses in preparing the ad. If the ad yields more than $150 in commission, then copy and layout should be free. All additional expenses—printing, artwork, photography, etc.—are billed to you at a 20 percent markup.

An agency will save you time and mistakes and give your ads a professional look. But until you're in the bucks, learn about advertising by doing it yourself—or with a little help from your friends.

WHERE TO ADVERTISE

Evaluate all media, and decide which ones reach your prospective market most effectively.

Newspapers

This category includes dailies, weeklies, biweeklies, Sunday editions, shoppers, neighborhood newspapers. Get rate sheets and circulation data on every publication in your area. See how well they report local news for a clue to the extent and nature of their readership. Look into special interest journals, foreign-language papers, publications of clubs, societies and churches, theater and summer stock programs.

Display ads can be a fraction of a page (a half-page, an eighth, a sixteenth, etc.) or sold by the column inch. A column inch is one-inch deep (fourteen lines) and the width of the column in the publication.

Rates decrease as you increase the volume of ads you place. Classified listings are usually money-wasters, unless the publication is particularly suited to them.

Newspaper advertising must be frequent. Consider what kind of schedule will be most effective for your business. Mondays and Tuesdays are good for services, Wednesdays through Sundays best for store advertising. Newspapers provide intensive coverage and quick response.

Before you sign a publication's space contract, make sure you understand the conditions, costs, and termination clause. Find out what it will cost if you decide you want to get out of the commitment.

Magazines

CONSUMER MAGAZINES

Many national magazines publish regional editions.* If your business has a large enough appeal, look into these. They may cover several states, a single state, or even a large metropolitan/suburban area.

And look into special interest magazines. If there is one that ties in with your product or service, it would be worth considering.

BUSINESS MAGAZINES

Business and trade publications are a good way of letting others know what you're doing. Consult the *Standard Rate and Data* (both the business publications issue and the consumer magazine book).†

If you're not familiar with the magazine you're considering,

---

* To acquire names and addresses, check your library for the following comprehensive publications: *Editor & Publisher International Yearbook*; *Ayer's Directory of Newspapers and Periodicals*; *Radio Annual and TV Yearbook*; *Bacon's Publicity Checker*; *The Gebbie Press House Magazine Directory* (lists house organs of large corporations); and *Standard Rate and Data*.

† Check your library, or try to get an old copy from an ad agency—they usually throw back issues out as new ones arrive. The Department of Commerce also publishes a state-by-state list of trade publications.

have them send you circulation data,* rates, and a copy of a back issue. Evaluate it for quality, number of advertisers, and decide whether it will be a good platform for your message.

LOCAL MAGAZINES

Look into local business publications, sponsored by the Chamber of Commerce and local trade associations. Also check out club, alumnae, college organization, and visitor magazines.

Magazine rates vary widely. Many offer discounts based on volume, frequency, and continuity. Magazine rates usually go by pages and fractions of pages, although some offer classified and column-inch rates.

Magazines have a longer reading life than newspapers, and special interest magazines are often kept on file, instead of being thrown out. General interest magazines attract more readers per copy, but their readership's interests are less carefully pinpointed.

Classified Directories

The Yellow Pages is the most famous of these. When you take out a business phone, you are allowed one free listing. But if you offer a variety of products or services, consider placing ads under more than one category. It costs extra, but people do use the Yellow Pages. A telephone company representative will give you a cost breakdown for bold-type listings, column-inch and display ads. (You can also pay to have bold type in your White Pages listing.) Instead of a flat yearly rate, you pay the telephone company in monthly installments.

Other classified media include general industrial directories for all industries or types of products.

Radio and Television

Many community stations offer reasonable rates for local time slots. Rates vary greatly, depending on the time of day and the

---

* Make sure the statistics quoted are audited or sworn-circulation statements.

length of the spot. Radio is apt to be less expensive, both in terms of production costs and media costs, but check with all your local stations for particulars.

Different types of shows reach different audiences. Aim for the market you want and the best time of day to reach it. A late-late-show time slot is inexpensive and fine if your product appeals to a college audience, but not worth the expense if you're trying to sell to pre-teen-agers.

To have any impact, you must advertise regularly. Don't waste your money on a one-shot radio ad.

Broadcast advertising makes a strong impression. If you are seriously considering TV and radio, don't rush into it. Start timing ads to see how much you can get effectively into a minute, thirty seconds, or ten seconds. Study the messages that get across to you, and break down their ingredients. Count the number of times the product's name is mentioned during a commercial.

In preparing a commercial for TV, you can keep costs down by using a series of still pictures with a voice-over announcer. Or rent videotape equipment and stage a mini-production. Use the same guideline you use in print advertising: keep it simple. Don't try to jam in too much.

Make sure the announcer's voice is easily understood; the less colloquial, the better. For radio, you can either tape an ad or submit copy to be read by the announcer or disc jockey on the air. In some local markets this can also be done with television.

Mailers and Brochures

Follow the same thought patterns and physical steps for preparing a print ad and producing a brochure, catalog, mailer, or flyer. Before you begin, talk to a printer about sizes. It's cheaper if the piece fits a standard envelope, preferably an envelope the size of your stationery. There are a number of shapes to consider, too—invitation, presentation, accordion, one page, etc. Ask to see samples of brochures, not only to evaluate printing quality but also to get ideas.

Get a price estimate. The printer will figure it for you based on the size of the piece, the paper stock you choose, the number of colors, and the quantity of the run. Standard sizes are less expensive, and the fewer colors you use, the less it will cost you (see Chapter 4, under the heading "Logo, Stationery, and Business Cards"). Don't forget the folding, which is also done and charged for by the printer.

Some printers offer lower prices for four-color printing by running a batch of orders together on a large press. This is economical, but it takes longer (the printer will wait until she has enough separate orders), and often you won't get perfect color matching. There is also a three-color for two process, which applies to two-sided printing. (The printer can print black plus one color on the first side, for example, and then black plus another color on the reverse. When folded properly, it can be very effective.)

Consider the possibility of designing self-mailers. These are brochures or other mailing pieces that can be sent without an envelope; they are simply folded, stamped, and addressed.

Catalogs

If you provide a number of products or services, or sell by mail order, put together a catalog. Catalogs must be well-organized, with items grouped according to category. (Some with multiple application may be repeated in several categories.) Products can also be classified by price range, seasonal sales, etc.

In the copy, be brief, accurate, and catchy. Use clear, simple illustration and an uncluttered layout. The cover of your catalog should be eye-grabbing and colorful, even if the inside contents are in black and white. If you offer many items, you might consider adding an index page for your customers' convenience.

Be sure to feature the company name and address, preferably on the front and back covers. If items can be ordered by mail, or additional information requested, include order cards or relevant instructions.

Print "catalog" on the outside of the mailing envelope. Make up a dummy catalog with the paper stock you will be using and have it priced at the Post Office; if you're just over one price plateau, maybe you can cut down the size a little. Postage adds up.

There is a lot of copy in a catalog and a lot of room for

typographical errors. When you have your copy ready for the printer, check it over thoroughly. Make copies of it and give them to friends to proofread. Catch mistakes before they go to press in order to avoid expensive and time-consuming resetting.

Shop-by-Mail Advertising

If you are selling a product, consider advertising in the shop-by-mail sections located in the backs of many consumer magazines. In this way, you can offer your product via direct mail, prepaid with postage costs included. Be sure to include a clear photo or sketch of the product you're offering. Check with your Post Office to obtain accurate shipping fees for the product (including all the packaging).

In order to gauge success with your ads, instigate a coding system to monitor your ads. With your mailing address, have the customer write to Dept. A (B, C, and so forth). Have a different code for each magazine and each issue you advertise in. This is how you will be able to keep track of publications (and months) which are bringing in the most orders. Shop-by-mail advertising is expensive, for the most part, so don't go overboard until you have determined the mail-order popularity of your product. Also, you must be set up to ship your product as soon as the orders start flowing in; current law stipulates that the order be filled within three weeks.

Direct Mail

This is advertising sent through the mail to a selected group of customers. It can be useful for soliciting mail- or phone-order business; announcing new products or services, and special events like sales; notification of price changes; and public relations via holiday greetings, etc.

Direct mail is expensive. An average piece of mailing costs about twenty-five cents for paper, printing, and postage. There is the chance of a full minute of someone's attention and the risk of an immediate throwaway. Keep it individual, personal, and never address it to "Occupant."

DIRECT RESPONSE MAIL

The aim is to get potential customers to respond *now*, via return postcard for orders or more information. You could also enclose a questionnaire or a quiz. There are ad agencies whose specialty is determining the best kind of direct response mailing for your needs.*

THE USE OF MAILING LISTS

A mailing is only as good as its mailing list. It can be costly and ineffective if you don't hit the right market for your product, or if three out of five persons have moved.

You can either build your own list (preferable and cheaper) or purchase one (desirable if you're looking for special groups of people).

To build your own, ask for lists from social clubs, or any organization you belong to, the Chamber of Commerce, charity groups, your child's school list, or the local college, and church lists. Noncompetitive organizations are easier to approach than the business community. You can also check directories and newspaper notices. Once you've started in business, get the names and addresses of all customers. Sponsor a contest or sweepstakes, in which the participants must provide name and address.

The rental or purchase of names from mailing list houses (and some magazine publishers) provides you with general lists of names or specialized lists according to categories of people. But it is expensive, and the lists go out of date quickly. Make sure you get recommendations for a reliable company before laying out money.† And make one person on your staff responsible for keeping the lists up to date.

---

* To obtain names of local members of the Women's Direct Response Group, contact, Beacon Direct Response, 666 Fifth Avenue, New York, New York 10019. For more information in general, contact Direct Mail Marketing Association, 6 East Forty-third Street, New York, New York 10017.

† The Small Business Administration publishes several useful booklets: Small Business Bibliography no. 29, *National Mailing List Houses;* Small Business Bibliography no. 3, *Selling by Mail Order*, Small Business Bibliography no. 13, *National Directories for Use in Marketing.* Available from the Small Business Administration, Washington, D.C. 20416, or your nearest local office. Mailing lists cost around twenty-five to thirty-five dollars per thousand names; returns are about 5 to 10 percent for selective lists, 2 percent for more general sets of names.

First class mail is automatically forwarded to a new address or returned to you (make sure to include the return address). It's expensive, so use it only for personalized mailing pieces. Third or fourth class (parcel post) provides cheaper rates, although you must pay an extra fee to have the mail forwarded or returned. Include on the envelope "Return or Forwarding Postage Guaranteed." For bulk mailings you must obtain a permit, and there are certain regulations to be complied with before you can get a bulk mailing license. Talk to the Post Office for current rates and rules.

Direct Advertising

This is distinguished from direct mail because it is distributed in person, from house to house (under doors or attached to knobs), or handed out in the street. It also includes "take-one" cards which are displayed by cash registers or on counters in stores. These handbills, flyers, and other types of throwaways are basically unsatisfactory and cause litter. Note that it is illegal to place direct advertising pieces in mail boxes.

Other Forms of Advertising

This category includes notices on bulletin boards, posters, billboard ads, transit ads, novelty giveaways (with your name imprinted) like matches, T-shirts, calendars, pens, memo books, buttons, ashtrays, and so forth. The best novelties are the ones that tie in with your business. For example, if you run a summer stock company, you might send out calendars featuring your production schedules. This kind of advertising can be expensive, but if it seems to answer your needs, it could be worthwhile.

PUBLIC RELATIONS AND PUBLICITY

A business has to keep its name in front of the public. Advertising is a constant, steadily building wave—publicity is the foam on top. It attracts attention, enhances your prestige, and it's free!

The snare is that people tend to become giddy in the limelight. Before they've used the publicity to their best advantage, it has floated away like a child's soap bubbles in the summer sky. People pay greatest heed to publicity when they can connect it with ads they've already seen. Publicity complements paid advertising but should never be a total substitute for it.

With ads, you are in control of what is said about your business. With publicity, you can be misquoted, or the wrong emphasis can be placed on your activities. It's rather like producing a play. When the reviews come out, they may be good or bad, but when you run ads afterward, you can assemble all the favorable quotes and present the show to its best advantage.

Visual Appearance of Shop or Office

The best long-term public relations for your business is the overall impression you give to your customers. A retail shop should maintain clean display windows, and see to it that displays are creative and changed frequently. The staff should be friendly and speak to each customer who enters. As the owner, make a point of introducing yourself and learning customers' names. The shop itself should be well-decorated, clean, bright, freshly painted, with good layout and sound (the type of background music you use should conform to your image; keep it low enough so as not to be intrusive).

The same rules apply to an office. The environment should be attractive; the staff, friendly and accommodating. Clients should be made to feel comfortable, especially if they have to wait to see you. Offer coffee, and keep up-to-date publications in your reception area.

Public Relations

Public relations is relating to the public—for recognition. It can be as seemingly insignificant as a smile or a thank-you note or as complex as staging a parade. PR is the sum total of everything that creates a favorable personality for your business.

Public relations must be planned. When handling PR, you or the person you designate must be confident, patient, friendly, and good with details and follow-through. This shouldn't be difficult; after all, you are selling something you believe in. There are seven basic steps to building a PR campaign:

1. Define your objectives (more specifically than "getting more clients"). What exactly are you after? What do people think of you? Exactly what can a campaign do for your business?
2. Create your central ideas. Then relate them to your needs, altering or expanding them. Keep in mind the people you are trying to reach.
3. Identify your public. Is it classified into age, sex, occupation, community, or a special interest group?
4. Select the media. Media does not just mean print or radio/television. It can be any form you use to reach your public with a message. Anything from printed brochures, special displays, door-to-door samples, contests, and giveaways to parades and press parties. *Always measure your ideas against your ability (and budget)* to execute them. A haphazardly planned, poorly executed scheme will work against your image. Be sure to notify the media well in advance of the event you want them to cover.
5. Set a timetable. It is important to know how much time the project will take, from start to finish.
6. Carry out the program. Schedule tasks with specific deadlines. Let each person know what she is to do and what it means to the overall project.
7. Evaluate results. Evaluation is the key factor to public relations. Check to see how effective your campaign has been and if it accomplished what you set out to do.

If you have information to share on any facet of your business, you might consider writing an article or even a short weekly column for a small local paper on a subject having nothing whatsoever to do with your business.

You can participate in community events, beautification programs, and so forth. Every positive intangible thing that you do, whether directly connected with your business or not, improves your image. And that's public relations—communications (subtle or otherwise) reflecting the public image of your business.

Hiring a PR Agency or Press Agent

Like everything else, a small-business owner must think in terms of getting her own publicity or hiring a talented freelancer. An agency would cost you anywhere from five hundred dollars a month on up. Besides, you have a key ingredient for success going for you: enthusiasm. No one will ever be able to love your business more, or sell your business better, than you.

Getting Publicity

Publicity comes in two packages. First, it swoops down from your lucky star: an editor or writer is intrigued by your ads or gets word through the grapevine that you're the only person in town who still weaves straw into gold. She calls you up for an interview or puts you on the local TV or radio talk show, and presto! Instant celebrity.

Remember, when you are interviewed, to accentuate your positives. This is no time for modesty. Make a list beforehand of things you want to emphasize, and stick to it. *You* control what you say during the interview; after that, the writer takes over. Don't say *anything* you wouldn't want printed. Good interviews come from good preparation—have answers ready for inevitable questions. You can psych out what an interviewer will ask by looking at your business as news. What aspects will make snappy reading?

Second, you can make your own luck. Come up with the most fascinating and newsworthy features of your business, and try to generate your own publicity. The points stressed might be you, what you do, who your clients are, or special announcements, like your grand opening.

Put it together into a friendly presentation, and call up

every local paper and talk show.* Don't hesitate to take advantage of any personal contacts for introductions to prestigious people at these places. Contact news, public affairs, and special feature departments at newspapers and radio and TV stations.

Tell them, in capsule form, why they should be interested in your business. Don't be shy about mentioning your potential fascination to their readers. In general, editors, columnists, talk show producers, and talent coordinators welcome news. If they think you've got something to say, they will be interested.

Don't hit just one place; go to every publication and station in town. Don't omit company employee newspapers (house organs) and alumnae magazines. If you get turned down, go back in six months, to another editor or department, or with a new twist.

Be wary, by the way, of any publication that offers you free publicity for advertising there.

Press (News) Releases

Another way to get written up is to issue press releases to local media. Be organized, and send them out as new developments occur. Anything you do that can be turned into a juicy news tidbit should be typed up and sent out. Develop your own editorial contacts, so that the releases can be directed to the proper people.

Keep an up-to-date press file of names and addresses of every media person in town who might be interested in your business or event. Find out deadline times for publications, and jot down this information as well. Get sample news releases from your local newspapers, and use them as a guideline for setting up your own format.

HOW TO WRITE A RELEASE

A press release is news, not an ad. So you must present your business as news. The content must be subtle, accurate, and

---

* If you think you have national, as well as local, appeal, get hold of *Bacon's Publicity Checker*, which lists every magazine and periodical in the United States and Canada, according to category. Check with your library, or write to H. R. Bacon and Co., 14 East Jackson Boulevard, Chicago, Illinois 60605.

never overstated. Avoid superlatives. Outline the most interesting side of your business in a few sentences. Aim for attracting the editor's immediate attention (or your carefully constructed chatter will be chucked into oblivion). Keep your release *brief and concise.* In the first paragraph, include the who, what, where, when, and how. Stress your major points, and back them up with facts. Then pep up the release with colorful descriptions, and round it out with minor details.

The release should be typed (double-spaced) on your company's stationery. At the top, type in caps "FOR IMMEDIATE RELEASE (date)." At the end, include your name as publicity director and a telephone number where you can be contacted for further information. Limit it to two pages, maximum.

Include a black-and-white glossy photograph whenever possible; the five-by-seven size is adequate. (Include a piece of cardboard in the envelope so that the photo won't be bent in the mail.) Type your name, address, and pertinent information (or caption) for the photo on a self-stick label, and attach it to the back of the picture. Don't write directly on the photo, or you may damage it for reproduction.

You would never let a child grow up without taking pictures of her development; the same should be true for your business. In general, think in terms of taking photos every six months or so. Never miss an opportunity to photograph a newsworthy business event.

Photographs can perk up your selling presentation and decorate your walls (people love to look at them). Often, a small publication will write about you but, lacking a photography budget, will request a picture from you to run with the piece. If you have one on hand, then you get twice as much space for the article.

Before a photography session, consider the most visual aspects of your business. Avoid sitting at a desk with telephone in hand. Action pictures are the most dynamic, even if the event has to be staged for the purpose of the photograph. And if you are hiring a professional photographer, plan your shots beforehand and don't waste time.

NEWS RELEASE OPPORTUNITIES

Keep inventing newsworthy extras that your business can offer. A gift shop might stock scissors for southpaws, and a pet store could add an aquarium-decorating service. For publicity's sake, a caterer could demonstrate ethnic hors d'oeuvres on a TV talk show.

In addition to your own imagination, there are standard events that merit press releases:

> Grand opening (or move to new headquarters)
> Adding new products or services
> Revealing a new business or manufacturing concept (for members of your trade or industry)
> Contests of all sorts
> Launching advertising or promotional campaigns
> Hirings and promotions
> Any publicity-worthy job or client
> Extracurricular events or community projects you are sponsoring
> Offering free brochures, informative booklets, or introductory kits
> Predictions of new trends (backed up by facts)
> Tie-ins with seasonal or charity events

Thinking up possible publicity angles should become as routine a consideration as advertising. Since publicity must be repetitive, like ads, it's a good idea to make up a yearly publicity calendar.

Maintain a relationship with your press and media contacts. Media people can change often—every six months or so. If you have specific names of contacts, call up every once in a while to check if they are still there or if they have been promoted. Be aware of their new titles, and always spell their names correctly.

Don't send one release and then forget it. Follow-up is important. The follow-up phone call should be short, informative, and cheerful. Remember, you're trying to make friends with another person. Keep up a dialogue with editors and media people. If they don't respond to your grand opening, hit them six months later with your expansion, after that with a new service, and later still, with a contest. Keep it rolling.

Once you have been written up or have appeared on a TV or radio show, call the person responsible to say how great the article or interview was. Or write a thank-you note.

Use your publicity and *keep on using it!* Have copies or

tearsheets prepared for special mailings, enclosures in billings, ads (especially the headlines or good quotes), and future press releases. Include publicity credits in your selling presentation. Once an editor sees that a story on you has been done elsewhere, he or she is more inclined not only to believe the story's authenticity, but also to follow up on it.

Publicity Stunts

It's often effective to come up with an unusual event or stunt; the more visual, the better. After all, everybody loves a parade, or someone dressed up as a gorilla, or whatever crazy scheme you can dream up and have the budget to afford. An offbeat visual stunt has a good chance of attracting TV film crews and newspaper photographers. Now that many TV news programs have expanded their air time, they are eager for local color stories to use as fillers.

The stunt should be related to your business or tied in with a season or community event. For example, if you own an antique clothes shop, why not throw an antique clothing fashion show and invite your customers and the press? If you want to charge admission to the event and donate the proceeds to charity, so much the better. Charity functions will get announced on radio community bulletin boards and written up in local community papers.

As always, send out a news release in plenty of time for the press to arrange for coverage. Make sure you include the subject of the event, date, time, and location, along with background information about the business for the editor's use in preparing the story.

Be imaginative. Remember, you are competing for press coverage with many other businesses and associations. Timing, as well as thorough planning, down to the last detail, is important. If the media covers an event that is poorly organized and doesn't quite come off, they are going to think twice about coming out next time. Again, remember Murphy's Law: what can go wrong will go wrong. Arrange for backup alternatives, including rain dates.

The Grand Opening Splash

Besides coordinating advertising and publicity with your opening, you might consider throwing a party for potential clients and members of the local media. Grand opening bashes are especially important for prestige businesses, like art galleries.

Hospitality wins admirers, and it doesn't have to cost a mint—beer and pretzels will do. Have it at your store or office; talk other businesses into furnishing you with supplies for credit or at discount. Or get local entertainment to help you out for the free publicity. Think of every angle. And reciprocate with other businesses throughout your career.

Other grand opening attention-getters might be a contest or raffle (give away a free product or service). You might have a car drive around town with a sign announcing your new existence. Have balloons or any other kind of giveaway printed with the name of your business.

Many newspapers and magazines have special sections or columns dealing with new products, new restaurants (reviews), or services. Find these and send a release to the editor. New-product columns are great for mail order as they will list your company name and address. And it's all *free!*

PUBLICITY CHECKLIST

Plan your publicity campaign well in advance, to allow the media enough time to arrange coverage.

Examine your campaign from every angle, to assure that it is zippy enough to attract coverage. Don't overlook any possibility for potential publicity. Be imaginative. If you can convince a local celebrity to attend your event, inform the press that he or she will be there. If you can tie your event in with another occasion or holiday celebration, so much the better.

Write a clear, informative press release, including the subject of the event, location, date, and time. Include the name and phone number of the person the press can contact for further information. (Try to designate one person to handle publicity, and cater to the needs of the press on the specific day of the event.)

Compile a mailing list of every possible person who can give you coverage. (This includes TV and radio news departments, public-affairs departments, talk shows, daily and regional newspapers and magazines, including alumnae magazines and company employee publications.)

Follow up the press release with phone calls to everyone on your list. Check to make sure they received your release, and offer assistance in setting up coverage.

Once you have been written up by local publications, have copies made of the article, and include it in future press release packages. (Send it to customers as well, in catalog mailings or billings.)

11

PROCEDURES AND PAPERWORK: RUNNING TRUE TO FORM

"The horror of that moment," the King went on, "I shall never, never forget!"
"You will though," the Queen said, "if you don't make a memorandum of it."
Lewis Carroll

Aside from the benefits of fulfillment and satisfaction, you are in business to make money. Besides your actual day-to-day endeavor, profits result from organized management. Plan, organize, direct, and control. Too often, business owner-managers get too bogged down in the daily routine. They are so overwhelmed by the "now" of things they can't tell whether they're situated on solid ground or teetering on the side of a cliff.

An owner has to develop her own visionary business bifocals. One minute she is dealing with a slothful supplier, the next with a crazy client who takes up an hour's time with nary a thank-you. Meanwhile, she is trying to keep track of receipts, balance the checkbook, reorder supplies, write ads, answer phones, and oversee the staff (if there is one).

All this is exhilarating, and not nearly as impossible as it sounds, so long as some commonsensical procedures are developed and followed. The complexity of organizational methods varies according to size and type of business. This chapter deals with a potpourri of basic guidelines to keep your feet on the ground and you on your feet.

First of all, set aside one day a week for the behind-the-scenes running of your business—billing, answering mail, re-ordering supplies, checking progress on current jobs, keeping the books up to date, and planning your advertising and selling campaigns.

Live your business from day to day, but plan ahead in blocks of time—three to six months or a year.

Periodically, reevaluate your systems and keep files and forms up to date. Know what everyone involved with your business is doing. Likewise, keep everyone advised on your activities.

TIME MANAGEMENT

Many women starting out in business make the mistake of trying to handle everything themselves in order to save money. Obviously, you have to pinch pennies, but time is money, too. You have to establish your priorities and stick to them. If you are going to manage your time prudently, you must be organized and map out a strategy plan. Here are some time-saving hints:

> Know your goals (daily, weekly, monthly, yearly), and keep them constantly before you.
>
> Make a list every morning, as well as an overall weekly list, outlining everything that needs to be done (including telephone calls, correspondence, record keeping, drumming up new business, and such). Arrange the items in order of priority, and get things done in that order. Lists mean nothing if you don't refer back to them constantly.
>
> Delegate responsibility. It may sometimes take longer to explain what you want done, but you must learn to differentiate between what must be done by you and what can be handled by others.
>
> Generate as little paperwork as possible. Many office forms are genuine time-savers, but don't get bogged down. Have a place for everything.

File papers immediately; don't let things pile up.

Use your business consultants to help you solve problems quickly.

Get as much done by phone as possible (ordering supplies, etc.). Or send a quick note to avoid a lengthy phone call with a chatty supplier or client.

Set specific times for specific tasks, e.g., telephoning and bill paying. Don't procrastinate.

Use waiting or traveling time to catch up on reading, think about solutions to problems, etc. Take taxis instead of buses (the Time = Money theory).

Go to lunch for pleasure. Business lunches are expensive and time-consuming and accomplish little. An office appointment takes less time and gets more done.

Don't spend precious office time making up your lists. Work on them on the way to work or the evening before.

In general, avoid busywork. Someone else should be doing it for you.

FILING

As your business grows, so will your need for additional filing space. Secondhand filing cabinets can be found cheaply at auctions or sales of used office equipment or can be floor samples from office supply stores.

Filing should be done alphabetically in manila file folders. Besides the alphabetical cataloging of clients and suppliers, there are general categories to be arranged: expenses, advertising (rate sheets, copies of ads, etc.), printing, publicity, photographs, bank statements, accounts receivable, paid bills, time sheets, general correspondence, and other informational sources related to your particular business.

Certain records must be stored safely, in case of fire or flooding. (Metal file cabinets are not fireproof.) You are also required by law to retain certain records for specific periods of time—financial records, tax returns, and so forth. (For a specific listing of what must be kept, for how long, see Chapter 6, page 68.) Keep these tucked away in a fireproof safe, in a bank safety deposit box, or on other premises.

Index Card Files

Index cards are an easy method of keeping track of various information: supplies and inventory, selling contacts, advertising and publicity sources, clients, and so forth.

Keep a card file by the telephone containing the names, addresses, phone numbers, and miscellaneous information on all clients and suppliers. Do up a card on your business, containing often-used information, like your sales tax resale number, Dun & Bradstreet number, tax Employer's Identification number, insurance policy information, and so forth.

Look at your business, and make up your own forms in areas where standardized information will be expedient. Visit office supply houses for preprinted forms of various types.

But don't bury yourself in forms. They are time-savers and memory aids, but too much paperwork can be counterproductive.

FORMS AND TIME-SAVERS

Everything should also be written down and filed in its proper place. As your business and staff grow, it becomes more and more necessary for all participants to have access to vital information.

Organization of the constant inflow of information is the only possible way to keep your business running efficiently.

Job Forms for Service or Manufacturing Businesses

Organization forms keep business flowing. Free-lance people or tiny businesses often get by in the beginning by using file cards. However, printed job forms grow with the business and eliminate the helter-skelter method of jotting down notes that can be misplaced or incomplete. Several copies should be made: the original should be kept in the master job form book or file, the copies in individual client folders and the bookkeeping record file. Until a job is completed, keep the client copy in a central location (on a bulletin board, for example) for quick reference.

No matter what sort of job data sheet you use, it must include the following information: date of call (order), date of job (or delivery), who took the call, client's name, address, and telephone number, the price quoted for job, form of payment, plus any other necessary description.

Each form should be numbered for reference, and a separate invoice number attached when the job is completed and billed. After that, it should be stamped and dated upon payment.

The master job file provides an at-a-glance record of past and current progress. If a job is canceled, the reason should be noted on the job form. If a client is difficult to deal with, it should be jotted down. The more people you have working for you, the more important it is for everyone to have access to this information.

Retail Business Forms

Stores must keep track of their orders from manufacturers and receipts to their own retail customers. You can purchase standard forms, or have them made up with your own logo or letterhead. Keep track of current stock with index file cards, and itemize all inventory purchases on a columnar pad (give every line of merchandise a number for easy identification), so you know when to restock and reorder. When inventory is replaced, keep track by entering the information on monthly on-order forms, listing the order number, date, manufacturer's name, style number, quantity, price, and shipping charges (if any).*

Daily Time Sheets

Any business whose fees are based on hours (services, crafts-makers, and the like) should rely heavily on time sheets for an

---

* For more information on retail record-keeping forms and stock control systems, see Leta Clark, *How to Open Your Own Shop or Gallery* (New York: St. Martin's Press). Also, Fairchild Publications (7 East Twelfth Street, New York, New York 10003) publishes informational books on all aspects of retailing.

accurate cost analysis per job and to see how time is being used. Both for yourself and others working with you, it is necessary to detect if you are working at capacity or wasting too much time.

Break the day down into hours, the hours into ten- or fifteen-minute slots. And write in everything—phone calls, coffee breaks, and details on activities for each and every job.

Petty Cash Records

A petty cash fund (a fixed amount of dollars) should be set up to make small payments in order to avoid having to write many checks. Every time money is taken from petty cash, a slip should be filled out, listing date, amount, purpose, and person to whom the money is given. Any invoices or receipts should be stapled to the slip. Every day the total of the petty cash slips should be balanced against the remaining money in the fund. Later, the slips are summarized according to type of expense and entered into the cash disbursements book.

CASH AND CREDIT ACCOUNTS

Cash Sales

If you run a store, you must write up the sales receipts for each sale (or use a cash register with tape receipts). Always give a copy to the customer. At the end of the day, all but a specified amount of money (for making change) should be taken out and deposited in your bank account. The cash should be tallied against the sales receipts to guard against errors. Try to go to the bank at different times of day so you won't be carrying the day's jackpot for deposit every afternoon at the same time.

Credit Card Sales

If you are willing to pay a small percentage (generally, 3 to 6 percent) of sales to credit card companies, you can allow your customers to use major credit cards. In exchange, they may make higher purchases. A drawback is that you don't get paid as fast and your cash flow is slowed down. Talk to your banker about setting up an association with credit card companies.

Charge Credit Sales

Some small retail stores and service businesses choose to boost business by establishing credit to regular customers. This is generally not advisable because of the time and expense. However, should you consider it, the key to not getting burned is to open every new account properly, according to a standard procedure. Obtain the following information from the customer (you can buy printed forms or make up your own): full name, address, home and work telephone numbers; place of business, job title, length of employment; former employer, if present employment is less than six months; names of companies/stores which already have extended credit (and obtain credit card numbers, where applicable).

Clear all applications through the credit bureau. Check with other creditors (some people promptly pay certain accounts and leave others in arrears). Some businesses limit charge customers to both the amount they can charge and the amount that must be paid on their monthly bill.

Accepting Checks

A retail business should place a ceiling on checks, require identification (usually two types), and compare signatures. In addition, make sure that (1) the customer's name, address, and phone number are written on back of the check; (2) the check is accurately dated, not postdated or more than thirty days old; (3) the bank's address and branch are on the check (never accept a blank check); (4) the check is made out for the exact amount of purchase (and not more, in exchange for cash); and (5) the numerical amount agrees with the written amount.

After you have received a check, stamp it immediately with your rubber bank deposit stamp—make sure your bank provides you with one—so that a thief can't cash it if you are robbed.

Your local Better Business Bureau, police, or bank may have a list of bad-check passers working in your area.

Most checks returned because of insufficient funds will clear the second time you deposit them. Notify the customer that you are redepositing the check. (Some banks will not allow you to redeposit more than twice; they also charge a service fee.)

If the check bounces a second time, call the client and request immediate payment, by cash or certified check. If you get an evasive response, then call a collection agency and have it get to work on the case.

Sources of Credit Information

Certain types of information are sold by credit agencies; some are available from them as a service. Find out about the available services of your local retail credit bureau, and talk to your banker. If you need daily credit information, then consider buying the services of a credit bureau. Acquaint yourself with the International Consumer Credit Association and general mercantile agencies, like Dun & Bradstreet and Equifax, Inc.

BILLING AND COLLECTING

Credit sales are as insubstantial as cotton candy until they have been paid. Often the most likable customers don't pay their bills. And small businesses are the most vulnerable prey since they can least afford loss. Nevertheless, extending customers credit usually peps up sales (especially for certain types of service businesses); your company's success depends on your ability to collect.

Send out bills at the beginning of each month, with terms of payment (due on the tenth of the month, or whenever). If a bill is unpaid, send a statement a month later, with another one following fifteen days after that. Next, two months after the original bill, send a letter politely requesting payment.

Follow up with a phone call, explaining that you must be

paid in order to pay your own bills. Inquire if the service, merchandise, invoice, etc., are in order and if there is any reason payment is being withheld. Ask for a date by which you can expect payment, and call back if it hasn't been received by that time. Remain polite during the second call, but find out what the matter is. (Be prepared for "The check was mailed several days ago; haven't you received it yet?" or one of the standard stalls.) Arrange another schedule for repayment. If that isn't met, call and say you must be paid in ten days or you will be forced to turn the matter over to your lawyer. And then do so.

Close off your credit line to deadbeats who will not pay on your terms. No client is worth the extensive time you spend cajoling and threatening her to pay up.

Only as a last resort will you want to hassle with a lawsuit or a collection agency to force payment. Discuss these methods with your accountant and lawyer. Collection agencies take a percentage of the monies they collect, but winding up with some of your money is better than none.

Should you have to sue a client for payment, represent yourself in small-claims court. This avoids exorbitant legal fees if your claim is under the designated monetary limit (generally, five hundred dollars or less).

PAYING BILLS

A new business establishes its credit rating by paying its bills on time. Be especially diligent about this the first six months you are in business and always with new suppliers. However, guard your cash flow, and never give up all your cash at once.

There is a priority of bill paying. In general, wait thirty to sixty days before paying bills in order to collect maximum interest on the money in your account. After that, banks and insurance companies must have the first consideration since loans or policies can be foreclosed or canceled. Next, pay your rent and utilities. From then on, pay according to commitments. Generally, the last people to be paid are creditors who are easy on you, and professional consultants—accountant, lawyer, etc.

If you are caught in a bind, be honest with your creditors.

Tell them you are waiting for accounts receivable, but *always honor your commitments*. Banks offer short-term loans (for thirty, sixty, or ninety days) to carry you over while you are waiting for a large payment.

After a check is written, mark the bill "paid," and add the date and check number. When a check is spoiled, mark it "void," tear off the signature portion, and staple it onto the back of its stub.

Every time you write a check, note the purpose as well as the date and amount. Keep a running balance, with deposits and check deductions up to date. Always reconcile your checkbook with your bank statement at the end of the month.

If a check is lost, call your bank immediately. Always stop payment on a check before issuing a duplicate.

PRODUCTION AND INVENTORY

If you manufacture products or make them by hand, keep an up-to-date inventory on all finished products as well as raw materials and tools. Your inventory of finished goods should provide a backlog of ready-to-sell items.

For retail, get advice from your suppliers on inventory. Stock small quantities, and see what sells best. In the long run, you will learn from experience what to stock in quantity, what to eliminate, and which are image items (not fast turnovers, but worth keeping in stock all the time). Aim toward a good merchandise turnover—have a variety of items so that customers can discover something different every time they visit your store. This involves organizing an active buying campaign on your part. The smaller the town, the more general and varied your merchandise will have to be.

Production Sequence (Manufacturing)

The physical layout of your working space should be planned for maximum efficiency. Plan each step in logical sequence, and have ample storage space for raw materials and finished products. The faster you turn out products, the more money you will make. Make sure you are performing every step the most expedient, commonsensical way. Avoid wasting time; keep up a steady work rhythm.

Stock Control

Know when to reorder so that deliveries are made before you are depleted of standard merchandise. Store stock on shelves with index cards showing amounts, sizes, colors, in front. As items are taken out of stock, write in the change on the index cards. Keep track of all inventory on a columnar pad, and give every line of merchandise a number for easy identification. Write down all transactions so that you will know when to restock and reorder. Physical inventory should be taken periodically to verify the balances you have on paper.

Keep track of raw materials and tools in the same way so that you don't run out. Always reorder when you get below a certain amount to allow time for shipment. A file card index is another useful way to keep track—every time you take an amount out of stock, write down the amount you take and subtract it from the original. Have a separate card for each line of merchandise.

INTERIOR DISPLAY (RETAIL)

The decoration and display of merchandise in your store should be unique—colorful, well-lighted, and imaginative. It should be functional as well as decorative; don't leave your merchandise tossed around as an easy mark for shoplifters, but don't keep it out of reach either. Look at other businesses for ideas on interior display. When you go on buying trips to other cities, look around while you're there. Pick up ideas you can adapt to your own location. Change interior displays periodically and window displays often, to attract attention.

Window displays should be original and imaginative ... wrap bracelets around loaves of french bread in picnic baskets, turn hardware supplies into *objets d'art*. Display the local sixth grade's art project, and throw a few of your products into the foreground.

Go to the window display decorator of a large department

store, and make friends with her. Stores like this always have leftovers and throwaways. Theaters and university prop shops have items to lend or rent. Borrow large plants from the local nursery in exchange for a free plug. Get Broadway or movie posters by writing away for them. Supplies and tie-ins are limitless. If you're too busy to deal with it, hire a free-lance display person to keep your store looking exciting and novel.

Protection Against Shoplifting

Shoplifting can be a major drain on the finances of any store.* With experience, you will intuitively spot potential shoplifters by their behavior. Of course, beware of shoppers with bulky coats and large pockets, umbrellas, and bulky packages. Many stores request that such paraphernalia be checked upon arrival.

There are a number of precautionary techniques: uniformed guards, convex mirrors in strategic locations, receipts stapled to bags, electronic pellets attached to expensive clothes, which must be removed by the cashier with special shears. Shoplifters also switch price labels; effective safeguards here are tamperproof gummed labels, plastic string on tags, and prices written in with ink or a rubber stamp.

Your shop's layout can discourage shoplifters. Keep small, high-priced items in locked cases. Allow only a certain number of garments in dressing rooms at one time. Don't leave enticing pocket-sized merchandise in unattended nooks. Inspect your store from a shoplifter's point of view, and rearrange any tempting displays.

Protection Against Robbery

Take out insurance. Keep up-to-date records of all inventory or equipment in case you are robbed. Talk to other small-business owners about their precautions. Sometimes a group

---

* Write for the SBA's booklet no. 129, *Reducing Shoplifting Losses*, for advice on detecting and dealing with shoplifters.

of merchants will get together and hire a private guard to patrol their block.

If your business warrants it, you can have a buzzer system installed with which you can unlock the door to let people in and out. This sort of thing sometimes discourages the casual customer, however, and is not recommended for a business that thrives on browsers. It is most effective for stores that specialize in small, high-priced merchandise, such as jewelers.

There are security systems ranging in price and sophistication that you can have installed in your office. Some are available that connect directly with a nearby police precinct house. A simpler and less expensive idea is to set up a secret buzzer with your next-door neighbors to enlist their aid in the event of a robbery while you are there. If you have an office, install a peephole on the main door, and keep the door locked when you are there alone. Another good deterrent is a guard dog. Even though it's dear old Fido, the family pet, if he's big enough, robbers will think twice about taking the chance of arousing his ire.

PACKING, SHIPPING, AND POSTAGE

Pack your merchandise well. Use sturdy corrugated containers, reinforced gummed tape (not masking tape), address labels, and string. Stuff inside with newspaper, tissue, styrofoam peanuts or popcorn, etc., to prevent sliding and breakage. Always enclose a list of contents inside the package or in an envelope enclosed on the outside.

For *Parcel Post*, the maximum weight is forty pounds, and the maximum size is 84 inches (length and girth combined). Rates depend on weight and destination. Insurance is extra but the only means of tracing a lost package.

United Parcel delivers almost everywhere in the continental United States. The maximum weight per package is fifty pounds and size is 108 inches (length and girth combined). Prices vary according to destination, and every parcel is automatically insured. For an extra charge, UPS will provide a pick-up service for packages.

Other means of shipping for larger packages are bus or

truck, the latter being generally too expensive for small businesses.

Postage meters are time-savers, but more costly than stamps because, in addition to the postage, you must pay a monthly rental on the machine itself. When the meter runs out of postage, it must be taken to the Post Office to be reset. The Post Office requires that you pay with cash or a certified check written for the amount for which the meter is to be set.

If you don't deal in mail orders or send out myriad catalogs and brochures, it's cheaper for a small business to stick with the personalized look of stamps.

There are any number of time-saving procedures to keep the behind-the-scenes of your business as pleasant to deal with as friendly customers. Talk to other business owners for additional tips. But, eventually, you will come up with your own individualized methods of smoothing out the edges.

Once you have become organized, don't let things slide. Reevaluate your systems as you go along—decide what to keep, what to drop, and what to add. Every business is different from every other one because of the individual personalities of the owners. Just remember to keep setting aside those few hours every week to feed the home fires. It's much easier to spot trouble and avoid it than to deal with it after the fact.

MARKETING: SELLING IT LIKE IT IS

Now, here, you see, it takes all the running you can do, to keep in the same place. If you want to get somewhere else, you must run at least twice as fast as that!

Lewis Carroll

Early in the life of every business, especially small ones, there comes a pause. The opening hoopla has begun to fade, and things are rolling along. You could almost be lulled into settling back into the business-as-usual phase. Instead, step out for a breath of air and stand far enough back to renew your perspective.

Word-of-mouth advertising about your business may be buzzing around town, the ads and publicity doing their magic. But you know there is an even bigger market out there. How do you tap it? It's time to design your active marketing campaign. In other words, get out there and hustle.

You've already conducted initial marketing research, before starting up and writing your first ads. Now, you have more facts about the people who are using your product or service. But people's needs keep changing, and you must adapt to them. Recognize change before it takes over. Be observant. Keep up with magazines, newspapers, and trade journals to stay ahead of the game and spot new trends. Maybe there are other markets you haven't explored, or new outlets that even your competition hasn't considered. This is no time to take a nap.

GOVERNMENT CONTRACTS

The government needs many things that are furnished by outside businesses—food, supplies, clothing, printing, writing, artwork, building, and much more. Securing a government contract could provide the entire financial base for your business—the jobs are generally large and can bring substantial money into your company.

It sounds ideal, but if you work for the government, you must submit to rigid requirements, strict time limitations, and masses of red tape. Many legal problems occur with government contracting (which must be unraveled by one of this country's three thousand lawyers who specialize in government contract work). For example, if you contract to do a job and don't deliver in time, the government will cancel without reimbursing your expenses for labor and supplies. If you are a manufacturer, you are required to provide a lifetime guarantee on your goods. And sometimes, as late as five years after the job is completed, the government may decide that you made too great a profit. You would then be required to put up a cash bond for the disputed amount (into an escrow account with the court of claims), until the matter is settled, no matter how long.

There are four basic types of contracts: "open for bid," advertised, negotiated, and rated. If the big bucks attract you and you are willing to go through the intensive rigmarole to qualify for government-contracted jobs, you can place your name on the government's list of producers and keep in contact with various government agencies.*

---

* For further information on obtaining government contracts, see *Anyone Can Do Business with the Government,* by Herman R. Holtz, available for $14.95 plus $1.50 postage from Government Marketing News, Inc., Suite 1109, 1001 Connecticut Avenue, N.W., Washington, D.C. 20036. It also publishes: *Directory of U.S. Government Buyers* ($11.95 plus $1.50 postage) and *Government Marketing News,* a monthly newsletter ($95/year). Also, check the *Commerce Business Daily,* available by subscription from the Government Printing Office (see appendix), for $105 per year (first-class mailing) or $85 per year (second-class mailing).

In addition, the SBA's Office of Procurement Assistance is now conducting a systematic search to locate and add to their source files the names of eligible women-owned small businesses that wish to seek government contracts.* Specialists within the SBA are available to counsel and advise business owners on how to obtain government contracts and how to prepare bids for major contracts and subcontracts. (Many government contractors depend on subcontractors to assist in getting the job done.) Also, the National Association of Women Business Owners and many local nonaffiliated women's business organizations are working to help women entrepreneurs secure these prime contracts.

MARKETING RESEARCH

Deeper probing into your market is a vital element in planning your sales campaign. Marketing is nothing more complicated than logic; it is the logical way to reach your customer or client. Just as market analysis helped direct the development of your original business concept and advertising, it is also the key to the future sales activities of your company.

Understanding your market is not just knowing who your customer is—you have to know where she's headed and her motivations as well. This involves increasing your perception of trends, your industry, competition, and your personal objectives for the business.

First, look at overall trends, and try to relate them to your business—for example, the growing economic independence of women, the escalating number of single people and unmarried couples, increased ethnic awareness and interest in origins, the ecology movement, etc. Observe how the economy encourages and affects these trends. Learn to recognize new directions, and investigate their potential in relation to you. Increase your awareness of what's going on all around you, at all levels of activity.

Second, understand your industry and how new trends affect it. A good example of what can happen if trends are

---

* "Small business" includes any service or retail business which grosses under $1.8 million in annual sales or any manufacturing company employing fewer than five hundred people.

ignored is the experience of the movie industry in the fifties. At that time, television sets were brought into millions of homes and movies almost died, owing to lack of accurate analysis and preparation for the real threat television posed. A major overhaul in motion picture production and marketing became necessary. Because the movie companies let competition steal their audience, they had to spend a fortune trying to gain the audience back.

Service industries have to be particularly in tune with the economy since services are always the first corners to be cut when money gets tight. If you deal in a leisure service, always be prepared to redirect your selling by emphasizing the fundamentals of your services.

Third, understand your competition. Identify them, and estimate how much of the market you share with them. Are they doing well, and why? Is it only they, or is your whole industry thriving? Defining the competition will help you evaluate your own strengths and weaknesses. Your problem could be as simple as inadequate parking space or as complex as a lack of customer identity and loyalty.

Next, be aware of your market—who your customer is and why she should buy from you. Is it a geographic decision (you're the only delicatessen for twenty blocks)? Or is she a customer-at-large (your homemade bagels bring people flocking from all over)? What factors are most important to your customer: price, availability, special service, unique products, location, quality, originality? How do you satisfy the customer's needs? What makes your business viable?

Finally, realize your personal objectives. Sit back, close your eyes and visualize where you want to be next year, in five years—not only within your business, but your entire lifestyle. If you have a partner or key staff members, communicate your objectives, and make sure you are all headed basically in the same direction. Have each person make a list of where she envisions the business flowing.

Research sources for defining your market in depth include the following:

> Local census bureaus. They can provide useful information on everything from income levels to geographic studies; also, talk to your local Chamber of Commerce or your state's department of economic

or industrial development, located in the state's capital city.

The Small Business Administration. Besides publishing a number of marketing booklets, it can provide marketing analysts to help you.

Libraries. These have numerous marketing reference directories.*

Universities and graduate schools. These are excellent sources of assistance. You might interest a student in doing her project study on your business or an entire class in conducting a market survey for you.

THE MARKETING PLAN

Your market having been researched, it's time to dive into all your statistics and come up with a marketing strategy. There are numerous approaches; by now you should have an indication of the best one for you. Your sales campaign might take a concentrated one-to-one selling approach, or it could involve stepping up your ad campaign by blasting out thirty-second radio spots around the clock. It might take a clown passing out balloons to children to lure their mothers into your toy store. Or you might decide to hire a graphic designer to create a spectacular new brochure and catalog.

In other words, marketing is highly personal to each business, and you must do what feels right, according to your budget. Be prepared to shift directions, if need be. The future is unpredictable, but partially under your control. Do everything in your power to understand and direct that control. And keep building your selling campaign—don't get lazy.

THE SELLING CAMPAIGN

The least complicated method of organizing your clients and contacts is to introduce a file card system. On large cards,

---

* Your librarian will help you locate what you need. See also: *Encyclopedia of Business Information Sources*, 2 vols., Gale Research Company, Book Tower, Detroit, Michigan 48226; Dun & Bradstreet's Marketing Services division (99 Church Street, New York, New York 10007) publishes many volumes on marketing.

keep a record of names, addresses, and phone numbers of current customers (be thinking up ways to increase *their* business), former clients (Why did they desert you? Can you win them back?), and companies or people you want to deal with (along with information on their products, services, main suppliers, ad agency, bank, or anything else that's pertinent to your needs).

Once you have instituted a card file, keep it up to date. Add new addresses, additional information, and notes of sales and inquiries. Fill in other transactions, phone calls, letters, etc., so that you will know at a glance exactly where you stand. Arrange (or cross-file) the names or categories of clients by alphabet, inactive or active clients, types of accounts, or regular calling dates.

Brainstorming: The Group Panel Discussion

Many ad agencies and marketing companies conceive new ideas, invent products, and evaluate services without lifting a creative finger. They enlist other people to do it for them. Not marketing Phi Beta Kappas but normal, just-us-folks kinds of people.

They put together a panel—a cross section of the right age, sex, and economic group, usually about eight to ten people—to discuss a specific subject. The panel has a moderator who tosses in leading questions and keeps the participants from digressing. Moderated panels are one of the most efficient methods of amassing relevant insights into particular problems.

This method can be adapted to solve some of your own business problems and chart out new courses for selling your product or service. Assemble your group in a comfortable environment, serve coffee, and let the ideas flow. Tape the discussion rather than take notes, so you can mull over it later. Don't ask direct yes or no questions. Toss in thought-provoking questions like: How would you go about this; What do you think we should do with that; or If you could create the perfect ———, what would it be like? You can glean valuable clues to refreshing every facet of your business, from prices to colors, new products to client relations.

If possible, hire an experienced panel moderator, because it takes talent to keep the dialogue pertinent, to draw out the quiet ones, and to keep any one person from monopolizing the floor.

Selling in Person

Before you can sell your product or service, the potential client has to be sold on you. Your approach should be friendly, confident, and direct. Relate to her on a one-to-one basis, and try to enjoy the meeting, regardless of the outcome. Play the moments, and the scene will play itself.

Look good. Your appearance must adhere generally to the expectations of the person to whom you are making your pitch. Whether your style is conventional or up-to-the-minute, your clothes and accessories should complement you.

Sound good; be articulate, poised, and enthusiastic. This becomes second nature when you are well-prepared and know what you are going to say and which items to stress. Use your imagination before you make a presentation of your product or service. Figure out how and why a specific client will be interested in what you are offering.

In addition, find out about your prospective client from her associates, trade journals, or your local newspaper. Assimilate facts on new promotions, products, areas toward which her business is heading. Then recycle this information into your presentation, and demonstrate logical tie-ins. Clients are flattered when you go out of your way to know who they are. Taking this initiative also makes you more assured and talking to your prospect easier.

Before entering the meeting, pause and assemble your mood. Even if you've had a rotten day, you have to radiate energy and goodwill. Remember, the show must go on. Be prepared to answer questions, but don't let the potential client batter down your stamina with a series of interruptions. A polite "I'm coming to that in a minute" will do.

Say what you have to say in twenty minutes or less, and if the person gets restless, cut it short. Don't oversell. Be in tune, and don't overwhelm the person. React and interact with her. If you make a sale right away, stop selling and change gears. If you cannot think fast enough on your feet, arrange to come back after you've mulled over the possibilities. Then go home, and redefine your pitch to the client's specific requirements.

Leave the door open for continuing contact. Plan another meeting, or phone with an estimate, send a brochure—in short, do anything that allows a follow-up. The more firmly fixed you are in a potential client's mind, the more likely she is to hire you.

Prospective clients are impressed if you're interested in both what they're doing and what you're selling. But they will buy your product only if they need it or think they can use it. If at first you don't succeed, periodically return—with new ideas, information, approaches. Often their needs will change, or a different person in charge may be more receptive to you. (Rapport has a great deal to do with it when all is said and done.) Hang in there, but never to the point of obnoxiousness.

The key to selling is backing up your sales with service. Always deliver what you promise, without delay, even if it means working overtime to do it. Once you have achieved a reputation for honest dealings, fair price, and prompt delivery, references from satisfied clients will help your business grow.

Keep your mind fertile. Think of new ways to present your business to the public. Never be complacent. Continue to woo new accounts, and expand existing ones. Exert extra effort to gear your product to meet the needs of new clients. Compete by giving better service, making a superior product, or marketing yourself more effectively.

Hold on to old clients by advising them of new ways to utilize your product or service. Do favors for them. Acknowledge their successes with personal congratulations. Old clients are like old friends—never underestimate their importance.

Sales Letters

The letter you send out to potential customers to attract their business or to pique their interest must be an attention-grabber. It must be simple, succinct. No matter how many copies of the same letter you mail out, each one must be typed separately and directed to a specific person. Call the company first for the name of its marketing director, or whomever you want to make your pitch to.

The letter must include an explanation of your business along with a few descriptive details or names of satisfied clients. Indicate briefly what you believe you can offer your prospective client. Allude to the ways you can help her improve her business.

By all means, keep it to one page. You can include a brochure, but generally it's best to save it, leaving it with the client after you've met with her.

THE FOLLOW-UP

A couple of days after you've sent your letter, phone and make an appointment. If you can't get through to the person in question, keep at it. If you hit a dead end, try another person at the same company. Sooner or later someone will open the door wide enough for you to get through. Don't ever forget the squeaky wheel philosophy; that's what selling's all about.

The Visual Presentation

Show and tell is usually the best way to sell your product or service. No matter how articulate and peppy your sales pitch, people like to have visual treats paraded in front of them. Besides, it makes your job easier to have a prop. Just make sure you know how to handle it. Don't fidget, or let the visual presentation take center stage away from you.

What kind of visual paraphernalia should you rely on? If your product is portable, then that, plus a brochure or catalog, is all you need to accompany your sales patter.

It's very professional to whip out a portable slide carousel and screen a well-edited series of convincing slides. But it is also costly and time-consuming; you have to keep reediting the slides to suit the particular client you are about to solicit. The equipment and slides (photographer, film, developing) are expensive, and they're heavy to lug around. But it looks terrific if you have a product or service that will really benefit from this sort of presentation.

For smaller budgets, there is a presentation book, usually a ring binder with plastic sheet protectors, which props up easel-style. It should complement your rhetoric, illustrating your enthusiasm with photographs of products, jobs completed, happy clients, along with letters of recommendation, publicity pieces, and anything else that will prove your point.

Lettering and headings in your presentation book should be done by hand, with press type or felt-tip pen. Use magic markers for underlining, and glue with rubber cement. First, rough it out on tracing paper; then paste up and print the presentation. Be consistent—have all material either vertical or horizontal. If you must have both, don't switch back and forth. Arrange verticals in one half, horizontals grouped together in the next section. Use only the right-hand side of the page, to avoid clutter.

WHAT TO ILLUSTRATE

List reasons, in order, why the potential client will want your service or product. Will it save the client money, enhance her image, or save time? Condense these reasons into headlines or captions. Then assemble all the points that support and prove your assumptions, along with photographs, letters, illustrations, charts, etc.

Selling in person is advertising in its most direct form. Gear your presentation book to special events and times of year and specific customers, just as you do your ads.

POLISH THE PITCH

Once you have your sales spiel and visual presentation, practice and polish it. Work it out on friends, family, and associates so that you become proficient and poised. Inject life into your soliloquy. A salesperson is really an actor, and every appointment like opening night. You have to know your lines, but be able to ad-lib if necessary.

HIRING A SALES REPRESENTATIVE

Sales reps provide a way for small wholesale or manufacturing businesses to keep costs down, but still have someone working to bring in more business. A sales representative usually handles lines of several manufacturers in a specified territory, on commission (and sometimes plus expenses). These salespeople generally stick to products of the same nature (various items sold in hardware stores, for example) on an exclusive basis for that area. (Occasionally, a small manufacturer will employ two reps—one to sell to boutiques, another to solicit the big chain or department stores.)

The amount of commission varies according to products, from about 10 percent to 20 percent (the commission percentage decreases for products which are expected to sell in greater volume). Commissions are generally paid monthly, after the order has been filled and received by the client.

Finding a Representative

Ask people in the same field as you, or place and check ads in trade journals. (You can also learn from these sources what percentage of commission is standard for your line of products.)*

Before taking on any sales representatives, check their references by telephone or in person—a letter may not give you the exact information you need. Look for someone with initiative, perseverance, reliability, and self-motivation.

Make sure your sales representative understands from the beginning exactly what you are looking for. She must be aware of all her duties and responsibilities. Remember, to buyers and consumers the salesperson doesn't just *represent* your company, she *is* your company.

Once you hire a rep, put your agreement of territory, commission, and payment terms in writing. Afterward, keep in touch with your sales rep, and keep her up to date on new developments, new products, etc. Find out how well your product is being received. If you're not getting a lot of orders, find out why. Is it your product or the representative? If the salesperson is a good one, she can report on the state of your market firsthand and probably send back good advice on future trends and competition.

---

* To locate a sales representative in your field, contact one of this nation's Merchandise Marts, located in Atlanta, Chicago, San Francisco, Dallas (World Trade Center), and Los Angeles (Pacific Design Center). Or check your Yellow Pages, under "Manufacturer's Agents and Representatives."

As a general precaution, send out confirmation notices to customers before filling and shipping the orders placed by your rep. This avoids any mix-ups and keeps you from getting burned should your representative be misrepresenting you.

CUSTOMER RELATIONS

You, as the owner, are the best salesperson for your business. *No one cares about it as much as you.* Keep in touch with your public. Be friendly and ask your customers' opinions about your business. Find out if there is a product or service you should add. Consider any suggestions from clients (and sales representatives or staff members), and act immediately to rectify any complaints. Build your business by increasing your rapport with the public.

A client's confidence in your talent and abilities is another stepping-stone to success. You must be able to offer quality products or service, at reasonable prices. Always deliver a service, product, or repair on time. (And reassure the client both before and during the job that it will be completed according to schedule. If you suspect that you will exceed a time or price estimate, notify the client immediately.)

People respond to courtesy and consideration. After completing a job of making a sale, try to provide finishing touches whenever possible. Wash the car you just repaired or gift-wrap packages at no extra charge. Don't be afraid to give free assistance to people—that extra something radiates goodwill. You have to make people *want* to see you and your business succeed; that's the key to reaping in the rewards of word-of-mouth advertising. If you lose one person's business, you usually lose other people's as well.

Be visible. Give talks; lead seminars; write articles; join trade associations. Let people regard you as an expert in your field.

Go forth into your community, too. Support charity drives, community activities, and improvements by contributing time and services. If you have a display window, give up space to posters for worthwhile causes. Initiate a community bulletin board. Salute the local rescue squad with a special window display .. anything to arouse attention and bring people into your place of business. Take the initiative for mini-events. Even if it's serving your customers or clients iced water on hot summer days, try to do a little extra all the time.

Most important of all, keep up to date. Be on a constant lookout in magazines, papers, and trade periodicals for new ideas, leads on new prospects, market trends, even advertising ideas from competitors. Keep updating your client and publicity list to show to new prospects.

And follow up. The potential client who is not interested in your product or services today may be ready for you in six months. Always follow up letters with phone calls.

TAXES: RENDERING UNTO SEIZURE

The weight of this sad time we must obey....
William Shakespeare

Every business owner is responsible for her company's federal, state, and local taxes, regardless of who actually does the bookkeeping and filing. Ignorance, as always, is no excuse; if you don't pay a tax, you'll have to pay a nasty penalty or answer ominous subpoenas. Have your accountant or tax attorney explain your obligations and provide you with a yearly tax calendar as a reminder of those deadly due dates. Consider having an extra bank account for tax monies (especially retail businesses with sales tax payments due quarterly), so that you won't accidentally spend money that should be allocated toward taxes.*

Keeping accurate, up-to-date business journals is the first step to computing taxes. The Internal Revenue Service (IRS) requires that a company's tax information be backed up by

---

* For tax advice and preparation, you may enlist the services of an *enrolled agent* instead of a tax lawyer or accountant. *Enrolled agents* can be both individuals who have passed the U.S. Treasury Department's arduous qualifying examination on tax laws and regulations and former IRS agents with more than five years' experience. (See the Yellow Pages, or contact your local IRS office for list of qualified enrolled agents.)

permanent records (for auditing, if need be). These records must verify income, deductions, credits, inventories (when applicable), and any sales or rentals subject to excise taxes. They must also include names, addresses, and social security numbers of owner(s) and staff, as well as your Employer Identification number.* (Taxes specifically relating to employees will be covered in Chapter 14.)

Since paying taxes is like walking a tightrope at best, check with the following sources for assistance and information on which taxes your business is subject to: the IRS, your state and local tax agencies, the public library, trade associations, your bank, or a tax information service. These places can fill you in on current tax regulations and offer suggestions on how to go about keeping the necessary tax records.

Major assistance will, of course, come from your accountant,† but, as in all other areas, the more you know yourself, the better off you'll be. Even if you plop these duties completely in your accountant's lap, make a point to understand your company's tax situation. If you do your own bookkeeping, you should obtain professional advice in the beginning on the accurate computation and filing of tax forms. Penalty fines on late- or nonpayment of taxes can be frustrating as well as costly, and they *are* avoidable so long as you know what's doing at the IRS.

First of all, sit down and read publication no. 334, *Tax Guide for Small Business*, published annually and obtainable from the IRS.‡ This guide will unclutter all the mysteries of federal income taxes. It is, in fact, a mini how-to book, explaining bookkeeping systems, tax laws, etc. for sole proprietorships, partnerships, and corporations, and it includes sample tax forms and all pertinent information required for the filing

---

* To obtain your taxpayer's identification number (also called Employer's Identification number), get Form SS-4 from the Internal Revenue Service.

† If you are ever faced by a complex tax question, you may require the advice of a tax lawyer or a tax consulting firm. This can be expensive, but if there is a lot at stake, it may be worth it.

‡ For important tips on tax-saving deductions, new tax rulings, etc., subscribe to the *Tax Angles Newsletter*. For subscription information, write Kephart Communications, Inc., 901 North Washington Street, Suite 200, Alexandria, Virginia 22314.

of your business tax returns. Whether you fill out the forms accurately yourself is another matter, but at least you will figure out what forms must be filed, why, and what deductions you can make.

FISCAL VERSUS CALENDAR YEAR

The following is a rundown of the taxes that each business structure is required to file. The filing dates depend on whether you register with the IRS by the *calendar* or *fiscal* year. A tax year is twelve consecutive months, ending on either December 31 (a calendar year) or at the end of any month of your choosing (a fiscal year). Your lawyer or accountant can advise you as to which date is most advantageous for your business. In general, filing returns fiscally allows the end of your fiscal year to coincide with the low point of your annual business cycle. Almost every business has a slow period, having to do with the very nature of the business. If you choose a fiscal year, ending at this point of least activity, then you will have more time to work on closing your books for the year and filing your tax returns. (Sole proprietors and unincorporated partnerships cannot file fiscally because business taxes must be paid on your personal income tax returns, due April 15 every year.)

TAX PLANNING

It is important to review profits and expenses toward the end of your tax year. In that way you can monitor your cash flow. You might want to accept payment from a client *after* the year's end, so the income will be taxed on the next year's return. Another way to get a deduction in a high-profit year is to prepay your loans or mortgages. In general, if you anticipate higher profits for next year, defer whatever *expenses* you can to that year's return. If you anticipate lower profits, defer whatever *income* you can. Your accountant should be on hand to advise you about your tax planning.

TAXES FOR INDIVIDUAL PROPRIETORS AND FREE-LANCERS

FEDERAL INCOME TAX

All business income and deductions* are to be filed on your individual tax return, Schedule C (Form 1040), available from your local IRS office. This is due on April 15. If you need an automatic sixty-day time extension (penalty-free) to prepare your taxes, use Form 4868 to request the extension; it must be filed on or before the original date that your taxes are due.

You must also file estimated tax returns quarterly during the tax year.† Form 1040-ES is used for this purpose and contains complete filing and payment instructions.

STATE INCOME TAX (FRANCHISE TAX)

You must pay individual state income tax (if your state requires it) to the franchise tax board of your state. Check with it on filing procedures.

---

* A full explanation of the status of, and difference between, part-time and free-lance people is available in the *Tax Guide for Small Business*.

Consult the *Tax Guide for Small Business* for specifics on deductions and what constitutes taxable income for each business structure—the proprietorship, partnership, or corporation. In general, the following are included as tax-deductibles: rent, interest, taxes, depreciation, incidental repairs (but not improvements), bad debts (if you can prove they won't be paid), equipment that is leased, salaries paid to owners of partnerships and corporations (but not single proprietors), answering service, business cards and brochures, etc. If you work at home, see IRS publication no. 587, *Business Use of Your Home*, for deduction requirements. There is a new liberalized child-care income tax credit for working mothers. The credit provides for a dollar-for-dollar reduction of income tax liability. It is equal to 20 percent of all annual household and child-care expenses incurred up to a maximum of $4,000 for two or more children, i.e., $500 of tax credit per year. The new law also allows women to claim the credit for child-care payments made to parents and has therefore been nicknamed the Grandmother Credit.

† Check with your local IRS office for updated information. Currently you are required to file a document of estimated taxes if your estimated income, not subject to withholding taxes, is more than four hundred dollars, and your estimated tax on that income is forty dollars or more.

Check with your city government to see which of the following is applicable to your business, and obtain the proper filing forms: individual city income tax, sales tax, business licenses, city and county real or personal property taxes.

PARTNERSHIP TAXES

FEDERAL INCOME TAX

Each partner must file her individual share of the company's income on her personal tax return (Schedule C, Form 1040). However, for informational purposes, partnerships are also required to report the company's income. This is to be filed on Form 1065 (U.S. Partnership Return of Income), and there are stiff penalties for failure to file this form. Since the partnership itself is not subject to income tax, no estimated tax returns are required. Filing dates (and extensions) are the same as those for sole proprietorships.

STATE INCOME TAX (FRANCHISE TAX)

Partnerships are required to file an informational return to the state franchise tax board (if your state requires it). In some states, each partner must file an individual state income tax return. Contact your state's franchise tax board.

CITY-COUNTY-LOCAL TAXES

Check with your local city government to see what taxes are required for partnerships. (See tax listing for local taxes for sole proprietorships.)

SELF-EMPLOYMENT TAX FOR SINGLE OWNER OR PARTNERSHIP

Owners or partners are not subject to federal payroll taxes (withholding taxes), but instead are required to pay self-employment tax, based on their business income. The computation is done on Schedule C-3 (Form 1040) and filed with your

individual federal income tax, even though the self-employment tax is not an income tax.

CORPORATE TAXES

FEDERAL INCOME TAX

Corporations must file their income tax returns on Form 1120,
as well as estimated tax returns, due quarterly. The actual
estimated tax payments are to be made to your bank (or any
authorized commercial or Federal Reserve bank); payments
are to be accompanied by Form 503.* Form 1120-W gives
complete information on figuring and filing the estimated tax.
By the end of the tax year you will have to have paid at least
80 percent of your taxes. If, at that time, you owe more than
20 percent, you may be penalized for not having paid enough.

Corporate taxes must be recorded on the books as business
expenses.

If a corporation is on a calendar year, then the federal
income tax is due on March 15. For a fiscal year, the return
must be filed on or before the fifteenth day of the third month
after the close of its fiscal year.

Corporations may receive an automatic three-month extension of time for filing their tax returns. Submit an application
for an extension on Form 7004, on or before the original due
date of the return.

Subchapter S Corporations

Small-business corporations opting for the Subchapter S status must file Form 2553, obtainable from your local IRS office.
It's a one-page form, indicating your corporation's election to
be treated as a small-business corporation for income tax
purposes. (As explained in Chapter 5, this election enables the
company to be taxed at individual rates. The owners may then

---

* Every company whose estimated tax is expected to exceed forty dollars must
file estimated tax returns and make estimated tax payments, quarterly during the business year. Refer to the *Tax Guide for Small Business* for additional information.

report their share of the company's profits or losses on their personal tax returns. If they have income from other sources, their whole tax may be reduced as a result of their business expenses.)

Subchapter S corporations must file their actual income tax return on Form 1120-S, according to the same time schedule as regular corporations.

Additional Corporate Taxes

Besides income taxes, certain manufacturers and retailers are subject to excise taxes. Corporations must also pay stamp taxes and death taxes, when applicable, as well as employment and social security taxes (see Chapter 14). Check with your local IRS office to find out if you are obligated to pay excise or stamp taxes imposed on the sale or use of certain items (such as liquor, firearms, certain equipment, etc.), and usually filed quarterly.

STATE INCOME TAX (FRANCHISE TAX)

Every corporation is required to pay an initial minimum franchise tax (the amount varies from state to state), due on the date of incorporation. Thereafter, the tax is paid annually, based on the company's net income for the preceding year. Contact the franchise tax board of your state for information on filing franchise tax returns.

Besides state income taxes, corporations are subjected to some or all of the following taxes, according to the nature of the particular business: gross receipts and sales taxes, business real and personal property taxes, capital stock taxes, business car or truck licenses and inspection fees, death taxes, "foreign" state business taxes, employment taxes, and Worker's Compensation insurance premiums.

CITY-COUNTY-LOCAL TAXES

Check with your city's government for specific corporate tax requirements. Corporations are subject to business real and personal property taxes, rental occupancy taxes, sales taxes, business license fees, etc., depending on the type of business.

SALES AND USE TAXES

All retailers must have a seller's permit. This allows you to purchase tangible property for resale without paying sales tax. To register, apply to the board of equalization for a seller's permit (resale tax) number. (Sometimes, the board requires a security deposit at the time of registration, the amount depending on the company's size.)

Taxes are paid to the board *after* the item has been resold.

Wholesalers or manufacturers must record transactions on resale certificates. These certificates plus instructions are available from the board of equalization.

PROPERTY TAXES

All businesses must pay annual personal property taxes on tangible personal property, including equipment and inventory. Real property taxes (on land, buildings), as well as rental occupancy tax, must be paid semiannually to your local tax authorities.

PAYROLL AND SOCIAL SECURITY TAXES

Once you begin hiring employees, your role as business owner becomes even more complex. There are strict regulations regarding personnel, including required insurance, federal and state unemployment taxes, and payroll and withholding taxes. (These will be explained in detail in Chapter 14.)

Everyone is familiar with Benjamin Franklin's pithy maxim "... In this world nothin is certain but death and taxes"; and he was probably ruminating on taxes again when he wrote, "The first mistake in public business is the going into it."

The responsibility here as elsewhere falls on the business owner, even if she's just supervising her bookkeeper or accountant. There is no salve to relieve the pain of taxes. The only way to alleviate the discomfort is by accurate recording, reporting, and remitting.

14

HIRING: HELP!

Woman is woman's natural ally.
Euripides

As your business flourishes, the day may arrive when you just can't do it all yourself. You need help, because it is no longer feasible, practical, or pleasant to go it alone. Sometimes it happens as suddenly as receiving an order too large to handle yourself. Or perhaps you've been letting some projects coast because you can't fit everything into the twenty-four-hour day.

Don't, however, take on any permanent workers until you are sure you are busy enough—*all* the time—to warrant the extra expense. Your increased business must be well-established, not just seasonal. Because employees mean not only salary, but withholding taxes, Worker's Compensation, social security, and the increased bookkeeping that goes along with these—not to mention the additional space, desks, telephone equipment, and supplies.

Before hiring anyone, figure out exactly what the job will entail and what duties will be included. Then, determine whether they can be performed by someone working full or part time. In general, small businesses can cut down on time wasting by hiring part-time or "new-time" workers, who tend not to loaf because of their shortened hours.* You also save money in salaries and benefits.

FREE-LANCE WORKERS

Free-lance help is a good way to save money if you have a temporarily heavy workload but cannot justify taking anyone on full time. Generally, you will pay on an hourly basis, although in some cases you may choose to pay a per project salary—a percentage of the profits of the job equal to the value of the free-lancer's service to you. State laws vary according to their tax and benefit requirements for free-lance or temporary workers.

WHOM TO HIRE

The job itself answers this question: What degree of experience is needed to fill it? Highly qualified people require high incentives—large salary, ample fringe benefits (longer paid vacations, hospitalization insurance, profit-sharing, etc.). And about the only way a small-business owner can afford to bring this sort of additional experience into the company is to take on a partner and give up a percentage of the business.

If intelligence and common sense are qualification enough, then look for these qualities in a less experienced, energetic person willing to buckle down and learn—for example, recent graduates of commerce schools, college students, a parent whose hours must coincide with school time, etc. The more flexible the hours, the more categories of workers open up.

It is good policy *not* to hire friends if you want to keep the friendship. At least evaluate the friend's ability to view your role as boss seriously and take orders without resentment. Before hiring a friend, consider whether you could *fire* her (without unpleasant repercussions) if things didn't work out.

HOW TO FIND HER

First of all, spread the word around that you are hiring. Announce what kind of person (and qualifications) you are

---

* New time is part time coinciding with school hours, designed for working mothers.

searching for to business associates and friends. This word-of-mouth network is often the most satisfactory way to find someone.

Using the services of an employment agency costs a fee, and if the person doesn't work out, there's no money-back guarantee. To save time, contact several recommended agencies, and interview people from all of them. Sometimes talking to a number of qualified applicants helps you to clarify your requirements.

Other sources for tracking down people are school placement offices, help-wanted notices on public bulletin boards, and paid ads in newspapers.

THE DESCRIPTION OF THE JOB

Before you start looking, chart out your requirements. List every duty you will want your staff member to perform. Try to envision what the job could grow into as business increases. That way, when interviewing, you can evaluate whether a person will grow with your company or is suited for only one level of activity. As a woman employer, you should try to redefine secretarial and other jobs which have traditionally been dead-ends for women.

Besides delineating job requirements, you must decide on salary, hours, number of sick days and vacation, plus fringe benefits (group health, discounts, etc.). Do this for every job to be filled, and make sure that every person you hire knows and understands exactly what she is to do.

WHAT THE JOB WILL PAY

The salary you offer will depend on the job to be filled and the going rates. Check your balance sheet, and discuss this with your accountant so that you know exactly what you can afford to pay. Contact your state's departments of labor and industrial relations or your local office of the United States Employment Service for minimum wage requirements, as well as contract and wage stipulations should you have to deal with a union. To attract top-notch help, you must offer reasonable salaries, adequate benefits, and pleasant working conditions.

For retail businesses, the amount spent on payroll should represent 15 percent of the store's total volume.

INTERVIEWING

No matter how highly recommended a person comes or how qualified she seems to be, you must interview her, formally or informally. Find out her qualifications for the job. Ask for references, and *check them*, no matter how excellent a judge of character you are.

Besides measuring her abilities, lean on your intuition and rapport. Consider whether you want to share close working quarters with this person, day in and day out.

You might want to include a bit of on-the-spot improvisation, where you see the interviewee relate to the work she must do. (Have her type a letter to check typing skills, wait on a customer, or check out your products, etc.)

The Job Application Form

Have typed application forms ready to be filled out at the beginning of the interview. The basic information you need is:

> Name
> Address and telephone number
> Social security number
> Previous job experience—where employed, for how long, and specific responsibilities
> References (other than previous employer)
> Any other skills, unusual qualifications, or pertinent information. (A person's marital status is not important, yet time schedules in relation to home life may be. A woman with children may need to arrange flexible afternoon hours.)
> Any other questions relevant to your specific business.

Be sure to leave adequate space for answers.

This should be filled out by all applicants as they arrive so that you can refer to it during the interview. Hold on to the applications, even after you have filled the job, in case you need someone else at a later date.

The Interview Procedure

After the prospective employee has filled out the application, explain exactly what you're looking for, what needs to be done. Besides experience, look for motivation—will she really enjoy the job or just stay until something better comes along? (Even so, you may still consider hiring her on a temporary basis.) The applicant's responses can help you predict her reliability and interest.

It is difficult to find perfection. Often, the person you intuitively like lacks certain skills that you require. You may have to compromise a bit and rely on on-the-job training to get what you want. If a person doesn't work out, you can always fire her, but that can be difficult (and expensive).

Don't rush the interview, unless you perceive immediately that the person has nothing to offer you. The more time you spend now, the better it will work out later. Interviewing becomes easier the more you do it. Just remember, trust your instincts as well as your intelligence. The right person will add a new dimension to your business and help you to increase sales and expand. The wrong one can waste time, materials, and lose customers.

ON-THE-JOB TRAINING

When a new person joins your staff, plan to take time from your own work to spend exclusively with her. Give her on-the-job instruction on every facet of her duties. Don't ever be too busy to answer questions. Explain the workings of the entire business, where things are, any rules and regulations, who the regular clients are, and other pertinent facts. Then keep observing her work and refining your instructions.

Each staff member must understand her job and how she relates to the overall scheme of the business. She must know her responsibilities, authority, and relationships. She must have the confidence that she can accomplish her assignments and that it is in her best interest to do so.

Everyone has different working methods. So long as a job is well-executed according to schedule, don't be upset if a staff member does it her way. Don't smother your co-workers or give them free rein to run amok. Be there to guide, but stand back and give your carefully selected associates the freedom to do things their own way.

SUPERVISING

Nearly 70 percent of all customer losses can be attributed to bad service by indifferent employees. At the root of most problems with employees is a business owner who is inept at handling personnel and delegating work and responsibility.

Throughout your entire working relationship, communicate what needs to be done, and when and how you want it. Be consistent in pointing out what's wrong (and what's *right*) about a person's work.

Don't forget that you are at the helm—giving instructions, gauging your success, building business, seeing clients, ordering supplies or inventory, charting new directions. After all, you are risking your money, and you have to make the decisions. Supervising your employees is just part of supervising your business. You must be willing to spend considerable time in hiring, training, and managing your personnel. You must emanate confidence in order to inspire it and to keep things flowing and growing.

DELEGATING WORK AND RESPONSIBILITY

Once you have delegated authority, allow key associates to take the initiative to run things, even during your absence. It is difficult for small-business owners to sit back and let anyone else shoulder responsibility, but you must resist the urge to thwart your staff and keep them from flourishing.*

Be available constantly for encouragement and guidance.

---

* Read the SBA's free pamphlet no. 191, *Delegating Work and Responsibility*, available at your local SBA office or the Government Printing Office. (See appendix.)

There must be individual motivation as well as team enthusiasm, but try to encourage cooperative, noncompetitive attitudes among your staff.

Switch perspectives periodically, too. Listen to your associates. Find out what *they* want out of their job. You may not be realizing their full potential. Ask for advice and suggestions—and act on them. Earn your employees' loyalty and respect by respecting them.

Don't forget to promote people, and raise their salaries as your business makes more money. Give each job a title.

FIRING

Since the standards of the business are yours, its ultimate success lies in your lap. If the quality starts faltering because of an indifferent or untalented employee, then you will have to let her go. Be kind to people, but not at the expense of your company's reputation and profits. If you do fire someone, try to be helpful in steering her into work for which she might be better suited.

STAFF MEETINGS

Keep well-informed on what everyone is doing; let everyone know what *you* are doing. The most effective procedure is to hold regular meetings, either daily or weekly, to review new jobs, policies, production, sales, and suggestions.

A small business must encourage camaraderie among the workers. As your business grows, so will you—from both the additional customers and the fresh ideas and opinions of your staff.

MAINTAINING GOOD OFFICE RELATIONS

Personnel management experts offer these tips for keeping behind-the-scenes office harmony:*

> Publicly praise the good work of staff members, and discuss grievances or criticism in private.

---

* Adapted from "Avoiding Management Pitfalls," *Small Business Reporter*, vol. 11, no. 5, Copyright © 1973, Bank of America, San Francisco, California 94137.

Actively solicit suggestions, opinions, and ideas from your staff. Adopt good ideas, giving full credit where it's due. Explain why other suggestions are not feasible.

Respect differences of opinion. Obviously, everyone views each situation differently.

Keep reassessing each job, with an eye toward keeping it interesting and challenging. Bored workers will not enhance your business' image.

Admit your own mistakes; your staff will respect you for it.

Keep your staff up to date with what's happening with the business, especially with matters concerning them.

Always explain why new policies are being put into effect.

Give promotions when they're due. Whenever possible, promote from within, rather than hire someone new. It's up to you to train employees so that they will be equipped to handle additional responsibilities.

Set up personnel guidelines, but don't be rigid. Deal with individual problems as they occur.

Be honest when dealing with your staff. Be consistent. Above all, be fair.

PAYROLL PAPERWORK PROCEDURES

Payroll Record Keeping

There are no legal requirements as to *how* employee records are to be maintained. There are numerous payroll record-keeping systems, and your bookkeeper or accountant can advise you on the simplest method for your needs. The following information must be recorded:

The employees' names, addresses, and social security numbers

Amount and date of salary payments subject to withholding taxes, and the amounts withheld

The periods of employment, including payments to employees during their absence owing to illness or injury

W-4 forms (income tax-withholding exemption certificates)

Your Employer Identification number. (File Form SS-4 with your Internal Revenue Service district director in order to obtain this number.)

Duplicate copies of tax returns that have been filed

Dates and amounts of deposits made with government depositories (your bank or a Federal Reserve bank)

PAYROLL TAXES

From the moment you hire your first employee you have taken on an added responsibility. Every business with one or more employees is required to withhold *federal income taxes* and social security taxes. This amount is taken out before the paycheck is issued.

First off, file Form SS-4 with your IRS district director to obtain your Employer Identification number (not to be confused with the social security number required on individual tax returns). Obtain specific information from the IRS on your type of business, as well as Circular E in the IRS's *Employer's Tax Guide*, which indicates the up-to-date deductions to withhold (taxes and social security) from every paycheck, based on the total salary amount. Contact the Department of Labor if you have any additional questions.

Withholding returns are to be filed quarterly on Form 941, available from the IRS or your bank.

At the beginning of each year (calendar) and when hiring someone new, you must furnish every employee with a W-4 Form (or W-4E, in some cases—check with the IRS to see who qualifies). This form, called the Employee's Withholding Allowance Certificate, also indicates the number of dependents she is deducting from her paycheck.

SOCIAL SECURITY TAXES

Social security taxes must also be withheld and matched equally by the company; the amounts change yearly. The IRS and Social Security Administration offices provide tables showing the exact amounts to withhold and match for different salary levels. This computation must be done on Schedule C-3 (Form 1040) and filed with the individual's return.

CITY AND STATE WITHHOLDING TAXES

Contact your local and state tax authorities for information about any payroll and withholding tax requirements under their jurisdictions.

SELF-EMPLOYMENT TAX

Instead of social security, proprietorship and partnership owners are required to pay a self-employment tax (see Chapter 13). Pension and profit-sharing plans for noncorporation owners are covered in Chapter 7.

FEDERAL UNEMPLOYMENT TAXES (FUTA) AND DISABILITY INSURANCE

Both FUTA and Disability insurance taxes are filed annually on Form 940. You are required to file it if (1) you pay wages of $1,500 or more in any quarter of your business year; and (2) you have hired one or more employees in each of twenty calendar weeks.

STATE UNEMPLOYMENT TAXES AND DISABILITY BENEFITS

Most states require the above if you have one or more employees, and are paying more than a hundred dollars per quarter in wages. (This unemployment tax cannot be collected or deducted from your employees' salaries.) If you qualify, you must register with the department of human resources development or other proper department of your state.

Disability benefits are deducted from the employee's paycheck, along with withholding and social security. This provides compensation for illness or injury unrelated to the job.

WORKER'S COMPENSATION AND
UNEMPLOYMENT INSURANCE

If you have full-time employees, you are required to take out Worker's Compensation, from a state insurance fund or private insurer. The applications of Worker's Compensation vary widely between states. (See Chapter 7.) This insurance is mandatory once a single employee is hired.

For unemployment insurance coverage, apply to the state department of human resources development within fifteen days of hiring your first employee.

15

BUYING A BUSINESS OR FRANCHISE: YOUR SLICE OF PIE IN THE SKY

If there were dreams to sell, what would you buy?
Thomas Lovell Beddoes

If you don't want to start a business from scratch, there are other ways to go. You can take over a going business or buy a franchise. Although the two parallel and overlap in many instances, they still remain very different concepts in owning your own business.

BUYING A BUSINESS

There are a number of good reasons for buying an already-existing business. You may not be able to come up with a lucrative new idea that will go over in your community. Or you may hear of a business for sale that is just what you're looking for. Perhaps you want to put your talent and experience to work for yourself, but don't want the hassles of starting from scratch.

Assuming you haven't spotted a "for sale" sign blinking just for you, the most obvious place to begin your search is the local newspaper under "Business Opportunities." Or you can advertise there yourself: "Looking to buy . . . (special interest)." Other excellent information sources are business realtors and your accountant or banker. They may be able to help, especially if you're open-minded about what you want to try.

Once you've found something that interests you, be prepared to spend time and money on investigating the scene behind the "for sale" sign. The nitty-gritty of the transaction will involve negotiating a fair price, evaluating the seller's facts and figures, and closing the deal.

Consult with a lawyer and an accountant. A lawyer, besides helping you arrive at a decision, must represent you in the final transaction. An accountant will not only verify the financial records, she will contribute valuable observations on market trends and the company's future profit potential. These professionals will also help you evaluate the answers to the questions that follow.

Why Is This Business for Sale?

Knowing the owner's (real) reasons for selling will help you negotiate the price and will give you an idea of the degree of experience and skill needed to continue the business profitably. It is possible that the seller is moving out of town, retiring, or simply ready to go on to something else. It's also possible that the new superhighway is scheduled to cut right down aisle four.

Get the facts, and be wary if the seller seems to hedge on certain information. The fewer unknowns, the better chance you will have of success. The things to check on and evaluate are:

> Debts or hidden (or unrecorded) obligations.
> Accounts receivable—how long do customers take to pay?
> Repeat business—what percentage of the billing is with steady clientele?
> Back taxes or employee withholdings—does the company owe any?
> Lawsuits—are there any pending?
> Length of lease—is it renewable or transferable to the new owner?

Property, fixtures, equipment—is there solid evidence of the seller's ownership of these things?

Trademarks, patents, copyrights—have they been granted, or are they pending?

State, federal, and city licensing—has the seller complied with all regulations?

Zoning laws—any new ones which will affect the business? Any pertinent construction or demolition in the neighborhood?

Competition—who and where are they?

Distribution—are there problems with outlets or suppliers?

Staff members—to what degree are they important to the business? Are they willing to stay on with the new ownership?

Most times, though, a business is for sale because it's losing money through the owner's inadequate managerial ability. This is not necessarily a bad prospect—if you have ability and managerial skills, you're in a good position to pull off a success.

Will This Business Make a Profit?

In arriving at a fair purchase price, the profit potential is the key factor in your negotiations. Check the records (annual profit-loss statements, balance sheets, tax returns) of past performance.

The simplest way to forecast profit trend is to assume that sales will continue to increase or decrease at the same percentage rate as they have in the past. If the profit trend is down, then either new money or special skills will be needed to improve the picture. If profits are up, the seller is in the best negotiating position. The final sale price will strongly depend on these trends.

How Strong Is the Market?

Learn all you can about the product or service. What is the demand for it; who are the customers? To what extent is the business affected by the overall economy? Is the location convenient to customers and suppliers? Is the business seasonal?

Does it thrive on word of mouth, or does it call for saturation advertising and active promotions? Buying a business without checking these things is like buying a house without looking in all the rooms.

What Are the Tangible Assets of the Business?

What is the actual, physical property you will be buying? Have a qualified appraiser evaluate the inventory of goods, fixtures, equipment, supplies, furniture and decoration, lease on the space, active client lists, and property ownership. All of these should be assessed at the real value to the buyer—are they usable or salable on today's market? How much additional inventory, supplies, and equipment will you have to put into the business? Calculate *everything*, including new stationery, logo, or brochures, interior design, expanded line of merchandise, and the like. The ongoing quality of the business is the strong determining factor in the cost appraisal of the tangibles.

What Are the Intangible Assets of the Business?

Often these are labeled the "goodwill" of the business, and it's much harder to place a price tag on that. It is the image under which the business operates: its reputation, financial standing, reliability of the product or service, and the favorable location. It also includes the company's relationships with suppliers, creditors, and the community at large. It is of real value to both the seller and the buyer if the business scores well above average in these areas.

What Are the Liabilities?

Liabilities are the risks involved in operating any business. Investigate them just as thoroughly as you do the assets. (Check out the company's credit rating and whether there are current loans outstanding.) Naturally, the seller will minimize the risk factors. If there is hesitation or evasion on her part to supply this information, you can assume that the risks are greater than the potentials.

Negotiating the Price

Despite a favorable image, if the business' profits have been sliding downhill, then the purchase price can be little more than the physical assets. If the company is healthy in spirit and profits, there are various formulas which can be used to determine a reasonable buying price. One of the simplest is to estimate the resale worth of the *tangible* assets. Then set a value on the *intangibles*. First, figure the average annual net profit, based on the company's tax records and financial statements.

Next, multiply that figure times *five*, if the business is well-established with a favorable name, product, or location; times *three*, for a moderately well-known business; or, times *one*, if the business has only a one-year profit picture.

Finally, add the tangible and intangible assets together to set the total price.

Closing the Deal

Both your lawyer and the seller's lawyer will negotiate a contract spelling out every term of the transaction, including:

1. A clear title to all physical property.
2. Agreeable finance terms. Remember, you will still need operating capital, so that purchase payments should not deplete your cash flow.
3. Protection against any false statements, inaccurate financial information, or hidden liabilities.
4. A provision giving you operating control between the time of agreement and actual takeover. This protects you from the seller depleting assets with a "going-out-of-business sale" or destroying the goodwill factor.

5. A statement of when and how the buyer is to take over the business, and specifications of the familiarization period.

Every buy-sell transaction has its own special and highly individual aspects that will dictate the negotiations. Money may not always be the deciding factor for the buyer or seller. For example, the seller may accept a lower bid in favor of the person she feels will best maintain the quality of the product or service. The buyer may rank the psychological factors of owning her own business far higher than the actual income of the business.

In the end, only you can understand and appreciate why you are buying (or selling), and the final price will rest heavily on your motivations.

BUYING A FRANCHISE

Basically, a franchise is a licensing and distribution agreement between a parent company and an independent businessperson. Franchising is a viable and often exciting way to get into business for yourself. There are pros and cons from both a business and personal angle; whether it is right for you depends on many considerations.

Advantages of Franchising

For people with little or no business experience, buying a franchise can be a godsend. A franchise offers a proven success formula. The groundwork has already been laid in image, advertising, and publicity. Often the franchisor will tailor ads and promotional campaigns to your community. You buy equipment, fixtures, products, and supplies through a centralized purchasing system, so that long months aren't spent in establishing credit. The cash outlay is often lower than what is required to set up a business from scratch. And the franchisor may be able to help you with financing, either through its own credit system or by arranging a loan through your bank.

More important, the franchisor can offer you training and continuing marketing advice. You automatically join a business community made up of people who operate similar businesses, and together you can learn from each other.

Disadvantages of Franchising

The misconception about franchising is that it guarantees profits on your investment. But franchising carries no more guarantee of success than any other investment. Success or failure ultimately rests with you, and you must be qualified to run the business.

You will be expected to work hard and to follow the systems and the set way of doing business. If you are a spontaneous person with strong innovative and creative talents, then franchising is probably not for you. Most contracts are restrictive and lean heavily on pretested methods and controls with no room for deviation. If you don't want to do business that way, then don't buy the franchise.

Finding a Franchise

First, assess how much money you have to invest. Understand that over and above the franchise fee, you will need financing for overhead and operational costs.

Now, what kind of business do you see yourself in? In selecting a franchise, your main concern is to make sure the business fits. It should involve you in the kind of physical environment you like and bring you into contact with the type of people you feel comfortable dealing with. What kind of service or product is needed in your area? Some services simply won't go over in a small conservative community the way they do in larger urban areas.

There are various ways to locate franchise opportunities. Start with the local and nearby city newspapers. Under "Business Opportunities" you will find listings of both businesses for sale and franchises. Other sources of information are trade associations and business organizations. There are franchise directories and publications, usually available in libraries.

Look up franchising in *The New York Times Reader's Guide*; write the editors of the *Wall Street Journal*; look up "business opportunities" or "women in business" in the *Guide to Periodicals*. If you're looking for an unusual business, something that isn't listed in the franchise guides, it's a sure bet it's been mentioned in one of these sources.

There are also franchise exhibitions held in major cities around the country. For information on these shows, write to convention centers in major cities.

Evaluating a Franchise

Once you've located a promising franchise operation, find out everything you can, not only about the franchise policy of the particular company but about the company itself. For instance, you will want to visit its home base, see its operation, meet the officers. Go see another franchisee—talk out the pros and cons of this business and the terms of agreement; find out if the company is available when needed. Does the company provide the ads and promotions it promises? What profits can you realistically expect? Hire a lawyer who can help you with the investigation and advise you on the contract.

This is not a one-sided proposition—the franchisor must accept you as well. The company will have a definite idea of the type of person and territory best suited to its product or service, and will start forming an impression of you from the very first letter of inquiry you write. Be aware of the image you are projecting; your letters should be clear, to the point, and typewritten. Correspondence should be answered promptly, and appointments kept on time.*

THE PARENT COMPANY

Does it have a good reputation? Is it known in your area? How long has it been in business? What are the histories and

---

* Contact the following organizations for advice or assistance in judging a franchise: Small Business Administration, and Office of Minority Business Enterprise (see appendix); International Franchise Association, 7315 Wisconsin Avenue, Bethesda, Maryland 20014; Council of Better Business Bureaus, Inc., 1150 Seventeenth Street, N.W., Washington, D.C. 20036; or, Small Business Guidance and Development Center, Howard University, 1420 N Street, N.W., Suite 5A, Washington, D.C. 20005.

backgrounds of the principals in the business? How has the product/service changed since its original inception? Is it a staple or a luxury, and how will the economy affect its marketability? How many other franchise operations are there, and are they successful?

The company should freely provide you with names and addresses of other franchisees. Any attempt on the part of the company representative to evade questions is highly suspect. So is the attempt to lay any pressure on you to "sign on now." Reputable firms don't engage in high-pressure tactics. They don't have to.

For further information on the company, check with the International Franchise Association, an organization which screens all franchisors who join. The IFA will answer all your questions pertaining to the standards and ethics of a company. If the company you are interested in is not listed there, ask for references that you and your lawyer can check. A bank credit reference is particularly important as an indication of how long it has been doing business and the strength of its credit. Other sources of information are the Better Business Bureau and the Small Business Administration.

THE TERRITORY

This can be critical. What is the territory, and is it clearly defined? Will you have options to expand? What is the competition in the territory? How protected are your exclusive rights?

THE MARKET

Has a market survey been done by the company? How does your territory measure up under that survey? Who is the consumer, in terms of age and income, and how is that consumer reached? Does the salability of the service or product depend on location? On advertising?

THE FRANCHISE FEE

Just what will you be getting for your money—is it clearly spelled out in the contract? Does the franchisor offer training, sales aids, national or local advertising, promotion, publicity? Does it help you pick your location and provide interior design and central purchasing of equipment? Does it offer continuing assistance and a strong operating system, and is it on call for unexpected emergencies?

THE COST

Discuss and consider the additional funds and operating capital you will need to get the business underway and to sustain it during the months when profits will be small and expenses high. Are there hidden costs? What professional help will you need—salespeople, accountants, etc.?

FINANCING AND PROFIT POTENTIAL

What percentage of the profits will you be required to pay the franchisor, and under what terms? Is this percentage reasonable when weighed against profit potential? Will the franchisor assist you if you should need a loan? Will you be extended long-term credit on equipment and/or products? Ask to see the profit figures of franchisees who operate on a level on which you expect to operate.

PERSONAL EVALUATION

Rely on your feelings as well as the facts. Are you happy with the people you have met? Have you understood the terms of agreement, and are you still enthusiastic about the venture? What about your ability, physically and emotionally, to do the work necessary to build this business, now that you've had a closer look? This is going to be your business, so before signing any agreements or making any payments, be sure you feel right about everything. Any nagging doubts you now have may come back to haunt you later on.

THE CONTRACT

Your lawyer will see things in (or not in) a contract that will never occur to you. She can uncover loopholes and can advise you on your own qualifications, both personal and financial.

Go over the contract with your lawyer, and make sure you have a clear understanding of it. Most contracts will read strongly in favor of the parent company; remember, business relationships are not social ones, no matter how nice the franchisor makes it seem. In the business world, as everywhere, it's the fittest who survive.

PART TWO

WOMEN IN BUSINESS - INTERVIEWS

16

INTRODUCTION

If you don't have a good idea—don't. If you don't have enough capital—don't. And if you think you are going to work at it part-time, for heaven's sake, don't. Because there is no more demanding job known to man—or woman—than working for oneself.

Guin Hall (former director of the
Women's Bureau, New York State
Department of Commerce)

The first section of this book dealt with the information and sources needed for striking out on your own. Part Two illustrates, via the experiences of successful women entrepreneurs, how it all becomes a day-to-day reality.

For many women, often the least considered reality of being in business is the repercussion that business will have on home, family, and social life. For most business owners there is no cutoff at five o'clock. Problems spill over from work to home, time becomes a precious commodity, and careful planning is essential if home life and professional life are to work together smoothly.

Married women and those with children all agreed that the support and back-up of the family were essential as priorities, schedules, and duties dramatically shifted when a new business was added to the family. Many women found that including their families in the day-to-day operations of the business was the answer to surviving the pressures of managing a public and private life. This mingling of two usually separate spheres, career with marriage and parenthood, seemed to benefit everyone. The children learn about the demands and responsibilities of the grown-up world, the business profits from the input of extra heads and hands, and women have more time to spend with their families and on their jobs—instead of being torn between the two.

Of course, there are pitfalls, too. No matter how hard one tries to plan ahead, working women simply will not have the time or freedom they had before. Obviously, this may present problems, often serious ones. As some marriages improved, others dissolved. But whether a business is going to be friend or foe to one's home life seems to depend most on the attitude of the business owner herself. The business needn't be disruptive, but it will most definitely cause a shifting of focus.

The following interviews cover a variety of businesses in urban and rural communities across the country. The aim, however, is not to outline business ideas, but to provide first-person insights that will be useful to anyone starting almost any business. The more you know about different kinds of businesses and the professional demands on other women, the easier it will be to focus your own energies. You can learn from other women's successes in order to create your own.

17

RETAILING

Successfully merchandising goods to the retail market is a talent. It's knowing what will sell and how to make it sell in a continuous cycle of buying from one source and selling to another. The merchandiser strives to appeal to her customers' individual needs while buying for the market as a whole. At the same time the retailer must wade through inventory control systems, timed delivery dates, credit extensions, and billings. Retailing is a highly visible business, and every store, no matter how large or small, must build a positive image through display, advertising, quality of product, service, and ambience.

More women head into retailing than any other kind of business. It's the business most people think they understand best because it's the kind of business they deal with most often. It all seems so simple—clothes neatly arranged in sizes, books displayed by author and category, beautiful paintings lit by subtle track lighting, exotic plants misted to perfect subtropical conditions. When a purchase is made, the salesperson jots down the sale, collects the money, and hands over the goods. What could be easier?

A lot of things. The mortality rate of retail businesses is

high. The Small Business Administration computes the failure rate of women's boutiques at 75 percent. Dun & Bradstreet found that 58 percent of all business failure in the United States was in the retail trade. Inexperience and undercapitalization are cited as the reasons why.

Retailing takes money as well as talent. A good location, inventory investment, buying trips, operating capital, store design, promotion, and fixtures are all costly. And these days the need for security systems has added another major expense to the initial outlay of money.

But if you don't have large sums of money to invest, there are other ways to go. Stalls in mini-malls and flea markets can cut overhead to a minimum while offering high-traffic locations and maximum security. Advertising becomes a collective effort, and you can test your merchandising skills without the same risks as when you go it alone.

Consignment is another possibility. It can save money on rounding out a basic inventory line or be the foundation for an entire operation. Consignment can mean everything from an elegant art gallery dealing in top artists to antiques, crafts, and any number of resale goods.

Retailing success depends on many things, outside your place of business as well as in. Trends, competition, and wholesale resources count for as much as image, style, and organization. The customer is fickle and may bypass quality for convenience, or convenience for quality, depending on the mood of the day. More important, the retailer is dependent on the wholesaler who must depend on the manufacturer, the mails, strikers, and sometimes the weather. Even in the best of times, orders can arrive late, damaged, incomplete, or left to mildew in far-flung customs outposts.

Finally, a large part of the retailer's success rests on customer relations. Any store owner must maintain a smile—even in the face of complaints, returns, and Junior's sticky fingers on the prized porcelain figurines. In the end, the customer *is* always right because if she isn't, she goes away—and takes her money with her.

But the rewards of retailing seem to outweigh these obstacles—why else would so many women be heading in this direction? The backbone of small business in America is in retail—an intensely people-oriented kind of business. Ideas quickly become tangible displays; activity and constant inter-action with others make up every business day.

And, as one store owner put it: "When a customer buys something you've especially picked out—and I don't care if it's a dress or an original painting—well, it's exhilarating!"

MURDER INK

Dilys Winn has been called the "mistress of mayhem." She mer-ited this title as chief proprietor of Murder Ink. Located on New York's Upper West Side, Murder Ink is the world's first bookstore devoted entirely to mysteries.

Many bookstores today specialize in one theme: children, sci-ence fiction, women, games, cookbooks, drama, the occult, and so on. Yet, as Winn is quick to point out, the bookstore business is marginal at best. Unable to increase her inventory because she already stocked every mystery in print, she cleverly expanded the life and financial income of the business with many satellite ventures, including her compendium of mystery lore, *Murder Ink*, published by Workman Publishing Company.

I was in advertising and really bored. For ten years I was one of those professional malcontents. Until one day it struck me that everybody said the same thing and nobody got off their ass. So I said, "Okay, I'm going to open a bookstore and specialize in murder mysteries." The idea had been churning around for some time—ever since I was little, I loved the idea of bookstores.

The next day, I looked around my neighborhood for a store, found it, and signed the lease. I opened Murder Ink six weeks later. I know it sounds incredible, but it was easy once I had made up my mind to do it.

I think the biggest deterrent when you start a business is getting advice from too many people. An idea is so fragile that it's easy to get talked out of it. My friends said, "What are you doing? You're throwing away all your money." What they didn't understand was that I very much wanted to open the bookstore, and I wanted to do it right then. If it had closed in six months, I would have spent my $15,000 very well. A lot of people can't handle that. I think maybe if you go into business just to make money, you might be in trouble.

I started with $15,000 in personal savings. Of that, $5,000

went for inventory, and about $3,000 for rent, telephone deposits, decoration and fixtures, business cards, and supplies. The rest was for living expenses until the shop began to show a profit. One thing I found out was that a business always costs more than you think it's going to cost. There is no way to stay within a conservative estimate because things go wrong or simply cost more than you think—hidden costs that you won't know about until you're operating. There was an ugly linoleum floor here when I moved in. I expected to rip it up and find nice wooden floors, but instead there were rotting timbers, and a new floor ended up costing me $1,200. It's one of those little caveats of business that's really true: you can never bring it in for your original estimate.

I registered the store and the name with the city, and then I opened a business bank account with my savings. To start a bookstore, the first step is to write the publishers for their catalogs and request to be put on their regional salesmen list. Go to the competition, and see what they're doing. I went to all the big bookstores on Fifth Avenue and copied down every mystery title they had, and that was my basic resource list. I still go to other bookstores to snoop new releases, and sometimes I'll discover a publisher I've never heard of. If you're small, you don't get the routine mailers the big stores get so that you can miss out on the more obscure publishing houses.

Because I had $15,000 in my business account, at least 60 percent of the publishing houses extended credit. The standard routine, though, is to pay cash for two shipments before you can get credit. With credit, you're allowed up to ninety days to pay, but you pay a little more the longer you wait. The bills come in with a current total, a thirty–sixty days' total, and a sixty–ninety days' total. After ninety days they close you out. The thing that hits you right off in this business is how badly the publishing business is run. You think everyone is very urbane and bright and they all have IQs of 140—well, forget it! They are in as much of a hassle as everyone else. Shipments come in wrong; billing is fouled up.

I'm a very compulsive bill payer. Bills come in, snap, I want to pay them. My accountant says to wait two months before paying, to let money earn interest. But in the beginning, I paid bills within three days of getting them. The publishing houses automatically bill the fifteenth and twenty-second of every month, so that I ended up paying the bills twice. It was a mess. I could never understand why I came up with no money at the end of the month. The smartest thing I ever did was to get my accountant, who then got me a bookkeeper; otherwise, I would have gone nuts. I did the bookkeeping for three months, and all I learned was that I had no talent for it.

I carry fire and liability insurance. I don't carry theft because when we looked into it, we found out it would cost me five hundred dollars per year against a five-hundred dollar loss. I don't keep money in the store, and I make my deposits every day. As for shoplifting, it's supposed to be chronic in bookstores, but I don't have much of a problem. The store is so specialized that the average customer who comes in is very protective of it. Also, the shop is small; there are no hidden corners or bookshelves to go behind, and I can see everywhere.

The standard way to arrange books is alphabetically by author in sections—fiction, nonfiction, travel, etc. But because this store only deals in one topic, I arrange according to style. Raymond Chandler has nothing to do with Agatha Christie, so why put them together? Raymond Chandler does have something in common with Dashiell Hammett. Agatha Christie has something in common with Dorothy Sayers, so I group them like that—stylistically. I keep my first editions either locked up or have them displayed on a top shelf: look but don't touch. People don't know how to handle books—they break the spines.

The bookstore business is one of those fantasy businesses. I had envisioned sitting here running a literary salon, serving my clientele glasses of sherry. But then the reality hits. Someone's got to cart those crates of books around, dust the shelves, and keep up with the reorders. People think I have such a cushy job, but they don't know I've got eleven cartons of books to uncrate a day.

On a typical day I get here about 8:30 A.M. to clean the store. Then I restock the shelves, and after that it takes me about three hours to answer the mail and ship the mail orders. Mail order is a good part of my business, and it all comes from the publicity I've received. I've never advertised the shop.

Publicity is what has made this shop as successful as it is. I made a profit in my first year of business, which is really incredible for a bookstore, but it was all because of the publicity. The day I opened, a *New York Times* reporter happened in because he was trying to find a laundromat. As it turned out, he was a great mystery buff, so he wrote up the shop for the *Times*. Someone from *New York* Magazine also lived in the neighborhood and within three weeks did an article. That started a whole series of out-of-town articles, which launched the mail orders. One bit of publicity fed another. I maintain a friendly relationship with the people who write about me because then I can call on them again. I write reporters thank-you notes, call them up for a friendly chat from time to time, and then, when the moment comes, you've got a whole raft of contacts that can help you. I had no press contacts before I started this business, and now I've got them all over the country.

The mortality rate in the book business is very high. More so than for other small businesses, because bookstore owners are notoriously bad managers. People walk into this business the way I did: they think it will be nice to sit and read a book and chat with customers, but you have to be organized. It's not a genteel business at all. I deal with forty different publishers, so that I'm ordering books all the time. If I were any bigger, I would have to keep inventory control cards, but I do what is called an "eyeball" inventory. If I see I have only five books left, I reorder. I have 5,000 covers in the shop and I can handle that in my head. Control cards list the titles and publishers of each book you have, plus the number shipped. Each time you sell a book, you mark it on the card, and when you get a certain low number, you reorder. As for knowing how many books to order at a time, you get a feel for it after a while, especially for your regular sellers. I hate to sound like the cook who says, "You'll know when the dough is right by the way it feels," but it is true in running a business. The formula I use for ordering my top sellers is this: thirty days in the month, you sell one book a day, plus an arbitrary ten. Delivery is approximately three weeks, so I order forty titles every three weeks. An interesting thing about the book business that's not true of other retail outlets is you've got a return policy with the publishers. You lose 20 percent on a return, but at least you're not stuck with inventory you can't move. The publisher sends you a special return form, and back they go. Everyone in the book business should subscribe to *Publish-*

ers Weekly. Aside from the book news, you'll find ads for fixtures and supplies plus ideas on display techniques. Also, once a year there is the American Booksellers Convention, which can give you new resources and lets you meet the publishers and many of the authors.

Bookstore profits are very low. Routinely, it's a 40 percent markup on current in-print titles. It swells to 100 percent or more for out-of-print titles and first editions, but even with 100 percent markup, it isn't much, especially if you're talking about a $1.50 paperback. To stay alive, you have to do a volume business or expand. In my case, there just aren't any more mystery books to be had—I stock all the titles. So I've figured out other ways to make money off the basic idea of this store. For the past two years I've organized the Murder Ink Lecture Series. It's one night a week for six weeks, and I hold it twice a year. Each lecture has a five-dollar admission charge, and I go after good speakers and fun, offbeat topics. For each series, I do a special mailing and go for publicity on it. The last series included the following:

"Want to buy the only Rembrandt painted in ballpoint?" Art frauds and art thefts, real and fictionalized. With John Canaday, art critic for *The New York Times*; Louis Goldenberg, president of the Wildenstein Gallery; Robert Volpe, founding member of the New York City Police Department's art squad.

"Ten fun things to do with arsenic." Suspicious soufflés, mordant mushrooms, and other very deadly recipes proposed by Lawrence Pardue of the Bronx Botanical Garden; Dr. Charles Joseph Umberger, eminent toxicologist.

"The urge to kill." Mass murderers, mind murderers, would-be murderers discussed by Dr. Glen Boles, psychotherapist and organizer of the tyranny of violence seminars; Dr. Harvey Bluestone, former chief of psychiatric services at Sing-Sing Prison.

"Who knows what evil lurks in the hearts of men . . ." The Shadow. With Walter Gibson, author, and selections from old Shadow radio shows and films.

"Meet me at the Morgue." A visit to the Specimen Museum and Office of the Chief Medical Examiner. With a forensic dentist and an Interpol consultant as our guides.

"Mystery Monday, literally." Secret comings and goings. One clue: Wear walking shoes and carry a big flashlight. Not for the timid. Smelling salts provided.

I've also instigated a two-week Murder Ink Mystery Tour of Britain, which will include a walking trip on the moors, haunted castles, visits to famous mystery sites, special English lectures, and shopping for rare books. Starting this year, I'm putting out a Murder Ink Quarterly for $6.50, containing mystery reviews and other related articles. All of this is great as it opens up the life of the business for me.

My biggest mistake has been my storage problem. I've collected books all my life, and I know there is never enough room for them. They seem to multiply in the night, and no one ever has enough bookshelf space. Yet I looked at this store and said, "That's adorable, it's just the right size, I'll take it." I never gave a thought to storage space. I would say you need almost the size of your selling space for your storage. Now I'm having to think about moving just for more storage space, and I hate to do that.

I don't think you can be money-hungry in the book business. I was in the black after the first year, but that's very unusual. Also, I'm not living the way I used to. In advertising, I made $35,000 a year, and now, after three years, I make $10,000. But the difference is that I love what I'm doing. There's no other bookstore quite like mine in the United States, and I've become the *expert* on mysteries.

THE KENTUCKY COFFEE COMPANY

The Kentucky Coffee Company specializes in imported coffees, teas, spices, and hundreds of related gift items and kitchenwares. In a country-store atmosphere of burlap-covered bins, wooden barrels filled with coffee beans and teas, hanging baskets of spice jars, potholders and mugs, rows of tea sets, coffeemakers, cookbooks, and utensils, customers can browse while sampling the many exotic beverage blends. Janine Shaw and her mother-in-law, Betty Shaw, first thought of opening their own shop early in 1975. They tossed ideas back and forth, but nothing clicked until one day on a trip to Dallas, Texas, Janine spotted a coffee and tea emporium—and that was it.

The Kentucky Coffee Company opened six months later in Lexington, Kentucky, in a small suburban shopping center. The total investment was $20,000. Late in 1976, when the business was operating safely in the black, they invested another $35,000 to open a second shop in an exclusive (and busy) downtown shopping mall.

Our original investment of $20,000 all came from family savings. My husband and I own two-thirds of the store, and my mother-in-law owns one-third. After seeing the shop in Dallas, I wrote to the owner and asked if she would help us set up our store for a consultation fee. In retrospect, this was one of the smartest things we did because, for the very reasonable fee of $1,500, she shared with us her business experience.

She gave us the names of reliable wholesale coffee, tea, and spice merchants, advice on how much to order and when to reorder, suggestions on fast-selling giftware items, display ideas, advertising and promotional hints, and general advice on management. All of which might have taken us a year or more to learn—but this way we learned from her expertise and mistakes, not ours.

Our first location was in a somewhat out-of-the-way shopping center, where the rents were cheaper but there was little in the way of walk-by traffic. Because we were unique to Lexington, I was able to attract newspaper publicity soon after we opened our doors. This launched the business with a steady stream of customers and saved us a great deal in advertising expenses.

We were operating in the black after a year, but when the new downtown Civic Center and Shopping Mall opened, I realized we should be in a prime location. My strongest advice for anyone going into the retail business is to go for a high-traffic location. Yes, it can be a great deal more expensive, but if you're serious about being in business, location is the key to success. Our sales tripled in the new store, because of impulse buying. In the first shop, customers had to go out of their way to visit us—here, because we have a large glass interior storefront, shoppers can see the displays and smell the aroma of freshly brewed coffee. That works better than advertising or publicity.

The cost breakdown on the original store was as follows:

> Consultation Fee: $1,500. This enabled us to open with confidence in our merchandise and a good sense of how to run a business. Neither my mother-in-law nor I had ever been in business before.
> Inventory: $7,000. Our initial stock consisted of eighteen coffees, twenty-four teas, fifty spices, and a

varied selection of tea sets, mugs, coffee grinders, canisters, cookbooks, spice racks, utensils, and much more. In the beginning, I went to a trade show in Columbia, South Carolina, and one in Atlanta, Georgia, to expand on our consultant's ideas, but now I do all my ordering from catalogs, from sales representatives, and through subscriptions to *The Tea and Coffee Trade Journal*, *The Gift and Decorative Accessories Magazine*, and *The Gifts and Tableware Reporter*.*

Store Design and Equipment: $6,500. The first shop was in excellent condition, and we saved money on construction because my husband and oldest son did the carpentry. I keep the coffee and tea in barrels purchased from the wholesalers and went to many garage sales for old shelving and antique jars and bottles. Most of this money was spent on a very expensive espresso machine imported from Italy, an electric coffee grinder, a cash register, and the tables, chairs, dishes and utensils we use to serve customers coffee and pastries.

Advertising/Promotion: $400. Small newspaper ads, brochures with mail-order coupons.

Rent: $600. For two months, paid in advance. Many landlords require three months in advance.

Expenses: $800. Gas, electricity, office supplies; buying trips and insurance ($200 for a three-year policy covering all liabilities—fire, theft, damages, personal injury).

Operating Capital: $3,000. This covered expenses for six months before profits established a cash flow.

The second shop cost a great deal more to open because it was totally raw space and we had to build an interior storefront, as

---

* *Directory of Conventions*, Successful Meetings Magazine, 633 Third Avenue, New York, New York 10017, lists exhibitions all over the country (gift shows, food shows, etc.).

Trade Directories of the World lists all industries, such as the coffee and tea industry, and the gifts and tablewares industry, with information on their publications. Check your local library, or write to Croner Publications, 211-05 Jamaica Avenue, Queens Village, New York 11428.

well as install flooring, bathrooms, and electrical wiring. But we did not have the outlay in inventory we'd had before, as our credit was well established by then.

We kept the suburban shop running for a year after the downtown store opened but closed it when profits proved so high in the new location. The first shop grossed $40,000 in sales per year, and the second shop grossed $104,000 in its first six months. That's why you go for location.

More than half our profits are made from the kitchenware and gift items which we sell at the standard 100 percent markup. The coffee, tea, and spices are priced according to the fluctuating market and competitive pricing. Here the profit margin is far less, but it's what brings the customers in.

We also make a nice profit on selling pastries and coffee by the cup. The only drawback with this is that by selling food eaten on the premises, we are classified a restaurant by the board of health, which means rigid restaurant inspections and compliance to special laws that really have nothing to do with us since we don't cook in the store. But again, a hot cup of coffee and a place to sit down bring in customers, and most don't leave without buying.

We also do a very lively mail-order business. I put one of our brochures in every package of goods I sell. It explains the various coffees and teas we sell and includes a mail-order coupon. I advertise in regional magazines, but most of our mail-order trade comes from the customers we get from the hotel that is also part of the Civic Center.

As far as promotion goes, we are written up occasionally in local publications. We were once featured in *Redbook* Magazine. Afterward, I was asked to speak at local women's clubs and civic clubs, which was excellent for public relations as well as publicity because I met people and the meetings were written up in bulletins and club newsletters.

This business is hard work, and it doesn't run itself. I work every morning, seven days a week, and am home in the afternoons and early evenings for my family. I then usually come back and work until the 10:00 P.M. closing time. My mother-in-law works in the afternoons, and we hire high school and college students for evenings, weekends, and the holiday season.

I do all the bookkeeping, reordering, checking of inventory, and taxes. Every day I check sales against stock, so I never run low, but I try not to order too much at any one time. I don't want to tie large amounts of money up in inventory, and with little storage space I can't store large shipments. Everything has to be carefully timed and watched because sometimes there are shipping delays, or orders come in only half filled. It keeps you on your toes.

The whole family takes a big interest in the business, and they are very supportive. My husband helps during the busy season, and my son, Brent, is a part-time employee after school. He's a senior in high school and has changed his major from dentistry to accounting. My being in business has made all four children aware that you have to work hard to achieve the goals you set. Nothing is handed to you without work, but the rewards are fantastic.

JANIE C. LEE GALLERY

Janie C. Lee is a pivotal figure in Houston's thriving art community. She is also the most visible symbol of the out-of-New-York gallery scene in this country. She opened her first gallery in Dallas—in her apartment—twelve years ago. There she developed her own taste and eye for contemporary art. After moving to Houston, she began to build a national reputation for handling the leading American contemporary painters and sculptors of the post–Abstract Expressionist generation.

A successful art gallery requires three things: a philosophical commitment to the art represented; an in-depth knowledge of the field, as well as expertise in a specific area; and a gift for promotion. Good art carries with it a special mystique, and a talented gallery owner must interpret that mystique and develop the public eye. It's all very personal, and much depends on your knowledge and taste.*

I studied stage lighting in college, and in my senior year traveled with a Broadway show starring George C. Scott. The

---

* *How to Open Your Own Shop or Gallery*, by Leta W. Clark (St. Martin's Press, New York), is an excellent manual for prospective gallery owners. In it she covers techniques for developing commercial and corporate clients as well as the specifics in mounting and promoting exhibitions.

experience inspired me to launch a business career as a producer. I formed a company with two partners, and we produced plays in New York. But after a few years I realized the avant-garde quality I wanted in the theater was, at that time, in the art world—with the painters and sculptors, not with the playwrights.

For six months I immersed myself in art. I went to all the shows, met a number of artists, studied the successful galleries, and talked to the owners. Then I moved to Dallas (a city I knew well) and opened my first gallery. To me it was a logical transition—producing plays and mounting exhibitions are quite similar.

I knew the only way I could succeed was to compete with New York. I set my standards high and was determined to maintain the quality of art I felt was important. The artists I wanted to represent were then virtually unknown in this part of the country. I remember driving a Frank Stella piece around in my pickup truck, and nobody would buy it. I still own it today, as a reminder of why you should stick to what you believe in.

The business was started in my apartment and then moved to an accessible but low-rent area of Dallas. Gallery space should be large and spare with solid, plain walls, unobtrusive flooring, and a ceiling that will house a movable track lighting system. Storage space and room for a small private office are also important.

The investment in starting a gallery is strictly your physical overhead: rent, insurance, and operating expenses.* All my inventory was on consignment from the large New York galleries, which lend pieces to gain exposure for artists in other parts of the country.† It took me three years to show a profit and five years before I could begin to acquire the art I represent.

After six years, I transferred the gallery to Houston because

---

* Standard year-round gallery insurance includes protection against fire, water damage, liability, and theft. In addition, a short-term Fine Arts Floater can be added to a regular insurance policy to cover all risks while artworks are in transit or on the premises.

† Financial arrangements vary, but a fifty-fifty split between the artist and dealer is most common.

it was then a more artistically active city. As in all art forms, you need a cultural atmosphere, a "scene," in order to stimulate and develop interest. If there's only one theater in town, chances are it struggles to stay open. The gallery world is the same—success relies on the whole artistic climate of the area. My gallery is located about five minutes from the Houston museums, in a block with a number of other good galleries.

I have approximately five openings a year, and the emphasis is on the major established modern American artists—Jasper Johns, Robert Rauschenberg, Nancy Graves, Helen Frankenthaler, Claes Oldenburg, and Robert Motherwell, to name a few. If there is a great modern American painting around, I will compete to get it.

I concentrate on making these shows elaborate and unique. I deal in a high-quality commodity, and my presentations of it reflect the image and importance of the works of art. The shows are a major connection with my clients. The relationship between a gallery owner and a client is a very personal one. Most retailers can function with a pleasant, surface relationship with their customers, but a gallery owner needs to build a personal image, become a trusted friend and recognized authority.

You have to be totally committed to the artists and their works. And you have to be highly visible—operating a gallery is a whole lifestyle devoted to being out there, to knowing your clients and potential clients, to developing in them an appreciation and taste for the kind of art you represent. I am trying to sell the art of serious ideas and trends as well as nationally important works.

You must be able to educate people into becoming your clients. And you must get to know them well so you can build a feeling of trust. They may be spending large sums of money in your gallery on things that will become a part of their lives, and you need to have a comfortable working relationship.

To open up the field for sales, many dealers also work with corporations, museums, and architects or designers of commercial buildings.

When I first moved to Houston, I was involved in a new art collection started by the First National City Bank, and I have placed paintings in many museums. This is a natural extension of a gallery's business, and often, especially when you're just starting out, it can bring in a steady year-round income that helps offset the fluctuating income from the exhibitions.

When I first started, it was hard to get people to take me seriously, to believe I knew what I was talking about. I earned the respect and attention of the business community when people began to realize I was consistent, reliable, and never promised anything I couldn't deliver. I always assumed if you did something, you should be the best at it. I am committed to bringing the best art I can find to the collectors in this area.

THE LEFT BANK

The Left Bank is a renovated bank building, originally built in the 1920s, in Cincinnati, Ohio. It houses eighteen tiny specialty shops selling everything from imported coffee to designer shoes. And although each shop owner leases space and operates as a separate retail business, the guiding force is Mary Sue Morris, who created the idea, bought the building, designed and supervised its conversion, and keeps the whole enterprise running.

Before my husband and I moved to Cincinnati, I had worked in New York as the head of the women's marketing for American Airlines. It was a fantastic job, but there was no way to transfer it to Ohio. My husband is a real estate developer and had never had a marketing department as a part of his company, so I got into business with him. We were putting up apartment complexes and European-type shopping villages in two cities near Cincinnati, and every day for one year I commuted a distance of about eighty miles. At the end of that year, I realized I did not know one soul in town, and I despised Cincinnati because I was so lonely.

Plus I had all the political problems of working within my husband's company. I mean you could kill yourself working, and it was never going to be what everyone wanted.

Then I met a woman who owned a shop on Hyde Park Square, and she told me about an old bank building that had been empty for years. It was a wonderful location but so expensive that no one business could afford to go into it. Hyde Park Square is the oldest shopping village in Cincinnati. It's the only area that has maintained its quality, and all the shops on the square are excellent specialty stores.

I looked at the building and loved it immediately. It was in pretty bad shape, though. The bank had put in three false ceilings, but it still had all the original fixtures, the bank cages, the old vault, and the original moldings.

I developed the idea of dividing it up so that a number of little specialty shops, each about ten-by-ten feet, could go in. I was simply at the right place with the right background in marketing and the construction business.

The first step was to take an option on the property. This would give me time to go out and sell other people on the idea, people who would agree to lease space and open shops after I had renovated the building.

To find people, I started out using word of mouth. I called every person who was already on the square, told them what I was trying to do and asked them to spread the word. I found out there was sort of a pent-up demand among people who had wanted to have a small shop in Hyde Park for years but found it too expensive.

I guess the trickiest part was getting the right mix of shops in here. I made up my mind that each shop would be unique. If one shop carries widgets, no other shop in the building can carry or sell widgets. I have this stated in the lease, and it's very strict: everything that each shop is going to sell is spelled out in the contract.

When a customer goes into the Left Bank, she knows that if she's seen one thing in a particular shop, she won't see it again. All eighteen shops are unique and individual, and I urge the shop owners to be very, very specialized.

As soon as I had a commitment on 50 percent of the leases, I felt I could afford to buy the building. And that meant going to the bank. To this day it makes my hands perspire, my heart beat faster, and I can hardly talk when I get there. I have a terrible fear of bankers. It's as if they can see through you and think you're going to use the money for some other motive than what you say. They make you feel that they are doing you a favor, and here you are ready to pay 12 percent interest!

My husband was not investing any money in this venture, but the bank wanted him to co-sign for me to buy the building. I felt it wasn't right, since he was not the one out leasing space and pulling this whole thing together. It was up to me to make the thing work, and the bank should believe in me as they would in any businessman applying for a loan. After all, my business credentials were very good. Finally, the bank said my husband would have to co-sign for 50 percent, and if he didn't, I couldn't have the loan. I didn't fight it any further because it was so necessary for me to get the building opened in time for Christmas.

In retail, the Christmas season can mean up to half your yearly sales, and to open a new place and miss Christmas would be foolish. I saw the building in June, bought it in July, and opened November 1.

The renovation of the bank was quite a saga. I'm a frustrated architect, so I laid out the basic interior design myself. Then I brought in an architect for exact proportions, special interior design, and, most important, to decipher the building codes.

The architect I hired came highly recommended, and when we initially sat down to talk, I thought I made it clear on how I wanted the place to look. Everything in there was to remain, the old feeling, the charm, and the classical facade. Well, we ended up in the biggest damned fight; it was just a nightmare. He came back with *lucite*! His plans had the entire front of the building ripped out and replaced with glass and lucite. He had planned the inside for an extremely contemporary look. I wanted the complete opposite; it was as if we spoke two different languages. The whole time you're in that position as a woman you're wondering if it's because you're the "little woman" that they're not hearing what you're saying. In the end, I had to pay his bill and mark that off as lesson number one.

It's almost impossible when renovating an old building to get anyone to say definitely what it's going to cost. It's hard to estimate, and a contractor doesn't want to lose money. On big expenses like plumbing, electricity, heating, and air-conditioning it is difficult to get a bid that will stick. *Always* assume it's going to cost more than the estimate.

My contractor turned out to be like 99 percent of the contractors you ever deal with; they assure you that you haven't got a thing to worry about, but during the last four weeks of the construction I was on the phone at 4:00 A.M., screaming about plaster, stairwells, bricklaying, and everything else. Contractors somehow never meet a deadline, and the pressure on me was tremendous because the shop owners had all been guaranteed the Christmas season. Their stock was arriving, and they needed to get into their space to decorate. In the end, I paid triple time to get the place finished.

I ask the highest rents in Cincinnati because I pay all the utilities and provide all the services in the building, including creative service for advertising and promotion. Practical services include insurance, security, trash removal, cleaning, window display cases, and all maintenance, repairs, and storage. The shop owners' only concern is their merchandise and sales.

The Left Bank is advertised as a whole. Each shop chips in fifteen dollars per month for advertising and promotion, which gives me the tiniest budget to work with.

The first year we ran small newspaper ads each month, but for the whole year we only have about $3500, which doesn't buy much in a city this size. I decided this year to go first class and shoot the works between November 1 and Christmas. The money was concentrated on television. We ran our ad in the local time slots on "The Today Show," "The Tonight Show," and the afternoon soaps. We wanted this campaign to reach a much larger market. We already had the upper-income bracket in Cincinnati, but we wanted people in surrounding areas to know about us and make an excursion to Hyde Park Square. And it worked: we had people coming in from more than a hundred miles away.

I did the ad the cheapest way possible. I had a good amateur photographer take a picture of each shop. Then I asked some friends in advertising to help me with the copy. The final product was a shot of each one of the shops shown in quick flashes while the voice-over recited a verse touching on all the different aspects of the bank, "Pots and pans and coffee beans/Socks and shoes for tennis teams . . ." and so on, for one minute. It ended with a shot of the bank from the front and the address. The ad cost sixty dollars to produce in all, and the rest of the money went to buy television time.

To launch the business, we held a huge promotional party when the bank opened, and got television and newspaper coverage. We've also appeared on all the local talk shows, displaying some of the unusual things you can buy here, and whenever a new shop opens, I send out a press release.

It has taken me a year to get the building running smoothly. In the first year there was no profit because I had to pay the construction bills, and there were the inevitable hidden costs and finishing touches. You can make a very good income from this kind of idea. Your income is fixed at the rents you charge and the amount of space you have to let. The cost of running the building runs close to the same each month, and now I only have to spend one day a week managing The Left Bank. This has left me free to start my next project: I've leased an old police station, built in 1901, which has been deserted for twenty years. The plan is to turn it into a restaurant and bar with a place for dancing.

THE HANDMADE STORE

The Handmade Store is a regional outlet for Appalachian crafts. Kathryn Horkan Campbell launched her store, located in the small town of Blacksburg, Virginia, in 1974. Building a retail business like this is not a matter of heading for the nearest wholesaler—it takes time to develop and an intense interest in the art and tradition of the craftspeople.

I had planned a career in photography, but I found myself in western Virginia, where my husband was finishing his studies at Virginia Tech. Blacksburg is a college town surrounded by the past. I realized what a rich area this was for crafts—yet there was no one store selling strictly handmade items. So the store grew out of a need—mine and the area's.

Up in the mountains near here there are people who have never learned to read and write, but the things they make with their hands are beautiful—their crafts are handed down from generation to generation. A Tennessee woman I know makes exquisite braided rugs. She rips the material, dyes, braids, and stitches it together herself—and she's ninety years old!

The shop stocks anything handmade—quilts, pottery, rugs, furniture, jewelry, and crafts made by children in school. We also have resident craftspeople working in leather, silver, candlemaking, and weaving.

I began by renting a space and setting my business up as a simple sole proprietorship. I made a profit after two years and then decided to incorporate because I wanted to get away from the one-person operation and into a self-perpetuating enterprise. I also wanted the structure of a corporation if and when I ever need to sell stock in the business.

Last year I bought a beautiful old building on Main Street and renovated it. I got complete financing from the bank. By then I had separated from my husband and used some of my own fuel stock as collateral. Owning a building gives me a great deal of leverage at the bank now. In a small town everybody likes to see a business grow.

My initial capital investment was $7,000—two-thirds was my own savings, and the rest was a loan. Today it would cost me about $45,000 to set up the size of operation I have now. Here we have much more merchandise, and I'm running the business much more professionally. I carry a great deal more insurance now and have set up a health insurance plan for myself and my three employees.

I hire only people who are intending to stay in the area. It's too hard, time-consuming, and expensive to teach new people the intricacies of the crafts and craftspeople. Of course, there is the basic problem that no one can ever know as much as I do about the business, but my employees work in all areas of managing the business—bookkeeping, display, sales, and advertising.

The record keeping kills us. We have to update shipments and sales for each craftsperson daily in a huge inventory book. I do the daily record keeping and have a CPA who does the taxes. At least half my time is spent on buying, dealing with the books, personnel, new construction, and bills. The rest of my time is spent finding new outlets for the business.

We're just now getting into mail order. Among people interested in crafts, the word spreads very quickly as to who is doing what. I get letters from as far away as North Dakota and California from people who want to buy or sell something. I have a simple catalog describing the things we sell and the craftspeople available to us. I expect this to become an important area for the business, but it is too soon now to estimate the percentage of profits from mail order.

I rely on word of mouth more than anything else to promote

the business. Advertising is minimal and directed only toward the crafts-oriented person through crafts publications. Making my location attractive and intriguing has increased business. I post signs on a chalkboard by the front door announcing the particular craft or artisan we're featuring that week.

Nothing in my background prepared me for running a business, and I was pretty naïve when I started. Now that I've developed a more businesslike attitude, I realize that there has to be a division between your personal life and business life. It's difficult because owning a business means you can't shut it out of your mind at five o'clock. It becomes a way of life, yet your time is not always entirely your own. It's especially important to realize this if you have a family. But it's possible to delegate too much authority to someone else. If you own a business, you've got to run it yourself. People just getting into business often don't realize the time, commitment, and dedication it takes.

Basically, I believe business is a matter of common sense and of not being afraid to take risks if you believe in your idea. Most important, you've got to be prepared to sacrifice immediate profits and put your money back into the business. When you go into business, be prepared for lean times and budget for them.

The main problem for me in starting The Handmade Store was getting people to take me seriously—to understand this was not a passing phase but an ongoing career. This doesn't mean I haven't made my share of mistakes. The first year I had no idea of the taxes I would need to pay and had to borrow money to meet them. The second year I overextended myself and was pinching pennies. After I bought the building, it was like starting all over again. I've made buying errors, too. I now forecast another four years in business before making a substantial profit, but I'm willing to give it time to grow naturally.

Business ownership definitely has two sides to the coin. It's at least three years of sacrificed freedom, having to put up with unsympathetic customers, a lot of money worries, and endless trial-and-error mistakes. But it's so very rewarding— the feeling of accomplishment against the odds. For me, the evolution of both the business and the owner has been incredible.

TRACK II

Until a few years ago Midway, Kentucky, was a sleepy hamlet off the interstate highway between Cincinnati, Ohio, and Lexington, Kentucky. Most of the small turn-of-the-century buildings on Main Street were boarded up or being used for storage. A grain and feed store, café, drugstore, and the poolhall maintained a semblance of business enterprise. Then Nancy Reeves turned the whole town around by opening a bright little gift shop called Something Special, followed by a sophisticated sportswear boutique—Track II. The novelty and charm of these two shops attracted other small retailers, and now the street is lined with newly renovated storefronts housing antique shops, interior decorators, an art gallery, a restaurant, an imported fabrics store, and many more. All this has turned Midway into a unique shopping village which attracts shoppers and tourists alike.

I had been the sportswear buyer for a large store in Lexington before opening Track II and therefore had years of experience in fashion merchandising. I was familiar with wholesale resources in New York and retailing in general, which made starting my own shop much easier.

Most boutiques fail because the owner doesn't know anything about the retailing business. It's a common fallacy to think it's fun and easy just because you love clothes. A flair for dressing yourself does not guarantee your success in running a clothing store. That's very different from knowing how to dress other people. My strongest advice to anyone would be to get some experience first. Otherwise, you just make too many mistakes, and for a small shop, one season's mistakes can put you out of business. You have to know about inventory controls, security, display, coordination of styles and colors, size ranges, delayed shipments. You have to keep on top of what credit extensions you're taking and keep in touch daily with your records.

You should know how to listen to your customer and to realize why she's buying or not buying. You can't just walk up to someone and say, "Why didn't you buy that dress?" You have to see that maybe it's a little too extravagant or impractical for her and translate that into your next buying trip. You have to walk the fine line between selling what the customer is used to and being creative—bringing new and exciting things to your clientele. If you don't, she'll never stick with you. No one wants to go into a shop and see the same thing season after season, or even week after week these days. And at the end of it all, you've got to be able to relate your sales to your expenses and figure out whether you're growing or standing still.

A boutique must be exclusive, personal, and original, yet you have to offer the customer a total look, too. If she comes in to buy trousers, you should have coordinating tops. Round out a line of swim suits with beach caftans and sunglasses. A boutique must provide a particular fashion look, concentrated in a room or two.

I think it is important to keep a few price ranges as well; if you're selling expensive trousers, you should have a choice of tops from expensive to moderate. The point is, you never want to lose a customer if you can help it. It's one thing if customers simply don't like the whole style of your shop—they're not going to buy anything anyway. But if they love the style and it's too expensive, you should be able to offer some alternative—fun jewelry in the midst of expensive clothes or little throwaway T-shirts next to imported trousers.

Track II carries sports clothes, and these days that can mean anything from trousers and tops to chiffon blouses and long skirts. We carry accessories, too—jewelry, espadrilles, scarves, hats, sunglasses, bags.*

The initial investment in Track II was $9,000, and out of that, $7,000 went for inventory. I went about building the stock carefully and slowly. By the way, Track II is not the name I would pick for our shop over again. We know what it means—it was the second shop by the tracks—but it says nothing about our image. People don't like to walk into a shop they have no feeling for. The name should help to define a shop.

Wholesale resources are the essential ingredient of any successful boutique, and you have to concentrate your major buying in a tight, often exhausting schedule. I do four buying trips to New York a year. The rest of the time I keep up with

---

* *Women's Wear Daily* advises a percentage breakdown of stock as follows: 15 percent is accessories (hats, bags, jewelry, etc.); 50 percent is the basic fashion look of the store; 25 percent is a seasonal or style look—things that keep the shop looking new—the changing display items; and 10 percent is promotional new look—French butcher shop smocks, Chinese slippers, whatever is different.

the changing trends and fashion forecasts through a subscription to *Women's Wear Daily* and all the fashion magazines. I also reach into other, seemingly unrelated areas for ideas. For example, a fashion look can come out of a popular movie as it did with *Annie Hall* or from sports or anything else the media spotlights.

Trade shows can ease the beginner's buying trips because they provide a concentrated source of wholesalers under one roof. The National Boutique Show is held twice a year in New York and once a year in Los Angeles. The organizers of the show also produce a boutique fashion magazine listing all the resources that exhibit with the show. A variety of merchandising shows are held in other major cities (Atlanta, Chicago, Dallas, Miami, Denver) which can simplify buying in specific areas. *Women's Wear Daily* provides an excellent information service which can direct you to wholesalers in every fashion category as well as to information on the various trade shows around the country.

I think it is very important that you set up a system whereby you are in touch with what is happening with the merchandise. It's officially called a "unit control system," and basically it directs you from one buying trip to the next. The unit control shows the activity of the merchandise from the minute it enters the shop to the time it leaves. Each piece is listed with the resource name, style description and order number, price at cost, price at retail, markdown (if any), color, and size.

When you begin to record the performance of your inventory, you are in a much better position to know what to buy or reorder. If the shop is tiny, you may not need such a detailed system: you'll know just by looking that none of your size fourteens sold. But believe me, when you get to New York and see hundreds of styles and scribble pages of notes that are somehow always illegible when you get back to your hotel room, you're going to be in much better shape if you've got a control system.

About a week in New York is all that a person's mind can handle, looking at things day after day. It's exhausting. Seventh Avenue is a form of madness in itself. The first visit there, you spend a great deal of time just trying to understand the language, or you wait hours before figuring out that you have to elbow your way onto the elevators. And even though you may arrive in New York with a composed list of showrooms to visit, your ears start picking up new resources from other buyers, and pretty soon you're racing around and are part of the madness, too.

What most new business owners don't realize is the money it takes to run a business before it begins to pay off. You have to pay taxes, salaries, and operational costs long before you reach the leveling-off period. You also need a pocket of extra cash for emergencies and for late changes or additions to your inventory. And you must plan for the inevitable mistakes you will make as well. No merchandiser can ever be 100 percent right on all the merchandise in a store, and at least 10 or 15 percent of your goods will go on sale.

All the shops in Midway work together in advertising and publicity, not only saving one money but adding a special aura and excitement about coming here to shop. Once a year we plan a special day with entertainment for the children, street vendors, an outdoor art show, music, and an open-house atmosphere in the shops. People come from hundreds of miles away, and the newspapers all over Kentucky and Ohio publicize it.

A few years ago every woman I knew took up tennis, last year it was jogging, and now it seems everyone wants to open her own business. My strongest advice is to be original and believe in what you're doing. Don't copy someone else's idea; otherwise, you'll have no inner resource to fall back on in the long and often tedious job of running a small business. You can't just want to get out of the house; you should want to be in business for the same reasons other professionals pick their work. It must say something to you.

SOAP OPERA

Marlo Kennedy moved from San Francisco to Santa Fe, New Mexico, six years ago with a savings of $5,000 and a notion to open a bath-and-body shop. She knew organic cosmetics were popular in California and felt that Santa Fe, with its resident artists and numerous tourists, would be the perfect place to start such a shop.

Soap Opera carries organic hand, face, hair, and bath products packaged under the Soap Opera label and features imported soaps, oils, herb creams, combs, brushes, sponges, and antique postcards, as well as ceramic soap dishes made by local craftspeople.

I had very little money to invest in a business and knew I would have to budget close to the bone. The first year I worked at night as a waitress, living on salary and tips so that I could put all the money in sales back into the shop.

My first location was on the ground floor of an old house within walking distance of the main shopping area. It was a lovely, quaint Victorian house, and people gravitated there because it was such a pleasant, cozy place. I used recycled fixtures and decorations to outfit the two tiny rooms. I found used shelves and old display cases in junk shops. Friends gave me furniture from their attics, and I covered old trunks and boxes with colorful wallpaper. The rest of the shop was filled with hanging plants and old-fashioned prints and posters.

After five years, the house was sold, and I moved to a busy shopping area, where I have more space and a lot more walk-by traffic. I've added baskets, mirrors, bath accessories, and hot tubs to the inventory. Business is booming here, but I miss the homelike atmosphere of the first place and think many of my old customers do, too.

The major portion of my capital went into cosmetics products. I ordered them in bulk from an organic cosmetics laboratory in Berkeley, California. I repackaged these under my own label, in simple bottles and jars ordered from a container manufacturer I found in the Yellow Pages.

The initial cost breakdown was as follows:

Inventory: $3,100. Two thousand dollars went for a basic line of organic lotions, shampoos and rinses, skin and face creams; $800 for sponges, combs, brushes, soaps, and oils; and $300 for ceramic soap dishes.

Equipment: $325. For bottles, jars, lids, and caps.

Store Improvements: $575. For painting, shelving, display cases and counters; furniture and decorations, including plants; and the storefront sign.

Rent: $400. For two months' rent.

Advertising/Promotion: $200. This included a listing in

the Yellow Pages, ads in local newspapers, promotional flyers, artwork with the Soap Opera logo, and printing of the labels.

Expenses: $100. For sales pads and office materials, gas and electricity, my business permit, and a first payment on my insurance policy which covers fire and damages.

Operating Capital: $500.

It wasn't at all difficult to build up my initial list of product distributors, importers, and wholesalers. I simply went to a large health-food store in San Francisco and jotted down the names of organic soaps and beauty products. I also asked the owners for names and advice, and they were very helpful. I then went to the laboratory in Berkeley and tested their various products, selecting those I knew would be good for Santa Fe's dry climate. Distributors and wholesalers can be incredibly useful when you're first going into any business as they can advise from a knowledge of what other retailers are doing.

I also wrote to the Merchandise Mart in Dallas and asked for a list of exhibitors that deal in my products.* And I wrote to distributors for catalogs. If they carried products I liked, I wrote back asking to be put on their sales representatives' routes. This way I never have to spend money on buying trips, and now I do all my ordering from catalogs or salesmen. Another good source for product ideas is the *Gift and Decorative Accessories* Magazine, which lists resources and trade shows throughout the country.†

Customers are another source of ideas. Ask them what they need and want. If they have a specific product in mind, ask them where they saw it, and if you do travel (especially to foreign countries), always be on the lookout for new products. So much of my trade is in repeat customers, and you always

---

* Merchandise Marts are located in Chicago, Atlanta, San Francisco, Dallas (World Trade Center), and Los Angeles (Pacific Design Center).

† Write to the Gift and Decorative Accessories Association of America, 51 Madison Avenue, New York, New York 10010. Ask for subscription rates on its monthly trade news magazine as well as its yearly Buyer's Directory.

See the bibliography for further listings on manufacturers, importers, trade and convention directories.

want your shop to have new and different items. It keeps the place fun and fresh.

Soap Opera is open from 10:00 A.M. to 6:00 P.M., six days a week. I am here every day but hire friends to help out during the busy seasons and as backup whenever I can't be in the shop. Look for initiative in the people you hire, and listen to their ideas. I'm a great believer in hiring friends, because they take almost the same interest in the business as you do.

I also believe in keeping the management routine simple, with a minimum amount of paperwork. At first keeping track of myriad suppliers, sales and shipments, reorders, and payment-due dates was a little overwhelming. But after a while the business fell into a rhythm. The important thing is never to let things slide. I have a loose-leaf ledger book in which I keep, on separate pages, each wholesaler, distributor, and supplier I deal with. Everything having to do with our transactions is recorded, and I keep in touch with this book daily, marking down sales so I'll know when to reorder and watching shipment and payment-due dates so I don't jeopardize my credit.

My bookkeeping consists of a simple list of expenses and sales. At year's end I send it all to the Internal Revenue Service, and they compute my taxes.*

When I started the shop, I had printed a simple one-page flyer that listed all my merchandise. I gave my friends a handful to distribute around town—to tack on bulletin boards, leave in restaurants and in the hotels and motels. And each summer we go over to the Santa Fe Opera's parking lot and put one on the windshield of each car.

The summer is our peak tourist season, and for those months I place ads in the local newspapers and in the opera programs. The rest of the year I rely on the Yellow Pages and on word of mouth, which in a small town like this is really the best advertising.

I sell all my products at a 100 percent markup, figuring in the costs of bottles, jars, and labels on the products I repack-

---

* If you are the sole proprietor of a small business whose profits are part of your personal income, the federal Internal Revenue Service and in some cases state income tax offices will do your taxes free. Inquire about the service at your local IRS.

age. I try out new products all the time, and if they don't sell quickly, I put them on sale and try something else. It's also important in a shop like this to put out sample displays and testers on many of the products, such as the lotions, scents, and cosmetics. When the customers can test the product, they are much more apt to buy.

As a rule, I sell out and reorder five to six times a year. And for me, sales triple at Christmas and during the tourist season. I'm now operating solidly in the black, but it took me three years to show a profit. My current inventory investment is around $15,000, and my yearly volume is $45,000 in sales.

SERVICES

Service businesses can loosely be divided into two areas: creative services which include everything in the realm of ideas, design, and the planning and coordination of events; and practical services—anything having to do with skills, organization, and placement.

The service industry is a product of our civilized condition. The more individualized and specialized we become, the more we look to professionals to get things done. It is basically an activities industry, even though a product may sometimes be necessary to perform the service. Performance is the key: the ability to do something better than someone else, or if not better, then either more imaginatively or more conveniently. You're in service if you're selling a talent or ability, an idea, or simply the willingness to perform a task.

A service business is one of the few types of enterprise that can still be started on a shoestring. Overhead expenses may be minimal if you work from home, and often your business can be launched for the initial price of a brochure and an answering service.

On the other hand, you may need the image of a good office

address, bustling staff, and sophisticated equipment in order to sell your talent to a prospective client. But whatever the investment, your business is largely a process of self-promotion because the product is you—your talent and skill to accommodate the needs of a particular market.

Sales techniques, image, and organization are the three basic elements of setting up your service business. And each of these must be well-thought through before the business is launched. Ask yourself the following questions:

1. *Will it work?* Describe the nature of the service, your skill, talent, or training that qualifies you to offer the service.
2. *Who will buy?* Identify your potential market—its needs and problems.
3. *How will it work?* Describe how the service will be delivered or administered. What will it take to sell the service to your clients—past performance, visuals, proof of efficiency, one-on-one sales calls, or blanket advertising?
4. *Will I make money at it?* Time is money. If your business is competitive, then you must price competitively, making sure you can fulfill the job at the same rate of time your competitor does. If it is not competitive, then you set fees on what the traffic will bear, the type of client you are going after, and his or her need of your service. Again, a clear understanding of the time it will take you to complete the job will direct you to a final fee.

Negotiation of price is very often called for in service businesses—especially in the creative or organizational areas.

To bid on a job, you must first estimate the amount of time the job will take. Be sure to include traveling and administrative time. Next, estimate the expenses you will incur on the job—labor, transportation, telephone, supplies, and so on. Next, figure the very least amount of money you need to survive (the money it takes to pay for your business and personal expenses). Break that down to an hourly income based on the amount of billable hours you can work. Lastly, estimate what you would like to get for the job—aim as high as you honestly think the job is worth.

You now know your negotiating range—the time and cost of the job, what you must have to survive, and what you professionally think the job is worth. Intuition takes over from here—who is the client, and how great is his or her need of your service? Do your background and experience warrant a high-, middle-, or low-range fee?

Present the details of the project in its fullest form to the client, giving yourself room to add and subtract elements of the job as negotiations proceed. Be confident of your initial price, but be prepared to quote a lower fee if necessary. Never quote a lower price without some alteration in the logistics of the project. In other words, you can give the client a reduced rate, but you must alter some aspect of the presentation (i.e., another grade of material, fewer staff, fewer frills, and so on). Present this positively—the job can be done equally well, for a lower price, but with some alternate solutions.

In time, setting fees becomes a natural skill. Just as the retailer learns merchandising systems and the manufacturer learns distribution tactics, the service entrepreneur learns negotiating and bidding.

Over the past decade, home services have offered new business ideas to women. Traditionally, women have worked as consultants in decorating and landscaping, but home services now include maintenance as well. As often as not it is women who paint rooms, paper walls, put up bookshelves, repair, glue, and fix whatever they can.

Yet when women take these skills into the marketplace, they are considered oddities. More often than not, men are hired to paint, scrape, hang, and repair. But women who have taken the plunge into maintenance services say that other women are their best customers. A sampling of women-owned maintenance services shows that playing up the fact you're a woman is a strong selling point: Lady Killers (exterminators); The Covergirls (interior wall painters and paperers); Universal Aunts (a clearinghouse for home services); Tinkerbell (auto repairs); Ms. Edison (electrician); The Plant Mistress (house calls to sick plants), to name a few.

Women are bringing new insights and expertise to numerous types of businesses—new and old. Emphasize the fact that you're a woman, especially if your service is a nontraditional one, and advertise or seek publicity in publications that appeal to women.

PORTFOLIO ASSOCIATES, INC.

Portfolio Associates is a creative consulting firm providing services in the areas of graphics, design, communications, and special projects. Specifically, the business has initiated a Black Film Festival, a poster campaign for the Post Office, and numerous surveys and studies to assist businesses and whole communities in management.

Beverly Harper started her company in Philadelphia, in 1969, unknown in the business community and decidedly unfunded. Today she has five full-time employees, fifteen special project people, and offices in a unique complex of modern commercial buildings.

My basic idea was to put together a team of highly creative people who could act as problem-solvers. Each staff member here has an area of specialty, which is a key to success; our skills collectively cover visual design, media development, research, selling, and a general account executive.

I worked out of my apartment for the first year and a half, and I think that was a good decision because if you're unfamiliar with business operation, especially with the long period of time it takes to get work on a regular basis, the last worry you need is meeting the expenses of a heavy monthly overhead.

I never went to anyone for financing, and this was a conscious decision. I felt that being black, a woman, having no business background, and needing money were four big strikes against me. I would have had to work four times as hard just to get to some neutral point, and I wasn't willing to do that; I didn't need negatives.

For the first three years, I took a minimal amount of money out of the business, as did everyone who worked here. That helped tremendously because it meant that we could afford an office after a year and a half and could create an image of a professional, competitive company.

When we started we had a Post Office Box and an answering service. I would arrange all my appointments outside the office (my apartment). Now that we have an office I try to have all initial meetings with a client here because it lets them know immediately that this is an established, ongoing business.

If you're cutting corners in the beginning by working from home, you should be doubly concerned with the image you're projecting and compensate for the lack of facilities in other ways. We've concentrated on our image through graphics—the letterhead, business cards, and written proposals. They have always been very exciting and very professional.

We were incorporated from the start, and I had a lawyer and an accountant to help set up the corporate structure. In looking for a lawyer and accountant, your special consideration should be to find people who are willing to work along with you. Don't go to anyone who is going to slap you with a fifty-dollar-per-hour professional fee. No new business needs that.

To launch the business, we sent a letter explaining our services and concepts to prospective clients. Then I would follow up with a phone call and hope to get an appointment. It is vitally important for a young company to look at its initial sales approach with an objective eye. Put yourself in the shoes of the person you're trying to reach. Think of the mail she or he must see every day: how can yours stand out and represent your company in the best possible light? A letter or a brochure is often a person's first impression of your company, and it should be easy to understand, to the point, friendly, but professional, too. It shouldn't ramble and by all means must be typed professionally.

Various business associations and service organizations are good sources for business contacts. The local Chamber of Commerce can be extremely helpful in providing mailing lists or people to talk to. The United Fund is another good source; most businesses belong or contribute to that organization, so that just by getting involved yourself you begin to make contacts. These kinds of contacts are vital to getting a new business off the ground.

You can waste a tremendous amount of precious time talking to the wrong people. Large organizations sometimes forget the kinds of problems they create when they string you along.

You just have to tell them diplomatically that it is impossible to keep meeting with them when you're not getting compensated for it.

Sales efforts for this business fall into two basic categories. First, we will see a need for something and go out and try to sell a client an idea that relates to that need. For instance, we instigated a citizen's participation campaign for a bank. They were opening an educational financing counseling center, and we sold them on the idea of working with the community and letting the consumers help identify their own individual and community needs. The bank was not soliciting ideas from us or from anyone; we just called them up and said we would like to meet with them.

The second area of sales is our ongoing marketing campaign in which we try to reach more and more people with a general presentation of what our company can do for them. We've done a lot of work for the Post Office in this area, and that's a good example of a general sales approach. In 1972 we found out that the government has something called the General Services Administration (GSA), and it publishes a list of approved businesses in various categories, which goes out to government offices throughout the country. To get on this list, a company has to write a proposal including its services and prices.

Once we were listed I did a mailing to all the regional offices in the area, sending samples of our graphic work with a letter. I followed up every piece with a phone call and perhaps a meeting. Out of all this, the Post Office said that it wanted a campaign developed to promote letter writing. We came up with a tremendously successful headline for a poster campaign: "When you say it in a letter it lasts a long, long time."

That phrase came out of a brainstorming session in which we came up with about twenty-five different ideas. You narrow that down to five to present to the client. Usually, out of the five there is one we all feel strongly about, the one we really believe in and try to sell to the client. But we cover ourselves with four other backup ideas.

One of our most fun and successful creations has been the Black Film Festival. I had met a man who told me about his idea for a film festival. He was new in Philadelphia and didn't have any contacts here, so we jointly came up with a working concept: he was to screen and select the films, while I was to provide the organization and planning, the fund raising, and the overall graphic image of the festival. Each year the festival has grown. The first year it was held at the University of Pennsylvania, and this year it goes out to six states.

The whole technique of selling is to be organized before you go into a meeting; have as much background on the company and the person as you can, and know exactly what you can do for them. Get to the point as soon as you can.

When we first started out, about 90 percent of our business was for community associations with a great many needs but not much money. It gave us a strong background in terms of planning and finding out what service organizations needed, and what the time and cost factors were on a variety of jobs. In that respect, it gave us our initial business experience, which was used later as our "track record" to interest clients who could pay. After two years, I phased out almost all our volunteer work and concentrated on clients with budgets. I have kept some of the original commitments over the years because I feel that it is important for a business to be involved in some phase of community life.

Each year we set financial goals. This can't be done from the first day, but certainly after six or twelve months of operation you should be able to sit down and say, "This is what I've done, and this is where I want to be next year." Establish your fixed expenses for the business—the basic needs and overhead. Then set a range of what you personally need to live on, a rock-bottom take-home salary. Both of these costs will then suggest to you what you have to sell yearly just to survive. What I do is break it down on a monthly basis so that any given month I know where I stand.

Every year I've been in business I've had to read twice as much as I did the year before. We subscribe to a lot of publications, and I've talked informally with the professors at the Wharton Business School about specific problems. I've found they are willing to give me free, extremely valuable advice—something I never could have paid for.

Once a year we rent a conference room at a hotel, and the staff and I go over there for one day and plan the activities for the next year. We set our goals and objectives and schedules for reaching them. The important thing is to get out of the familiar office environment to a place where you can really focus on ideas and schedules.

Setting fees is always difficult in the beginning. You just have to believe that it will get easier. You find that in order to get work in the beginning, you have to price low, which adds to the difficulty of getting the business on its feet. But a lot of times that's the only way you're going to get work. Price low, and develop a track record.

Most new businesses don't realize the amount of time that goes into planning. For a five-day week, I spend perhaps a day planning and organizing my time. Usually I do this over the weekend, and I set up a list of things that have to be done. During the week, as new things come in, I keep adding to the list.

The other part of planning—the part that most often goes unattended—is evaluating. For instance, consider your sales meetings or weekly events: what was good, bad, how can it be improved upon, and so on. One of my weaknesses is not delegating authority, and I know this from analyzing myself in relation to the business. It's important for the person running the business to know her strengths and weaknesses. Once you are able to isolate what they are you can start working on improving them or using them to better advantage.

DIMENSION TALENT

The measure of success in business is growth and the measure of the true entrepreneur is the ability to expand on the basic idea: to develop the scope of the business and to stimulate new activities in promotion and creative planning. Expansion is the goal of any business.

Joan Solomon was just twenty-one when she started her business in Minneapolis, but she had a strong sense of promotion and a particular ability to take her original idea and move it into new areas during each of the six years she was in business.

In 1974 she sold the business and got into marketing and television production, eventually moving to Los Angeles, where she is currently writing a movie about her days at Dimension Talent.

First of all, let me say, never start a business thinking you're going to get out of work. I thought that if I started my own business, it would be just great—set my own hours, come and go as I please. Believe me, you work twice as hard as anybody else, and your hours are set by the demand of the business. You are committed to respond to that demand.

I was just out of college and looking for a job, an exciting job, something stimulating, and I wasn't finding it in the Minneapolis job market. In my frantic search, I had registered with the one and only model agency in town. The owner had been in business for fifteen years and wasn't doing anything creative in the field because she didn't have to. Some of the biggest corporations are located here, General Mills, IBM, 3M, and models were in demand; but she would send out the same five models on every job that came in, and you would see their faces over and over again.

My intuition told me that a creative, young, innovative talent agency would go over in a big way. My initial plan was to find ten new models and see if I could get them work. I dreamed up the name for the business and ran an ad for models in the paper.

The response was tremendous. Over two hundred models called and wanted to come by! I was using my apartment as my office, and there I sat, alone, trying to manage this rush of girls, pictures, and résumés.

I had $500 of my own, which paid for the initial expenses. The investment amounted to the advertisement, the application forms, a few pencils, and my telephone. A well-thought-out application form is the essential tool of any agency business. Aside from the basic information, you need to know a lot of specifics to match a model to a client's needs. There are shoe models and hand models, for instance, high fashion and all-American, character models and straight models. I went through all the magazines looking at the picture layouts to see what kinds of activities a model is required to do. Does she play tennis, ski, horseback ride, dance? All those things can be important to the job.

So I had the models. That was the first step in putting the business in motion. To get jobs, I compiled a list of advertising agencies in town through the Yellow Pages. Then I called and made an appointment to see the creative art directors at each agency.

I had a composite brochure made up with my best models' pictures in it, and I sent that around to every company and person I thought might be hiring. After six months I had enough business to ease up on sales calls and put my profits behind promotional techniques.

The astrology craze was just blossoming across the country, and I came up with the idea for a huge calendar with a photograph of the Horoscope Girl of the Month. The photographs were spectacular. Each month I brought in a new photographer who did the work for free because these calendars went to every creative director in town. It was a great promotion because the calendars hung in every office and were a reminder for the whole year of our agency. We even won an art directors' award for them.

I made sure every promotion that I did was new to this area. I tried new ideas all the time. And I'll have to say a lot of them flopped, but it doesn't seem profitable to limit yourself in scope, for you never know what doors are going to open. Try new angles, even if they seem remote from your daily operation. A business has got to be flexible in order to grow.

As I began to understand the media market in this city, I realized that radio and television weren't being tapped at all. The Guthrie Theatre and the Walker Art Center had pulled in a great deal of East and West Coast talent, and there was no one here organizing and representing that talent for commercial and voice-over work. So I rounded up thirty-five actors from the Guthrie Theatre and rented time in a sound studio to make a demonstration tape. Each actor did two minutes of commercials, and I made quite a production out of this by inviting several directors from the advertising agencies to come in and take a turn at directing the actors.

I also thought it would make good publicity and called the paper. A columnist came to the recording studio and did a great article on us. Clients started asking to hear this tape and, suddenly, phase two of the business: radio and commercial television work.

I discovered that I had an agent's eye for what would sell. And I could translate this to the actors and models, helping them develop a commercial style—what clothes to wear, what photographs "sold" them best.

From this basic talent base, I began to go into other areas. I set up a photography studio and a props and styling service, designed and staffed conventions and exhibits, and, for a while, put together rock concerts.

In the meantime, I developed a staff of four women to be in

charge of various aspects of the business: the talent agency, prop finding and styling, the convention market, and day-to-day organization. I did this because I wanted to be free to develop new areas. My talent for the business was innovation. Once a new area of business opened up, I found the right person to run it.

The business had begun to show a profit after a year, and I never had to go looking for capital. In retrospect, I think having to look for money, while difficult for women, does force you to sit down and analyze your business. You have to figure out what's absolutely necessary and what's not, and whether you're going to friends or family or the bank. It's important to define the needs of business. I was never happy with administrative work and was lucky. Because there was such a need in Minneapolis for this service, I could afford my mistakes.

I was, however, careful never to spend money I didn't have, and I learned to get things done for next to nothing. Even when we didn't have money problems, I believed in this because that's a real danger, getting your head into spending money.

I was very gutsy when it came to setting fees. For my models, I knew the other agency was charging the client twenty-five dollars per hour and paying the women fifteen. So I immediately raised my rates: we were better, had better people, and the client should pay for it. As for the commercial actors, no one in this town had ever paid more than minimum AFTRA scale, but talent from the Guthrie was major talent, so I charged double scale. I mean you have to take chances, and I had to backtrack on that fee many times, but I had nothing to lose in trying to create a new price. Remember, I had very little competition.

I think in the course of six years I moved to a new office every year, but the best office I ever had was a storefront. We set the front area up as sort of a clubhouse for the actors and models. Because the space was so large and fun, I decided to throw a big party, my first business party. I wanted all the ad agency and media people to meet the actors and models in an informal atmosphere rather than the awkward interview/audition basis.

Behind the scenes, I had all the proper advisors—lawyer, accountant, banker, and insurance broker—so that we weren't running just on my steam. I got a tremendous amount of help and advice from my bank. I had gone to the biggest bank in town when I started, and really, they couldn't have cared less about me. I never got to talk to anyone higher than the second clerk, so I went to a small local bank, and it was all on a first-name basis, even with the president; they leaned over backwards with service and advice.

I always wanted a partner, desperately. But when I finally got around to finding one, it was a disaster. I made a serious error in judgment and went into partnership with a personal friend, a man who had been in business before. I really wanted someone who was interested in business administration. I was just too involved in the creative angles and figured that a *man* would know all about business, let's get a man in here. So I made him a partner, and it all took a nose dive.

The adage that a business partner is a marriage partner has never been truer. Conciliation, compromise, and flexibility are all things women by nature should be pretty good at. But the tough part is not getting steamrollered if you've chosen a male partner, and learning to stand up for your own ideas—not pushing, just standing.

It simply didn't work. I know now that in order for me to perform best, I have to go it alone. I started taking more and more time away from the business. Consequently, the business suffered.

Eventually, I decided to sell out my half. It took a long time to reach that decision, but I realized that there was no way to make the business work for me anymore. I had always maintained a sense of humor, which to me is a very important part of running a business. I laughed my way through six years; the seventh year I cried, and that was it, I knew it was over.

When it came to dividing the business, it was the same again as marriage. Only this time it's likely to be more like divorce—and who gets the kids?

My lawyer and accountant figured a rate of profit based on the last three years of business and from that average made a projection on the future probability of income. I negotiated my final sale price based on the projection, and because the business was basically on solid footing, I got my price.

I think if my temperament had been different, I'd have been able to stay with Dimension Talent and to continue to make the company grow; but my strong point is innovation, and I had already gone about as far as I could along the lines of developing talent in Minneapolis. I wanted to try something new and decided to take a giant step into the bright lights of Los Angeles.

I am now living in L.A. and have just sold my first TV series and am working on writing a feature film about guess what—my days at Dimension Talent. I've come full circle and have learned over and over: nothing is wasted. Every experience, "good" or "bad," serves some purpose.

Success is a matter of timing and doing what feels right. Women have great instincts, and we shouldn't limit ourselves, especially at the beginning of a career. I would say my success came from starting a business directly after college. You have strong ideals and a lot of gall coming out of school. It's a golden time to try your luck in business, and it just might be the only time you'll ever have the nerve. Youth and enthusiasm and, really, an overall lack of experience can be the things most strongly in your favor.

Starting a business opens up a flood of possibilities. No matter what the business does, it can provide you with a limitless world of people, places, and adventure.

THE ORGANIZING PRINCIPLE

Stephanie Winston gets paid $200 a day to organize other people's messy lives. Everyone knows people who are chronically late or whose offices, files, kitchens, and closets are in a hopeless shambles. A photographer's slides sit month after month in a large box gathering dust; a free-lance writer can't meet her deadline as children swarm around her working area; a library needs cataloging; bills need paying; office systems which seem efficient in theory don't work in practice. Working fulltime in New York, Stephanie has turned her talent for organization into a lucrative business, and although she doesn't claim the slightest formal credentials for this work, people are eager to pay. In 1978 she published a book on how to organize yourself, appropriately called *Getting Organized: The Easy Way to Put Your Life in Order.*

Being organized is not necessarily being neat. Being organized is being able to find what you want, when you want it, and being able to do what you want efficiently. I had no idea how many people felt truly uncomfortable because some system in their lives wasn't working. Some people just don't know how to go about getting organized; others simply let things get out of hand. The trick is to come up with solutions and systems so simple and helpful that people will stick to them.

The concept of organization is fascinating. Some people fear it because they feel that if they conform to conventional standards of neatness, they will somehow lose their individuality. Others feel they don't have to bother with the mundane chores of cleaning up and keeping order. Some people are chronically depressed and unable to cope with mess. Whatever the reason for disorder, bringing order into people's lives helps to ease tensions; it's definitely a positive business.

People who appear organized sometimes aren't. One client was a doctor whose office library was neatly shelved and alphabetized by author. Yet the book he needed most often was on the top shelf out of easy reach, simply because the author's name began with A. I set up a special, easily accessible shelf for frequently consulted books.

One project was for a psychotherapist who works at home. Her office was meticulously neat, but she hadn't any idea which patients had paid their bills, nor was she able to keep up with her own monthly bills. All her correspondence—business and personal, bills, and professional materials—was stuffed into shopping bags in the closet. She had no system for maintaining her client's accounts, for keeping track of her finances, or for using her time efficiently. The disarray was causing her considerable distress.

We started from scratch, going through her materials piece by piece, and I set up a very simple filing system and method of checking off client's names as they paid their bills.

I've reorganized an office for Xerox so that the secretary and her boss could see each other. If you have to get up to talk to your secretary or boss, it can be a constant irritation. And nobody likes to be buzzed.

I do a lot of work for small businesses, unscrambling their files. I would say that this is my most frequent business assignment. The most common filing mistake is excessive complexity. One company had a system so complicated, you needed a code book. There were markings like "PO-33." The secretaries were in tears because they couldn't find anything, so I just made it very simple. If something started with an A, I put it in the A file. Nobody had considered this before.

My original orientation was working with individuals—sometimes housewives at home, sometimes in large or small businesses, but the individual was still in focus. I'm moving into a more "problem-solving" focus for businesses. That is, if something isn't working, why isn't it? What can be done to improve the situation? Within a large corporation, The Organizing Principle works primarily on the departmental level, as opposed to the traditional management consultant who works with the company as a whole.

I love every aspect of this business, but I'm particularly fascinated with household organization because it's been so neglected. Running a household is a true executive-administrative enterprise. People may sniff at housewifery, but I'd like to see the reactions of a typical executive were he suddenly faced with coordinating the activities of three to five people and maintaining life support systems for them, and all of this very often on top of a regular job.

I go in and work with them if they feel disorganized, whether in terms of their personal time, their paperwork, their closets, their kitchens, or management of their family's logistics.

In most cases I work along with the client, solving the immediate problem, and then devise a maintenance system so that the person won't slip back into the old habits. My original fees were $100 per day, or $400 for a thirty-five-hour week. After doing this for over four years, realizing how much need there is for my services, I've been able to raise my rates. My average fee is $200 per day. Of course, negotiation comes into it, and there can be no hard-set formula, but those are the figures I try to stay with.

I conduct a preliminary interview with the client and then estimate the job. All this is without charge. It is understood that my final bill may not come out to be what the estimate was. In this kind of work it is impossible to know exactly how much time things will take to organize; I can come close, but I don't lock myself into any prearranged figure. If it looks as if it will take considerably more time, I renegotiate with the client.

My start-up investment was very low. I work from my apartment and do most of the selling, paperwork, accounting, and, of course, consulting myself. I now have one associate, and we have begun to give seminars on personal management to the staffs of large corporations. I also consult with people who want to start similar businesses in organization, but only with people outside the greater New York metropolitan area.

To launch the business, I tried different approaches. I made up a brochure and did a mailing, and that was no good. It brought me no customers. Through personal contacts, friends and word of mouth, I began building up a track record, and having done that, I went after publicity. I was on a few local television talk shows, and the *Village Voice*, *The New York Times* and the *Wall Street Journal* did articles. Most of my business has come from the publicity. I had the news articles reprinted, and then wrote a letter and included tearsheets of the publicity, which I sent to a number of businesses and corporations in town.

Currently, I would estimate about one-fourth of my time is spent in finding new clients. I read business magazines and all the local newspapers regularly to get ideas and names of people to see. I know a market for an immense business is out there if I make the effort to tap it. For the moment, I'm developing what I've got, and in the process, it's been an exhilarating experience. I've met so many interesting people and know I've been instrumental in helping people change their lives.

I'm not obsessive about order and organization, but I do believe it's an instrument and technique for saving time and living more easily. I find it continually stimulating, even organizing someone's closet, and I'm the only person I know who enjoys doing income taxes. It's fun.

EXEC-U-TOURS OF BOSTON

Ellen McKenney Fahey specializes in hospitality, information, and events planning. Her brainchild—Exec-U-Tours—is a combined guided tour, executive relocation service, and convention coordinating business.

Working through the area's corporations, hotels, and convention bureau, she and her guides plan historical and cultural tours, help relocate newcomers to the city, supervise and sell conventions and sales meetings, and, in general, solve problems and handle any of the many events that occur in the business and tourist community of Boston.

My original idea was to offer a personalized tour service in Boston. I knew from firsthand experience traveling in Europe that a tour guide can make all the difference in how a person views a city. It can be either a boring recitation of facts or an exciting intimate experience. I'm a native Bostonian and love the city. I wanted to make it come alive for visitors.

My first step was to talk informally to the public relations people in the better hotels and to executives in large corporations, asking if they could use a VIP tour service. The response was very encouraging. I checked into other tour services in town and found only the Grey Line Company, so it was a wide-open field.

Next, I called six of my friends, women like me without jobs or young children to tie them down. (I have four children, and all were living at home when I started the business.) I knew from working with these women in charity drives and volunteer work that they could fulfill a commitment. Together we educated ourselves on Boston: we took bus trips and attended lectures, films, and classes on various Boston themes. We talked to historical societies, architects, art professors, museum curators. We talked to everyone who knew anything about Boston and came up with names of little-known restaurants and shops, private collectors, and antique specialists.

In no time we had an incredible storehouse of information. At this point, the official business had not opened. No one was paid; no business expenses were incurred. It was a time to investigate and grow with the idea until it became a firm business concept.

On my own, I worked on marketing ideas, pricing, brochures, and a general budget to launch the business. I dreamed of an office overlooking the Common, all decorated in early New England furniture. But I had only the barest funds to start with and found myself on opening day cutting a blue ribbon which we had hung across the door to my den at home.

In the beginning, I hesitated telling clients that I worked from my home. But over the years I found that if you deliver a sound, reliable service, then it doesn't matter at all. Mainly I liked working from home so I could be near my children and their activities. My children have all gotten involved in one way or another in the business and have given me some great ideas. We've worked together on many projects, and I think involving them has taught them the meaning of work and helped them understand the responsibility one has to a job. It gave them a better idea of what the grown-up world they would someday have to face is all about.

The second part of the Exec-U-Tour business, the relocation service for executives and their families, came about from a firsthand experience. Just about the time I was ready to launch the tour business, my husband was offered a job in Baton Rouge, Louisiana. Well, there went my business, and along with it came a sudden panic! We not only knew no one in Baton Rouge; I didn't know anything about that part of the United States—the schools, the climate, places to live, or what there was to do. Anyone who has moved knows how terrifying a new city can be, especially for the wife without an office to buffer the initial loneliness and guesswork. In the end, my husband decided against the job, so the tour business was back on, and along with it another concept, a relocation service in Boston for executives and their families.

I wrote a letter to all the personnel directors of every major corporation in the area explaining the service. Exec-U-Tours would act as a welcoming committee as well as a qualified agency to handle any and all relocation problems. As it turned out, there was a definite need for the service. More than ever corporations are responsive to the personal needs of their employees, yet no one personnel office is set up to handle the myriad details involved in getting a family settled in a new area.

Once a company hires us, we send the relocating family a four-page questionnaire. It covers every aspect of their needs and personnel preferences. If a daughter wants to continue her horseback riding lessons, we've got a list of stables. If a child was with a speech therapist in his old town, we can arrange the same here. Houses, clubs, schools, activities, and special needs are all covered. After we get the answered questionnaire, we block out a daily program to solve the individual problems. This is billed to the company at $100 per day, plus all expenses. We pick up the clients at the airport, book them into a hotel, schedule house-hunting tours, advise on schools, introduce them to clubs, conduct shopping excursions, and generally acclimate each family to the city.

We've relocated almost three hundred families for Gillette alone since 1969. Other corporations in the area use us exclusively for this service as well. I have women who are knowledgeable in every facet of real estate, including apartments, condominiums, and private houses. But our service extends into personal areas as well. We give suppers to introduce newcomers to the neighborhood, arrange for teen-agers to meet students from the schools they are to attend, take wives on shopping tours, or see to special interests. We have bilingual guides and host delegations and individuals from all over the world.

Working through the convention bureau and Chamber of Commerce, we offer services in setting up conventions, exhibits, and sales meetings. Often we are called upon to "sell" Boston to potential convention clients.

I have thirty-five part-time guides now, each working on a per job basis. There are three full-time employees who work with me on the sales and marketing of Exec-U-Tours as well as coordinating conventions and schedules.

I have kept my overhead expenses minimal. I bought an IBM electric typewriter because I think that if you're dealing with executives and corporations, you have to meet their image. Everything else I need is rented or leased for the particular job. My logo, stationery, business cards, and brochure are very straightforward and conservative and printed in tones of brown and beige. I rely a great deal on a letter introducing myself and the service and a follow-up appointment. For the tour business, I've tried advertising in many different places, but over the years I've discovered that the Yellow Pages brings in the most work. I run a display ad and plan a much bigger one this year. It's well worth the money.

My business is still small and personal, and I like it that way. The selling point is that we are a highly personalized service. We've gotten the most wonderful fan letters sent to us and to the companies who retain us, and I can't tell you how much that means to me and the people who work with me. It's like a glass of champagne.

HOME BINDERY, INC.

In 1967 Myrna Vincent created the Home Bindery business, in Columbus, Ohio, based on an idea she had gleaned from working part-time as a typist for a printing company. A bindery handles any kind of work that involves paper after it comes off the presses: gluing, stapling, folding, collating, multiple-piece mailing, and stamping. Many jobs cannot be done by machines, like stuffing odd-sized folders into odd-sized envelopes, or gathering sheets of paper together for assembly of a booklet, or hand-folding large posters. The key in starting this type of business is a source of inexpensive labor.

I started this business on a shoestring with very little knowledge about the bindery business. The only thing I knew was that there was a need.

Printers and agencies traditionally run behind schedule with advertising literature. As a result, a lot of work is done on a crash basis that will cost the printer a great deal in overtime in order to deliver on the required due date. I knew that if I could offer a bindery service that promised speedy delivery and a lower price, I just might have a job for myself. I was right.

I sent a letter to all the printers in my area offering a home bindery service. The letter stated our position of being able to help with rush hand-bindery jobs. The name "Home Bindery" was decided on because it said we worked at home doing bindery work. That also implied that we were not expensive, which we weren't at the time. The first letter was immediately answered by a telephone call, and within one month we (my family, neighbors, and friends) were collating printed material into large envelopes.

Our first slogan was "If it's done by hand, it's done by Home." We later changed from the letter format to clever mailers and used other catchy phrases such as "ninety nimble fingers."

My business has boomed. The company now bills over $300,000 a year. I employ about twenty women with families who can make their own hours. For the first years we worked out of my house, but finally got too big for the space, and I now own a building which houses the business. Having built up experience and capital over the years, I've expanded the service of the business. We now own addressing and labeling machinery and three printing presses. I decided to get into printing, too, as there were just too many times that we were delayed by the printers.

But starting this kind of service as we did is easy. It's a matter of placing an ad, going to talk to printers and advertising agencies, or sending a letter of inquiry the way I did. In order to keep the price down, which is one of the key issues, you will probably want to work from home. You will need space, a large clean work table, and good light. You need people you can rely on to help you when a large rush project comes in: your service promises speed, and you must deliver when you say you will.

Estimating your fee is the tough part in the beginning, and you may lose money on a few jobs before you get the hang of it. Printers prefer their prices in units of a thousand. Only experience will tell you how long it will take to stuff a brochure into an odd-sized envelope. Even today our estimating is done by trial and error on hand-bindery jobs. If a printer calls and asks for a quote on five sheets of paper to be gathered and stuffed into an envelope and the flaps of this envelope tucked inside, we actually try some samples to develop our hourly cost. Our present base rate is eight dollars per hour.

Methods of paying your workers are extremely important. Workers should be told in advance what they will get for doing the job and that you will pay them when you get paid. All workers are considered subcontractors, and they become responsible for reporting their income. In other words, they are self-employed just like you.

A subcontractor's contract is signed by them before they get a job. This contract lists their fixed pay on that particular job, states that they are responsible for reporting their income, and has a liability clause that releases you from any damage that could occur while they are working on a bindery job. A general subcontractor's form is available from most office supply dealers.

NANCY PALMER PHOTO AGENCY

Nancy Palmer is an agent. She represents commercial photographers and has been in the business for twenty years in New York City. The business offers two services to a wide assortment of clients—talented photographers for hire on photography projects, and a large stock file of photographs for immediate use in print.

An agent's job is an active one, requiring an in-depth knowledge of her field, contacts, and an ability to sell and negotiate. It's a middleman's job, and to be effective, one must have a steady hand at the bargaining table, a perceptive view of trends, and the ability to develop ideas in a competitive marketplace.

Entertainers, writers, inventors, designers, and all types of artisans can serve as the basis for a representative's business.

The agent is the link between the creative arts and the commercial world. For the writer, actor, painter, designer, and (in my case) photographer, an agent is a vital person who both sells and develops the work of the artist in the marketplace. I am the go-between. I know the needs of my clients and what their interests are from long experience. I know where my photographers are and what they can do. My business is a matter of coordinating two elements—the photographer's works and the client's needs.

I handle any existing pictures the photographer has, but the interesting part of my work is getting an assignment for a photographer. Sometimes the photographer and I develop an idea, and sometimes I can interest a client in a photographer's work enough to have an assignment commissioned.

A client is any source using pictures: magazines, book publishers, ad agencies, newspapers, and television. I use the published works of my photographers as a sales tool and spend most of my days seeing clients. It's a constant process of seeing the buyer, tuning in on his or her likes and dislikes, finding out what projects are coming up, and listening for clues to what *might* be coming up.

I was originally a journalist, but was not successful, so I became a photographer. I had a talent for it, and I felt it satisfied my ambitions in journalism. I had always been interested in education, and in looking at textbooks, I found their pictures sadly lacking in just about everything I thought good pictures should be. So I developed an idea for supplying good contemporary photographs to textbook publishers.

I went to a woman who was in the picture agency business. She found the idea interesting and asked me to develop it under her umbrella. From that experience I found I could sell other people's works far better than I could sell my own.

I also realized I had a really good sense for placing pictures. I could talk photography and could talk to editors. So, with very little capital and a lot of knowledge, I became a photographer's representative. My business developed out of a basic interest in the field. Over the years it has continued to stimulate me because I work with creative people and I have to be creative in my approach as well. We stimulate each other.

I started very simply, although I did rent an office. I must have a place to go every day—some place away from my house—but this sort of business could very well be started at home. You go out to see clients, and the photographers certainly don't care where you set up, so that it's a business that can be launched on very little funds.

I had stationery and cards printed up and had an answering service installed. My highest operational costs are telephone and postage—mailing packages of pictures to clients is costly because of the insurance.

It's a very competitive market, and I have to be flexible in setting fees. Many times if I simply don't know what the price should be, I'll ask the client what his budget is or what he would like to pay for a certain project. Then, if the quote is too low, I'll negotiate, offering a counterprice. But the main thing is to be flexible and never to refuse a fair offer. Your initial prices will be based on the competition and the demand; with experience you'll soon know what things are worth.

Each job is then put into contract form. If I know the client, I put it all into a letter stating the details of the job, the advance on expenses, and the fee. I usually require an advance on estimated expenses so the photographer is never out-of-pocket.

A representative needn't be aggressive in personality. I like the soft sell. I respond to it myself, and although I may drive a hard bargain in the end, my selling approach is low-key. I like my clients, and I appreciate the photographers I handle. I couldn't sell for selling's sake; because I like what I sell, I can sell it.

My fee for representing a photographer is on a percentage basis. That, too, is flexible and depends on the experience of the photographer and the market for the work. The basic range for me is between 40 and 50 percent, but it varies widely in the industry. For instance, a talent representative may work at 10 or 15 percent.

One of my biggest problems is saying no to a talented photographer, and there's occasionally a conflict between the appreciation of talent and business. Sometimes the portfolio may be great but there will be no market for it.

There is a tremendous amount of paperwork in this business. I have purposely kept my operation small, and I prefer to keep my own books and do my own taxes. It's the best way to keep in touch with the business. Working with the books, I can tell how much money each photographer brings in, the price ranges certain clients are in, and how prices are holding.

I am incorporated for protection against lawsuits and carry damage insurance as well. I'm very aware of the fact that I hold other people's property.

My strongest advice to anyone going into business is to keep your overhead down. I don't spend anything on appearances. My office is small; none of my furniture matches; I'm located off the mainstream of New York activity. This business is a matter of legwork, studying the market, and selling. People want my product, not my decorating ability.

WOMANKIND EMPLOYMENT AGENCY

Womankind is dedicated to finding good middle-management and executive jobs for qualified women.

The competition in this field is fierce. New York has over two hundred personnel and temporary employment agencies that scramble for jobs in the employment marketplace. In a business that seems to have about as much sympathy for the human condition as a cold germ, Beverly Ibes has managed to create a small haven for the foot-weary and the unemployed.

I was a secretary but always thought of it as something I would do until I got married. Suddenly, I was forty years old, and I was still in the typing pool. I suspected it was doing a lot of damage to me, and I was right. I had always wanted to open a personnel agency, but because you have to have two years of personnel background before you qualify for a license, I decided to open a temporary employment agency, which doesn't require a license. Working in so many offices, I had seen the standards of other temporary agencies, and I was sure I could do better.

I ran the business from my apartment in the East Village. Without an office rental fee, my initial expenses were minimal: typewriter, business telephone, office supplies, business cards and stationery, flyers, and an advertising budget. I launched the business with a $5,000 loan from a friend. Initially, I put an ad in the *Times* for temporary office workers, and the response was tremendous. In the beginning, I certainly didn't have enough clients to fill the demand for jobs. I didn't realize when I started how difficult it was to get clients. I thought all you had to do was send out a beautiful flyer printed in bright colors. But it was amazing to me how loyal people would be even if I couldn't place them. For some reason, when people walked into my office, which was my living room, we became friends. Six months later we would get a call from one of the applicants who was working with a company and who would want to hire one of our temporaries. We've gotten more business this way than through our brochures or advertising.

The name "Womankind" helped attract superior people, and because of them, I knew we were a superior service. Once I had the name, things were expected of me that were not expected of other agencies. Womankind became my conscience, and I think I can safely say that we were the first woman-oriented middle-management employment agency. I was able to get my personnel license sooner than I thought and moved into executive placement.

The best thing that happened in getting the business off the ground was meeting a woman who worked for a competitor. She was a tremendous help, and virtually put me through a mini-course on how to operate a personnel agency—what kind of insurance I needed, how to set up the payroll systems, and so forth. If you're setting up a business, you should get out and talk to people, try to build up a network of contacts, and find other women doing things. People are always willing to help.

People say that running a personnel agency is the roughest business you can be in. It's worse than selling insurance because your prospective customer is going to fight to get away from you. It's a very competitive business, and you have to know what your competition is doing. They may suddenly drop their rates, and you have to find out how much by calling other agencies and pretending to be a client. They do this to us; we do it to them. You also have two clients to please instead of one so that there is a double effort behind each match.

I would never have been able to survive if it hadn't been for the fact that I started out so small. After a year, when I really began to understand my business, I moved to a midtown office.

I broke even the first year and then dropped into the red because of the move. I bought $5,000 worth of furniture and equipment. Every time I would make money I would spend more money, and I had to learn that I was the enemy. I had to watch myself.

Operational costs include rent, telephones (that's a major expense because this is a telephone business), advertising, promotion, and insurance. We carry liability up to $500,000, but if something happens to one of our temporaries, we are named co-insurers with the office that has hired her. My advertising and promotion budget is less now than it was in the beginning—word of mouth is inevitable because people are always looking for good employees. If we're getting more job orders than our pool of people, we just run an ad in the paper. We maintain a display ad in the Yellow Pages as well.

Once we were having trouble getting good secretaries. None of our ads was bringing in enough qualified people for the jobs we had to fill. One day I was walking home from the office and noticed a parked van with loudspeakers blaring, asking addicts to come inside and sign up for methadone programs. I have a friend with a van, which I borrowed and decorated with balloons and signs and parked in front of Gimbels on Eighty-sixth Street. We had a typewriter inside for the typing test and applications. And we got a fantastic response plus some free publicity out of it, too. The newspapers and one television station covered us.

For temporary work, you have to give a typing test to ensure that you have qualified people. I used to be overly cautious and got all hyped if someone made five mistakes in five minutes, but now I say, "Never mind the speed test," and have the applicant sit down and write me a letter telling me why she is here. And that seems to work very well. I've gotten many brilliant letters, and it worked to my advantage because I discovered really talented people who could do special projects for me, writing my promotional literature.

I also go out and see clients; we mail a brochure first and then follow up and try to get an appointment. We call a company once, and if they say no, that's it; we may wait anywhere from two to six months before contacting them again. But there are employment agencies that, as a policy, call the same client three times a week, get three rejections, but keep at it until they get a yes. That works, by the way, but I myself could never subject anyone to that kind of treatment. I feel it would alienate people.

Both the temporary personnel and the clients sign a contract stating they will not negotiate a permanent job unless it is through our office. It's supposed to scare people off from stealing our people, but there's not a judge in the world who will grant in favor of an agency. The agreement is a formality, but if a company steals your people, you can send their name to the Employment Agency Association so that other people are aware of the company.

For specialized and executive placement our recruiting is more sophisticated. When we get a job description, we first check to see if we have someone in our files. If we don't, we start calling women who work in that particular field and ask them if they know anyone who fits the requirements. It works nine out of ten times, and this is the part that's exciting to me. It's a treasure hunt! I love being in business. Sex was the joy of my youth, and business is the joy of my middle years. I can't remember the person I was before I started Womankind, and there is no job I can think of I would rather have than running my own business. I've learned that you can't know what there is to learn unless you've tried something completely on your own. I'm very optimistic about the future; the economy worries me, but I don't think we'll be badly affected. If clients know they can get the best people here—good service and qualified help—we won't suffer. There is always a market.

I've made a special point to attend any activities being set up for women in business. I think that in any community women should seek each other out because they can help each other a great deal.

As for general advice to women starting any business, I would say don't be afraid of your own ideas. Most people think that if they're going to start a business, they have to follow a blueprint, but that way you lose the greatest aid to success— innovation. Perhaps the one advantage women have is a fresher approach, and because of this can come up with new and better ways of doing things.

TRAVELMANIA

You need more than wanderlust to make it in the travel agency business. When Oliva Posada opened Travelmania in a fashionable brownstone office building in New York City, she had had many years' experience working in travel.

Getting started in a travel agency business is tricky. It's a highly registration. First of all, you have to be approved by both the IATA (International Air Transport Association) and the ATC (Air Traffic Conference), the domestic regulatory board. An agency must be licensed before the airlines will allow it to hold blank tickets or will extend a credit line on the tickets.

But in order to apply for a license, you have to be set up in business. They want to see your office, check out your investment and operating capital, and investigate your experience in the business. In order to be approved, either the owner or an office manager must have at least two years' experience in the travel business. It doesn't have to be the owners because it's the agency that's licensed, not the agents themselves. So you can hire an office manager who has had experience.

In addition, a minimum investment of $15,000 is required plus minimum bonding insurance of $10,000. The margin of profit in a travel agency is not large. Business depends on volume and clients who will pay quickly. The airlines only allow a ten-day credit line, so if clients don't pay right away, which they don't, I'm out that money. That's why they require that you have a large operating capital.

So setting up an agency is time and investment. IATA only meets twice a year, in August and February, and the smartest thing to do is to apply within three months of one of these dates. That way you won't be waiting half the year to get your ticket-writing license and credit extensions. During the time between your application and licensing, all the airlines pay you a visit. IATA and ATC drop in, too, but you don't know who they are. They check to see that you're serious and competent to run an agency.

I learned the travel business initially by working for a small southern airline in Florida. Then I came to New York and worked for TWA as a ticket agent and spent several more years agency hopping. I began to pick up a following of clients and finally decided I could do it myself.

The first step was to find a suitable office. The airlines prefer that you have a storefront operation because they don't want to have to handle the walk-in street traffic. For them, it's a big bother if their ticketing agents have to take time arranging a whole itinerary, and that's why the 7 to 10 percent an agent makes back on each ticket is so readily given.

Be prepared to send eight-by-ten glossies of your office, safe, and equipment, and proof of advertising and promotion. Also, acquire a minimum of three letters from customers verifying that they have done and will continue to do business with you. To qualify, you have to prove that you can generate a volume of at least $100,000 a year.

It's a lot easier to buy an already-existing agency, but then you pay for the clientele, and there's no guarantee that those clients will stay with you. I had a following who sent me all their business in the beginning, and from them I got a lot of clients through word of mouth. Most of my accounts are commercial, which is the backbone of the travel industry, especially these days. People just aren't going off on faraway holidays, but the business community still has to travel. They may not go first class or travel as many times a year, but they have to travel.

For the most part, the business is a matter of building accounts and selling the package tours already arranged by the airlines. They do all the advertising. But I am also putting together tours for women. Men can travel alone and go to exotic places without much of a problem, but for women, especially in some foreign countries, they just can't be by themselves with any ease. I want to organize exciting tours for women to offbeat places. One idea is a boat trip down the Amazon. Another, called "Great Is Diana," has been designed to rediscover the historic origins and mythological roots of women. Travelmania also arranges inexpensive villa accommodations in the Caribbean, plans camping trips, rafting excursions on the Colorado River, and salmon fishing in Alaska.

To get an excursion idea off the ground, I first go to one of the airlines and present my idea. If they like it, they will take over, create the package, and have a brochure printed up. I then do a mailing to my clients. We can also advertise and may give a wine-and-cheese party to introduce people to the idea, showing slides narrated by a speaker.

Mailings are really the best way to promote an agency.

There are too many special tour packages put out by the airlines and advertised by them in a big way for the small agencies to compete.

The worst reason for getting into the travel business is wanting to travel. It's very much a service business, and you have to put effort into it. If you just want to travel, you're going to take very little interest in the client. You have to be in business a year, and producing revenue for the airlines, before they start extending travel privileges. First, you get discounts on tickets, and then you are invited on free trips. The agent is invited only if the agency is. doing business and bringing in clients. So it's not an automatic thing. You have to work to maintain your status.

Some people don't know what a good travel agency can offer. An experienced agent can give you a wider choice of everything, at the best available prices. And for anyone whose time means money, an agency is a necessary convenience. Corporate accounts are clearly the most lucrative clients to go after; their steady repeat business is the backbone of the travel industry. From these accounts I've also gained many individual clients for whom I plan holiday trips. These are the most interesting clients as well as the most demanding. I take a personal interest in my clients and always follow up to make sure their trip and my arrangements were a success.

FOOD

The food business is extraordinarily appealing. Nearly everyone loves good food and the discussion of it: favorite dishes, restaurants, cookbooks, and ethnic taste discoveries. It's no wonder that the selling of food and drink is the number one retail business in the United States. Women have traditionally gravitated to the food business, and while images of The Lilac Tearoom and Flo's Truck Stop die hard, women are branching out.

Restaurants, specialty prepared foods, catering services, pushcarts, cooking schools, and wholesale foods all are areas in which women are starting businesses. The food business is one of the most closely regulated you can enter. The board of health is a formidable presence lurking in the background ready to pounce on you with unwritten rules and unscheduled inspections. Restaurants must also be licensed and cleared by the fire department, city and state licensing bureaus, local zoning and special occupancy agencies. In addition, you must be licensed to sell liquor and other taxable items. But almost any vendor needs a license of some sort, so check (and double-check) to find out what you can, and cannot, do before you start cooking.

RESTAURANTS

Of all the food businesses, starting a restaurant is perhaps the most appealing, yet one of the most difficult businesses to run at a profit. So much so that there are numerous trade books on the market, filled with markup formulas, percentage margins, equipment information, licensing information, kitchen planning, and food technology.

But restaurateurs are a strange breed of people. Most prefer to run full steam ahead on intuition and enthusiasm. It's only after the fact, when she finds herself slaving for sixteen hours a day, seven days a week, for a self-imposed nominal salary, watching the nice, tidy little investment stagger under the weight of unforeseen expenses, that the small restaurateur begins to study up on industry guidelines. The epicurean dream turns into a nightmare for 50 percent of new restaurant owners. Most of the rest will make livable profits, with only a very few ending up wealthy. Still and all, the psychological pull of restaurant ownership remains one of the overwhelming drawing cards of the business.

Below is a brief survey of industry rules of thumb and averages.*

> *Location:* As in any retail business, go for a high-traffic location rather than pinch pennies on rent. Ideally, try to lease an existing restaurant facility requiring only interior decorations rather than total refurbishing.
>
> *Size:* Your profits are directly related to your seating capacity and rate of turnover. To estimate gross sales, multiply number of seats by the average meal-check figure. Multiply this by turnover (number of times you expect each seat to be occupied each day). Then multiply that figure by the number of days that you will be open each year.
>
> *Profits:* Your profit should be 20 percent of your gross sales. Operational costs break down as follows: 33 percent for payroll; 33 percent for food and beverages; 12 to 15 percent for overhead.
>
> *Pricing:* In low-rent restaurants, the markup standard is three times the price of food costs. In high-rent

---

* Write the National Restaurant Association, 1 IBM Plaza, Chicago, Illinois 60611, for trade publications.

operations, it is four times the price of food. After that, it's anything the market will bear.

Liquor: Because the margins are so slim between profit and loss, most restaurant owners lean heavily on wine and beer, or full liquor service, for profits. This can mean up to 20 percent of the gross. The markup for a bottle of wine generally runs double the wholesale price, plus one dollar. Mixed-drink markup varies with the style of the restaurant but can be marked up as high as 500 percent over the cost of the bottle.

Of course, numbers mean nothing if your establishment doesn't catch on. Another common mistake a new restaurant owner can make is to assume that everyone in town will flock to her door. They may—the first week or month, but the eating public is a notoriously fickle lot. You must always work for new customers. Publicity, restaurant reviews, catering, private parties, giveaway dinners, complimentary wine to newcomers, gimmicks such as summer picnic baskets or a Sunday morning jogger's special, and advertising all are part of a restaurant owner's busy, exhausting day.

CATERING

Caterers come in all sizes, from those who do parties for hundreds to those who specialize in one dish. There is a woman in Atlanta who bakes birthday cakes for nearby Georgia Tech students. She gets the names and home addresses of the students, writes to their parents, enclosing an order form, and, if hired, delivers a cake on the appointed day.

Catering prices are based on two formulas: marking up the food costs, quoted on a per person basis (for example, a cocktail party for one hundred might be quoted at $10 per person, including liquor and hors d'oeuvres), or charging for time and talent at an hourly rate, adding the cost of food and expenses.

Laws vary state by state as to whether you can prepare food for commercial consumption in your own home facilities or not. Check with your local board of health.

COOKING CLASSES

The essential ingredient for teaching a cooking class is a kitchen facility conducive to teaching, with counters and room for students to sit and take notes or gather about the stove. Pricing depends on your credentials, the length of the course, and the competition.

Often gourmet shops and department stores will have cooking facilities, and you might try building a clientele by demonstrating a dish that will help the store sell a product—for example, crêpes or homemade pasta can sell crêpe pans and pasta machines.

Many organizations and clubs will also have cooking facilities, and you might find your audience there. Or teach at home, promoting yourself with a letter to a chosen segment of the community. Your mailer should include a statement of your qualifications and a brief outline of what will be taught in the course. Include a registration blank, and request a deposit.

Be sure you enjoy getting up in front of people and talking. A good cook is not necessarily a good teacher.

WHOLESALING

The dream of wholesaling is to market a product, such as your great-grandma's secret salad dressing with such success that a big manufacturer and distributor come begging at your door, check in hand, to make you as rich and famous as Sara Lee. Or you can dream about baking quiches in your oven for a local restaurant, building up to a fleet of trucks, selling your goods to every specialty shop on the East Coast.

Producing wholesale foods combines strict food regulations with manufacturing and wholesaling basics (see Chapter 20). The product must be prepared under approved conditions, and it must maintain its stability as it goes from manufacturer to wholesaler to shelf to consumer. Study what other independent food manufacturers have done, through trade journals and general articles written for magazines and newspapers.

A CUT ABOVE

Pat Rosende is building a sandwich empire in Atlanta. In seven years she has watched her initial investment of $15,000 in one specialty sandwich restaurant grow into a million-dollar enterprise which maintains seven restaurants, a central food commissary, and forty employees.

She started with no practical knowledge in the food business or

Sandwiches are as American as the proverbial apple pie. Anybody can make a sandwich, yet the legendary New York "deli" sandwich is rare in most parts of the country. After many years of my wanting to start a business and searching for a good idea, the thought of a delicious and interesting sandwich was the one that clicked. I knew it would work, and I felt I knew how to make it work. It was simply a matter of getting in there and doing it.

The real inspiration was my choice of location. None of my restaurants is in a commercial shopping area. Instead, they all are located on the ground floors of office buildings in Office Parks, which are suburban office complexes. In many cities, especially those that have experienced fast growth, like Atlanta, the business community is no longer concentrated in one area. It's scattered all over, and the concept of Office Parks seems to have taken hold. Yet none of these buildings offers much in the way of services or shops for their people. Each can house thousands of employees and executives, but lunchtime was a matter of bringing it in or getting in the car and driving to the nearest restaurant. With all this in mind, I simply looked for the tallest office building for my first location.

A Cut Above sells wholesome deli sandwiches, homemade soups, salads, fresh baked desserts and breads, and a hot special of the day. Each restaurant seats from fifty to one hundred, with an all-glass storefront facing the interior lobby of the building. I've decorated each place with hanging plants, antiques, and good prints and paintings.

And it worked! I had a hard time convincing my first landlord to rent me the space, but now everyone in Atlanta would like to be my partner.

That first shop was an instant success, which was not exactly what I had counted on. I had expected a slow start, giving me time to learn the skills I lacked; but from the first day it was simply the right idea in the right place, and there was no looking back. I paid for my ignorance by making mistakes, but that initial rush also made me stretch my abilities to the limits. When you're in a position like that, it's astounding how capable you can be.

The initial investment of $15,000 (it would take about $25,000 today) went toward equipment, rent, and the design of the shop. I hired a professional designer to build the counters and outfit the kitchen area because I really had no concept of what I needed. I had never worked at anything even remotely connected to the restaurant business before.

Initial costs went to refrigeration, work tables, cold and hot counters, cooking facilities, and, of course, all the necessary utensils and facilities for dining. Once I had convinced the landlord that A Cut Above would work, he was willing to work with me and absorb some of the installation costs. When I opened, I had $3,000 left for operating expenses.

I was especially lucky in the beginning because the sales manager for the wholesale food distributor I was working with took a major interest in my idea. He worked along with me and offered an enormous amount of advice as to the purchasing and handling of food. For example, I had no idea of the shelf life of certain foods, which is tremendously important in pricing, ordering, and menu planning. I think it's very important when you're on unfamiliar ground to seek out professional advice from people whom you can work with and depend on when you need them.

Business is not an impersonal interaction of goods; it's an interaction of people. Much of your success is based on how well you can work with the people who are necessary to operating your business.

I had originally planned for only the lunch trade, but what I didn't realize is that hardly anybody eats breakfast at home anymore. As they arrived for work in the morning, customers could smell delicious aromas coming from the kitchen, and suddenly, on opening day, there were seventy people outside the door, all clamoring for morning coffee and pastries. I had hired only two women to help me, and that first week was a nightmare, trying to adopt a breakfast schedule when I was still a novice at the idea of lunch. But I had the attitude that I could do anything, and I was totally committed to making this business work.

I opened my second shop eighteen months later with profits from the first, and the third shop with profits from the second. After that, I was able to open four more shops in thirteen months. Running seven restaurants is quite a bit different from running just one. I established a central office and commissary, which supplies all the restaurants, and I am now able to buy wholesale supplies from food brokers in volume. I work with one main food supplier but have numerous backup suppliers in case something goes wrong. I try to protect all areas of operation with alternate solutions. When you're dealing at this level, you must envision the potential problems and be prepared for them.

People are starved for quality, and I make an effort to produce the highest standard of food. I have created and tested each recipe and sandwich. We now have thirty variations on the menu. My soup cook is a genius, and I am constantly trying new ideas in home-baked goods. In the morning we bake fresh biscuits, something unheard of in most restaurants. I do cheesecake, cookies, and brownies, but the greatest dessert success has been fruit cobbler. It's something people remember from childhood, but I have yet to see it in any other restaurant. Always try new things, especially in a restaurant business. It keeps you active and interested in the daily process of the business. Variety is a sure way to keep customers.

It is vitally important to maintain strict controls. There is little margin for mistakes in a food business. Everything must be priced down to the last ingredient and cost of operation. It takes time before you can estimate daily sales volume, but after seven outlets, I've worked out very close estimates.

Each sandwich is a formula—so many ounces of filling—so that there is no guesswork on the part of employees. It's a tight business, and you literally have to watch every penny and every part of the process. My working area is in the middle of the commissary, so I can follow every stage of getting the food to the restaurants.

Each shop has a manager, who, in turn, reports to an area supervisor, who reports to me. The central office handles all the hiring and training of employees. Every person who works for me is familiarized with the business by working in the central commissary before she goes into a restaurant. My managers have the authority to fire an employee, which I think is important. But I do all the screening and hiring, so I am closely associated with anyone who works for me.

One of my major problems has to do with employee turnover. About 80 percent of my people have been with the business a year or longer, but that other 20 percent is constantly on the move. That means we're forever coming up one or two employees short. It's just one of the facts of life in this kind of business.

I am married and have two teen-age children, and my family life has changed quite a bit. You must have the cooperation of your family if you're going to start a business because it means you will not have the same time you had before to spend with the family. It took them all a while to get used to the fact that I love the business and have a great personal need for it. I could spend every day here, from dawn until midnight, but I curtail my working hours so that I am home in the evenings.

My son is now fifteen and is very interested in the business. He works with me in all areas, and that's great—I'm especially proud of that. My daughter, who is seventeen, is less enthusiastic. And that's okay, too. She knows how much it means to me and appreciates my love for it.

I think there are still very subtle obstacles for a woman in business. Maybe it's just the southern tradition of the helpless woman, but I've discovered that men love you until you're a success. The turning point came for me when I bought myself a new Mercedes. It was a purchase totally for me, independent of anyone else. The minute I had the car, attitudes changed. I was no longer someone to be encouraged, but someone to be challenged. The old friendly relationships altered, and there seemed less respect for what I was doing and more resentment.

For myself, I've learned to operate as an individual. I have the confidence to argue and stand up for my ideas. I trust my decisions, and I like the freedom of putting my ideas into operation. If I make a mistake, it's my mistake. For these reasons, I'm glad I'm not in partnership. It would be frustrating for me to have to clear everything through someone else.

I also ran into problems as a woman getting a bank loan. The original investment was my own money, and I used profits to start the second and third shops. By the time I went to the bank I had a good track record. All I wanted was $2,000 to buy an exhaust fan. No problem they said, as long as my husband co-signed. I refused and gave them all sorts of lectures on the changing laws and equal rights. So they agreed, and I got my money. But I found out they had sent the papers to my husband anyway and he had signed them. Well, I walked in there and raised hell. Ironically, I was depositing more than $2,000 a day into the business account, yet the old prejudice against women outweighed the facts.

After a two-year leveling-off period, plans are in motion for a series of new shops. I'll be going to the bank soon for financing, and this time they seem ready to deal with me as a businesswoman.

THE SOHO CHARCUTERIE

In the past ten years, the Soho area of New York City has been transformed. Originally the warehouse and factory district south of Greenwich Village, it has become one of the most active and interesting communities on Manhattan Island. Artists' lofts, galleries, off-off Broadway theaters, restaurants, and unusual shops now line the streets.

Among them you can find The Soho Charcuterie—an unusual food store stocked with freshly baked breads, imported cheeses, homemade preserves and pickled vegetables, and a wide array of meat and salad specialties, all from original recipes created by the owners, Madeline Poley and Francine Scherer.

I used to be in the student travel business and spent several months a year in Paris. That's where I got the idea of a charcuterie. In France, a *charcuterie* originally meant a shop specializing in pork products. Later *charcuteries* branched into pâtés, cold salads, and other prepared foods. Our shop could be called a delicatessen, but we wanted a new image and a new attitude toward our products. The foods we make are special, and we have customers who come all the way from Westchester and Long Island to buy them. We have a variety of pâtés, eight different kinds of quiche, coquille Saint-Jacques, and a house specialty of brioche stuffed with chicken tarragon. Salads are a large part of our sales and include everything from antipasto to our original green apples and curried tuna fish. We also carry breads, desserts, imported canned goods, pure maple syrup, imported teas and coffees, cheeses, and pastas.

My partner, Fran, has always been interested in cooking. When Mother Courage, the feminist restaurant, opened, she made quiches and pâtés for them. I told Fran she ought to open a specialty food shop. I had no intention of getting into it, but then I thought: why not do it, too? I kept my travel job for a few months after we opened, but quit when the charcuterie started to involve me more.

We started the business with $8,000 cash and a lot more in credit—a lot. The day we opened our doors we had $88 left in the bank, which was crazy, but it worked out for us because from the first day the shop was a success. We got tremendous support from the neighborhood. And shortly after we opened, we were written up in *New York* Magazine, which attracted people from all over the city and the suburbs.

The most important thing we did in the beginning was to establish credit with our suppliers; otherwise, we could never have scraped together the initial investment. The basic $8,000 came from all sources—family loans, personal savings (we each put in $2,000 of our own money)—and I also extended two loans I had taken out when I had the travel job. I never could have gotten the extensions if I had told the bank what the money was really for.

The first thing we needed was refrigeration and a cold-storage counter. We talked to a man who was running a similar type of shop, and he gave us the name of a good supplier. We were lucky because the company was extremely helpful. I think in cases like this it helps being a woman because men will lean over backwards to give you good deals and advice. It's an ego thing for them.

The cost of the counter we wanted was $5,000, which was impossible for us. So he offered us a $1,000 down and $100-per-month payment plan, which turned out to be a good deal in more ways than one. After establishing credit with him, we could use his company as a credit reference to buy other equipment. You have to owe money to get credit. By the time we opened, we had all the references we needed to approach the import food supply houses. The entire shop was started on a credit basis.

At first we only knew about A & A Distributors and Liberty Imports, which are the two biggest wholesalers in town for quality goods, but once a year, there is a Fancy Foods Show at the Coliseum, and we've since discovered new resources.

Our concept is to sell quality foods and our prices reflect

that. Before we started, we gave our friends lists of foods we planned to carry and had them do comparative shopping all over town. Now we set our fees based on our clientele and the time it takes to prepare dishes.

Passing the board of health inspection is the biggest issue in opening a food business. They offer no guidelines but come around without fail to inspect. We had been storing our spices in giant jars placed on the floor in the kitchen and after our first inspection had to build a platform to raise them off the floor. We also had an exposed brick wall—the whole shop is exposed brick—and we had to put tiles over it where our cutting board is. There were other minor adjustments, but for us it wasn't too bad. But you might have to redo entire floor plans before passing inspection. The best thing is to talk to people in similar businesses to get some idea of what other people have gone through.

The charcuterie did so well that after two years we expanded the whole operation and now run a restaurant—so we are now The Soho Charcuterie and Restaurant. Opening a restaurant was an incredible jump for us in investment and commitment, but operating the charcuterie first gave us the confidence and business experience to take on the really mammoth responsibility of a restaurant.

Also, with our credit and general contacts in the food industry in New York, we were able to keep our initial outlay of money to a minimum. We opened the restaurant on $25,000, which is only a third of what the actual cost would have been, had we not been in the business already.

And like everything, luck and timing helped. We were in a great location. We had already built up a reputation for quality, and we knew our customers and what competition we would be up against. The decision was to open an elegant, expensive restaurant rather than a casual neighborhood bar. We went after the "uptown" trade, so to speak, and it worked. Last year *New York* Magazine featured us as one of the ten best restaurants in the city.

ALFALFA

Alfalfa is a small restaurant featuring home-style cooking with a bias toward health foods. Oddly assorted furniture, hanging plants, local art displays, and a community bulletin board create a casual, earth-movement ambience.

Marina McCulloch, Ann Holson, and Arthur Howard, three graduates of the University of Kentucky, own and operate Alfalfa, located only steps from the campus of their alma mater.

Our initial investment was $5,000, which was almost exactly what it took to open the doors. This place was an old luncheonette, but we had to do so much renovation that it might as well have been a dry cleaner's. The kitchen was poorly placed, the floor was rotting, and none of the equipment was worth a dime except the dishwasher and exhaust fan. The reasons we rented the space were the location and the low rent. We knew that being right across from the university campus would guarantee our clientele.

All of us had worked in a restaurant before as waiters or cooks, which is why we got together and decided to open our own restaurant.

We found the space first and began to remodel it. We did all the work ourselves, including putting down a new floor in the kitchen. The first thing you have to do in opening a restaurant is to get everything cleared with the health inspector and the fire department. It's weird—they don't have any written rules; you pass or you don't, according to the inspector. One will look only at your exhaust and refrigeration; then six months later another one will come along and get you for plumbing or trash disposal. There is no way to know what they are looking for, so the best thing is to be nice. If the inspector likes you, he'll help you and make suggestions; if he doesn't, then things can really get involved. We've had two inspectors, and they were like night and day. Each one had a totally different concept of the rules.

The health department requires that you draw up a floor plan showing everything about your kitchen and seating arrangements, the entrance, back exits, and bathrooms. You have to list all electrical outlets, the plumbing diagram, and the storefront design (whether it's plate glass or not), which way the doors open, etc. We seat over fifty, so we are required to have two bathrooms. In Kentucky, you must have a partition between the sink and toilets, and you have to provide soap and towels. This is taken to the city inspector, who stamps and approves it, and then to the state inspector. It takes a lot of time because each one looks at the same thing differently. One says it's okay; the other questions it. You need patience.

Next comes the fire inspector. In our case, the requirements were an exhaust hood over both the stove and sink, and the front and exit doors had to open out. They also wanted a street plan indicating the stores on either side of us. I've heard fire inspections can be much tougher than this.

Then there's this little guy who comes around from local licensing. You're required to buy special licenses to serve ice cream, soft drinks, liquor, and cigarettes. Alfalfa serves none of these, so we were spared that extra expense.

Our entire restaurant is outfitted with secondhand equipment. We got a lot of kitchen equipment from a church that was being torn down and from restaurants going out of business. The kitchen has a restaurant stove and oven, steam table, four-door refrigerator, freezer, dishwasher, exhaust hoods and fans, a cold table for keeping salads and dressing, two work tables, and a dough-mixing machine. Our soup pots, lasagna trays, and baking pans all came from the church sale. And we finally got an espresso machine from a secondhand place in New York for $1,000.

The restaurant seats seventy-five; the tables and chairs come from garage sales and junk shops, any place we could pick them up. On opening day we were still short at least twenty chairs, so we advertised, "A free meal for a sturdy chair," and made up the rest that way.

We solved the rotting floor problem in the kitchen by building a platform over it; the landlady provided the lumber. She also put in air-conditioning and proper heating, which was provided for in the lease. That was a lucky break, since it cost almost $2,000, and we never could have afforded it.

The restaurant is open for lunch and dinner and organized in two shifts. On the first shift, we start at 8:00 A.M. and cook till 11:00 A.M. From 11:00 A.M. to 2:00 P.M. we serve lunch. Then, from 2:00 P.M. till 4:30 P.M., we work on management—payroll, ordering food, whatever needs doing. The second shift comes in at 2:00 P.M. and starts cooking for the evening meal.

Lunch includes two soups, three salads, three specials (usually a chili plus two other dishes), four home-baked desserts, home-baked breads, and beverages (spiced teas, espresso, fruit drinks). Dinner offers the soups and salads plus five specials, six homemade desserts and breads, and beverages.

About 75 percent of our supplies come from one foods wholesaler (spices, cheeses, meats, canned goods, frozen goods, and staples), and we have two other suppliers for dairy products and fresh vegetables and fruits. A general rule of thumb for ordering is to plan thirty people to a dish in a restaurant of our size.

Our pricing is based on the cost of the food times five, but we feel this is high. Our general breakdown is 40 percent food, 40 percent labor, and 20 percent everything else, including profit. What it *should* be is approximately 30 percent food, 33 percent labor, 37 percent all other expenses and profit.

The difference between profit and loss in a restaurant like this is very small, especially if you're operating without liquor The reason our food cost is high is that we go for fresh foods and don't cook to order. In other words, we spend more for supplies and estimate our crowd, with food going to waste at the end of the day if we've overestimated.

Our biggest mistake has been in not costing out each dish to the penny, right down to how much spice or how many drops of milk we put in. But since our menu changes every day, it might be months before we repeat a dish. The whole idea of the restaurant is to experiment with cooking, but our constant menu-changing makes it hell to keep track of costs.

The way to keep food costs down is have a fairly standardized menu. We've started keeping a detailed record of each dish: the exact ingredients and their cost, which varies with the seasons and the economy, and any other notes about preparation and cooking time. If we cost out a dish and divide it into servings, then in time, we'll have a better grip on where each penny goes.

Our labor cost is high, but because we all worked in restaurants, we know firsthand how underpaid the help usually is. We didn't want to start that whole thing all over again, so our people are paid fairly well: $3.00 per hour plus a guaranteed 40-cent tip per hour. All the tips are thrown into the same box and divided up per person for the hours worked.

The day-to-day running of the business is easy. Each day's take is recorded at the end of the day. The cash register records the price of each ticket, and we keep those receipts along with the guest checks on file. The cash register is tallied against the guest checks each day. Our bookkeeper is in the University of Kentucky Business School and works here as a waiter as well.

Last year, our first year, we brought in $110,000, but that was a break-even number. This year all our equipment and renovation expenses are paid up, so we expect to make a profit.

We incorporated for our own protection, and took out full insurance coverage—fire, plate glass damage (our entire storefront is glass), a three-month compensation policy for business interruption, and personal liability.

We do very little advertising because of the expense, but we do run a regular ad in the university paper, and when school is not in session, we advertise in the Lexington daily paper. We tried *not* advertising for a while to see if it really mattered and couldn't believe how much less business we did.

MOM

MOM has gone into the fast-food business. MOM sells over-the-counter main-dish meat and vegetable pies and a variety of fruit pies. And they are selling like hotcakes.

Behind MOM stand Judith Choate and her partner, Steven Pool. Judith had wanted to be involved with food since she learned all about cooking from her own mom at a very young age. She has written two cookbooks and many articles on food. However, it wasn't until her seven-year job as director of a national foundation ended that she decided to launch a takeout pie shop.

Located on Manhattan's Upper West Side, MOM lives up to its name, dispensing nourishing food from a cozy, copper kitchen.

There is no reason why quality food cannot be offered on a fast-food basis. It doesn't have to be bad, yet most of it is. I have always baked pies for friends and family, and it seemed to be the answer to convenience food. They are something everyone likes, yet at the same time they can be served quickly and cheaply, without sacrificing good quality.

Pies are perfect for working mothers. They can be frozen. Kids can heat them up themselves or eat them cold, if need be. I can't think of a better meal. The day MOM opened it was an instant success, not only as an attractive food but as a service.

When we started, we made only main-course pies—a meat pie, a chicken pie, a patchwork pie, and a vegetable pie. Now we've branched into dessert pies, quiches, cheesecake, and at Christmas, we do a fruitcake.

The main-dish pies come in two sizes—a six-serving large size for $6.95 and a one-serving small size for $1.95. We cook an average of three hundred pies a day.

Our only problem was that we started too small. The idea was to get into business and test our skills, so we took a tiny space on a side street to save on overhead. We were less prepared for success than we were prepared for failure and consequently were too cautious in the beginning. You've really got to believe in what you're doing before you start and then not work against yourself by trying to squeak into business.

On the other hand, I personally needed to start small. I couldn't handle the idea of a big business in the beginning. I wanted to try my hand on a less demanding scale.

Now, with a proven success formula, we're ready to expand. The first step will be to open outlet shops all around New York, with one central food kitchen. The next step is franchising nationwide, but I have a hard time in letting go. Franchising will mean losing control, and it's important to all of us to maintain the quality of our products.

Our initial investment was $25,000, funded from my partner's and my personal savings. The money went for equipment, renovations, supplies, operating capital, and a car, which we needed to make deliveries and pick up supplies at the wholesale markets.

The equipment needed was a stove (we have an ordinary Sears oven), a good-sized freezer, a refrigerator, an electric dough mixer, a pie press, work tables, storage bins, and a heavy exhaust unit. I now see we should have leased the heavy equipment until we could see how the store was doing, and put more of our money into a better location. Volume is the key to profits in this business, and location is the key to volume.

It took us a good six months to iron out the kinks of the business. The most difficult part was learning to cook in quantity. Developing the recipes for mass production meant careful testing. When you're cooking in volume, it's not just a matter of doubling or tripling the recipe. Food quality and taste change as the portions increase. This meant I had to spend far too much time testing pie fillings and not enough time directing the business.

Another difficult area was promoting the business. Because we were off the main shopping area and because advertising was too expensive, we went after publicity. Or rather publicity came after us. Right after we opened, we sent a pie to every food person in town. The reviews were fantastic. So much so that a local television station decided to do a story on us. The next day I arrived to find more than four hundred people eagerly waiting to buy pies, and there was no way we could handle the trade. Many had come out of their way, and you can imagine the ill will they felt for us as they went away empty-handed.

This is all hindsight now. MOM operates solidly in the black, and we are working to full capacity. Word of mouth and repeat customers make up a steady trade, and we know we have a proven success. People just can't get this quality anywhere else. As a small business, the operation could make a nice profit for anyone as it is, but our idea is to move into a much bigger picture.

I think some people are born entrepreneurs—they have an idea or see an opportunity and plunge right in. Others, like me, need to learn and find out about their business through trial and error. It's just a matter of how much time and money you have, not to mention patience, before both types arrive at the same spot.

It is very important to have good advisors when you're setting up a business because how you establish your business is later reflected in how you grow. I think many of our problems stemmed from the fact that we could never find an accountant who was good for us. I needed financial advice, not just someone to set up the books, but someone who could tell me which areas to put my money in, and when.

Our lawyer, on the other hand, is a personal friend, so we got things from him that you couldn't buy—special care and advice, based on a real desire to see us succeed. He set us up as two companies—both incorporated. He believed, if perhaps we didn't, that this business could move quickly into a large field of operation. One company owns the idea, the recipes, and the logo. The other company owns this shop. Fifteen percent of the shop is owned by our three employees. One is the pastry chef, and the other two work the counters, assist in filling the pies, and do the ordering.

The work starts in the shop at 7:00 A.M., with the baking and filling of pies. Everything is baked fresh daily. The store opens at 11:00 A.M. and closes at 8:30 P.M. Usually I am here on into the evenings, checking the sales, making lists for supplies and ingredients, and overseeing the cooking for the next day's pie fillings. The weekend trade is much heavier than the weekdays, and we often work until midnight. Holidays are frantic—we work all through the night, and even at that can't keep ahead of orders.

Wholesale prices fluctuate constantly, and you have to watch every dime carefully. Already we've had to raise our prices. So far our customers don't mind; they're still getting a good price for the quality of food.

My advice to any woman thinking of getting into business is that you must have an idea you believe in. You can make anything happen if you *think* it can happen. The odds were so against a tiny homemade pie shop, located on a side street, making it and going on to make it in a big way. And yet here we are.

THE HAPPY COOKERS

The Happy Cookers have reason to be happy. The catering service they started three years ago in Greenwich, Connecticut, is booming. Timmie Mason and her partner Betsy Buddy began their business at first as an informal extension of their love of cooking, catering small dinners on a part-time basis for friends.

Working from their own kitchens made start-up capital minimal. But as their reputation and profits grew, they quickly committed themselves to a full-time operation and now offer a complete events planning and catering service to both Connecticut clients and New York City businesses.

I had worked for a few years in New York for a creative promotional agency. Then I moved to San Francisco, where I continued to plan corporate promotional events on a freelance basis. Finding good caterers was always a problem. The big commercial companies trot out the same old standbys—

tray upon tray of strange little sandwiches or the familiar and boring Boeuf Bourguignon.

When I moved back to Connecticut to run a supper theater, a friend called, saying she was having thirty people to dinner and did I know of a good caterer? It sounded like fun, so I said, "Yes—me." I then called Betsy, who was a longtime friend, and roped her into helping me. We created an incredibly exotic meal, one that I would never repeat because most of it required split-second timing between stove and table.

I believe that cooking is a highly creative act. As in any art, there is a certain magic in the relationship between the cook and her ingredients and I discovered in that first dinner party how much more I enjoyed my command post in the kitchen than I had liked socializing out front. I had always loved to cook for my own guests, but cooking took on a whole new dimension, when I no longer had to play hostess.

So it began—slowly and by word of mouth. Betsy was teaching school and raising a family. My job at the supper theater was ending. Within a few months, we had done enough parties to feel comfortable with the process of catering. We had enough clients to know that we could have a lucrative business, if and when we wanted to push it.

Finally, we sat down and figured it out. Combining the experience I had had in planning promotional parties and corporate functions with the social whirl in Greenwich, we imagined every type of catering situation and what we would need in equipment and staff to bring it off.

Between us, we had enough basic equipment to handle small parties. Large equipment and extra serving utensils could be rented from a supplier in nearby Stamford. I negotiated a standard 10 percent professional discount with the rental company.

Our fee is based on time and talent, rather than a markup on the cost of food. I charge according to the number of people, plus cost of food, plus expenses. The fee is between $10 and $20 per hour—$10 for basic shopping and preparations, and $20 for full party arrangement services.

I buy very few wholesale food supplies—some basics, such as spices, dried goods, sugar, olive oil—but as I don't make any money off the cost of food, it doesn't benefit me to buy in bulk. I want absolutely fresh foods and the best quality, so I don't go out of my way to look for bargains. My butcher, greengrocer, and florist all give me 20 percent discounts when I buy in quantity.

We have no set menus, no preplanned meals. And to date, we've been able to do anything asked of us. Living so close to New York, we have a ready market for unusual ingredients and supplies. Every time I go to a good restaurant I bring home a menu for ideas. We have between us dozens of cookbooks, and we subscribe to *Gourmet* Magazine. *Gourmet* has an information and reprint service which is invaluable if you're researching a particular food from any part of the world.

I also look for talented people to make specialty goods, such as pastries, French breads, scones, preserves, and so on. Again, this is a service to my clients—finding the very best in food.

I keep files on each party we do. Ingredients, food costs, copies of the bills, instructions for serving, equipment needed, serving utensils—every element of each function is recorded for informal reference.

Depending on the size of the party, one or both of us will supervise the last-minute preparations. Both friends and professionals are hired to help with serving and cleanup. I keep an up-to-date file on where to find people and always plan for last-minute replacements. You can't imagine how many times people can't show at the eleventh hour.

Usually one meeting with the client is enough. We decide on the menu, set the arrangements, and I check out the facilities—regardless of whether it's in someone's house, club, yacht, or even if it's a picnic in a park. This, of course, minimizes any surprises. We did a large dinner for sixty one time and discovered all six burners on the host's stove would heat up only to half capacity. Luckily, a friend of mine lived two houses away. There we were, dashing through back lawns like bandits, trying to get everything to the table hot.

Most people giving parties are jittery, so you can expect lots of phone calls right up until the last minute. If there's anything you need in this business, it's the ability to *sound* calm and cool. I have developed my own special crisis style, and even as I pull a ghastly disaster out of the oven, I can sound as though things are going so smoothly that I'm about to sit down and flip through a magazine.

Once we were doing an extravaganza for two hundred and I arrived with God knows how many pounds of salad, freshly washed in a large plastic bag. It would have taken me hours to dry it, so I popped the whole thing in the clothes dryer. As luck would have it, the hostess rushed in to check on things, and you can't imagine the look on her face when she saw the entire salad spinning away on "cool." I announced it was the latest idea from *Gourmet* Magazine, and that seemed to reassure her.

Word of mouth continues to be our best advertising, but now I actively solicit business farther afield. I work with many law firms and corporations in the city, catering in-house luncheons and planning corporate dinners and promotional parties. We are beginning to advertise in local publications, but I feel most people respond if they can taste your food or see you preparing it. I've been on local talk shows, preparing and talking about special dishes, and I demonstrate cooking in department stores. I also teach cooking at the Y. The interest in cooking is tremendous, and many of my students will recommend me to their friends.

Bookkeeping is difficult mainly because we both hate to do it. You not only have to keep track of all the obvious expenses but have to estimate gasoline, heat, electricity, wear and tear on equipment, and staples. It's easy to forget the cup of flour you used or a last-minute dash for more ice, but somewhere those things have to be taken into account.

Anyone starting a catering service must maintain a high standard of quality, service, and reliability. This is particularly important when you're dealing with food. Things will go wrong; there will always be emergencies. Anticipating problems and planning for alternatives are essential.

People must have confidence in you, and I find the way to gain their confidence is to present myself more as a friend and partner than as a formal business operation. I am always available to my clients. They know they can call me at midnight, if need be. I ask for advance deposits only on major expenditures, and I quote my estimates verbally, rather than in writing. The final bill is carefully itemized, and so far, there have been no misunderstandings. The point is to stay in touch with your clients by working *with* them, not for them.

20

MANUFACTURING—WHOLESALING—MAIL ORDER—INVENTIONS—DESIGN

New products come on the market all the time, and behind them are designers, inventors, and everyday dreamers who are not content to let their inspirations fade into oblivion. The question is: how can you turn ideas into reality? How do you get your idea out of your head and onto the shelf?

As in any business, you must establish the marketability of the product. There must be a *need* before you manufacture, wholesale, or mail order a product. Need does not always mean necessity. Need can also be based on luxury, originality, price, and novelty. Test market your idea. Show it to friends and potential buyers, and get their reactions.

Establishing a market will lead you to distribution ideas, and distribution is the key to profits. The simple facts of business are that anything can be a profitable business as long as there's a market for it and the price is right.

Pricing is everything at this end of business. In production, you must not only think of your own profits but consider the retailer's final selling price as well. Your price must cover all production and marketing costs—raw materials, equipment, overhead, labor, and sales—as well as your profit. Then you must determine whether the final price to the individual retail buyer is in line with the quality of the product. A standard rule of thumb is: 20 percent to the manufacturer, 40 percent to the wholesaler, and 100 percent to the retailer. If the gadget you've invented will cost $5 to produce, and you sell it to the wholesaler for $6, who, in turn, sells it to the retailer for $8.40, can the retailer sell it to the customer for $16.80?

To produce and sell a profitable product, you must understand the many steps it will take to get that product to the general public.

MANUFACTURING

Your bibles are the Yellow Pages of your town, the nearest big city, and the surrounding area. They are required reading for anyone who needs raw materials and labor to make a particular product. Shop around. The woman making plastic boxes in her garage may suit your needs and budget better than a large manufacturer.

You should also have the New York City Yellow Pages. As a source guide it is invaluable. For example, New York's wholesale bead market is fabulous and much cheaper to buy from than a local crafts shop. Send for catalogs and free samples. You can get the Yellow Pages for any city in the country by calling the business office of your telephone company.

Another important source guide is the *Thomas Register*. It is an enormous catalog, listing manufacturers and dealers all over the United States. Everything is categorized: the *Thomas Register* tells you what products are produced by which company and also lists industrial design houses, suppliers, manufactured parts, and addresses.

Timing is important in manufacturing. Production should be closely timed to distribution and sales. It's a common mistake to think that you can manufacture to order, that you can take around a sample, write up orders, and then with guaranteed sales in hand, head back to the factory, where your orders will be made up.

Manufacturing usually means committing yourself to a run of goods, even if you're making them yourself. It's a calculated risk, but like anything in business, risk is the only route to profits. In manufacturing, risk can take on impressive stature because you may end up with a whole warehouse of ingenious gadgets only to find that no one but you thinks they will revolutionize the world.

WHOLESALING

Here you can often eliminate one risk because you can deal in samples. The product is made. It already exists. You buy a product or sample line from the manufacturer and take it around to retail buyers. Your concern is finding the buyers and presenting the product line in an attractive way. This can mean opening up new markets or jumping ahead of the competition with service, delivery, and a better price.

Often, however, the wholesaler will commission the manufacturer to make a special run of goods. In this case the wholesaler is committed to that run.

MAIL ORDER

The misunderstanding in mail order is that you can place an ad in a magazine, or buy a mailing list, and make a million dollars overnight. You can't. Competition is heavy in the mail-order business, and mailing charges, advertising costs, and methodical organization are prime considerations. It's a slow, demanding, and relatively risky business. In mail order, you never see your customer. Your ads must be carefully placed and laid out to catch the reader's eye. On mailing lists, a 1 or 2 percent return is not uncommon.

The cost for getting and filling each order is high, and it's difficult to buy goods at prices low enough to allow for a markup that will cover all your costs. Aside from the cost of inventory, you have the added charge of packaging—boxes, labels, and labor. And a mail-order business should never be run from the kitchen table. A good working area is essential.

INVENTIONS

New inventions can either be patented and manufactured by the inventor or sold in design form to a large company. Patents can cost up to $1,000 to obtain and may take two or three years to be approved by the Patent Office. A patent gives its owner the right to exclude others from making the same product. However, a few minor changes by a competitor often can circumvent your protection. "Patent Pending" offers no protection since the patent must be issued before you can take out suit against a copy. However, if you believe your formula is revolutionary, then consult with a patent lawyer. She will instigate a patent search and file the necessary application papers with the Patent Office.

The U.S. Department of Commerce publishes a directory of qualified patent attorneys. You can also check with your local bar association for this information, and general information on patents is available from the Library of Congress, Washington, D.C. 20540.

Often a designer or inventor considers selling her idea or sample product to a large company. It sounds ideal: you then sit back and wait for the royalty checks to arrive. However, your product's future is out of your control, and once behind corporate doors, it may even cease to exist. Before submitting an idea or design to a company, protect yourself by retaining a dated, witnessed copy of the written or drawn presentation.

DESIGN

Designs, as in greeting cards, posters, and the like, should be copyrighted. Copyrighting is relatively easy and can be done yourself. The Library of Congress publishes general information on how to obtain a copyright. Write to it, Washington, D.C. 20540.

In production, you must know your seasons. For example, it's futile to attempt to sell Christmas gift items, decorations, cards, etc., to department stores after October 1. Stores usually run over their Christmas budgets early in the fall and can't buy anything else, no matter how spectacular your product.

Seasonal articles and ads must be submitted to monthly magazines at least three months in advance of publication date; to weeklies, two to three weeks ahead. Greeting cards and gift wrap designs often must be submitted one year in advance.

In sales, you must nag. If you think the distributor or store buyer can use your products, keep after her. She may not have liked them in April, but perhaps she will in September, especially if you've added something new to the line or can assure her that Julia Child plans to use your product on her next show. On the other hand, just because she bought from you before does not mean she'll remember you forever. Keep reminding her of your existence, or hire an agent to do it for you.

Get on mailing lists. Find your field's professional organization, and even if you don't join, get on its list. If the item you manufacture requires raw materials, write the companies that make them, asking for free samples or news of new products.

Read the trade journals. Have your own business cards and stationery printed. Always look professional.

All in all, getting a product from your head to the shelf is not really so awesome and mysterious. If your product is worthy, there will always be a market for it. You just have to be prepared to study the market, learn its methodology, and devise step-by-step distribution plans.

THE AMERICAN NATURAL BEVERAGE COMPANY

Sophia Collier is a rather startling young woman. At the age of twenty-two, she wrote her own autobiography—*Soul Rush* published by William Morrow & Company—which tells of, among many things, her life for three years in the Divine Life Mission, a spiritual commune. Now, having followed Margaret Mead's dictum to get one's religious experience over with at an early age, she is the president of the American Natural Beverage Company in Brooklyn, New York. The company produces a natural soft drink called Soho.

Her partner, Connie Best, joins her in the manufacturing and distribution of Soho on the East Coast and a sales representative in Denver, Colorado, handles distribution in the Mountain States.

You may not want to manufacture a soft drink, but the saga of Soho is one which clearly outlines the many steps it will take to get any product from concept to shelf.

The food business has always been attractive to me. Soda is, of course, a nonessential food, but it's a fun product, and Americans are soda drinkers. They might as well be drinking something that isn't bad for them. Soho is a light, fruity, bubbly, all-natural drink, sweetened with fructose. A ten-ounce bottle of Soho has less sugar in it than an apple.

Soho came about not so much because I had suddenly invented a new drink, but because of my basic interest in how things are made. I had tried making beer at home and had an idea of how flavors are put together.

I like finding a need and creating the organization that produces a final result to fill the need. I think one of the real satisfactions of being in manufacturing is having to do the whole thing: to create something out of raw materials and then to channel it down the right road to its final market.

When you start to deal with any industry, you should know how to talk shop. For us, the profession was the beverage industry, which includes the bottlers, the flavor companies, the soft-drink distributors, and the supermarkets. I had to know as much as or more than the people I was going to be dealing with, so first I subscribed to all the beverage industry trade magazines. It was a fantastic way for me to learn everything I could, from names and resources for suppliers and dealers right down to the history of carbonated drinks.

My father had a friend who owned a beverage plant and arranged for me to spend a day there, talking to the foremen and the managers, learning exactly how a soft drink is made, bottled, and distributed. I think it was an important moment; it made everything seem as though it could be done. There was no longer any mystery involved.

Which is not to say that it's simple. Getting any invention, design, or formula to a final, salable form can be very complex. There are a million details in manufacturing a product. Add those to the million more details of distribution and promotion, and you can see that you've got to be pretty interested in the entire process if you want an ongoing business.

The first step is to get the idea into a manufacturing system. I first talked to a flavor chemist who gave me a lot of advice on how to keep flavors stable. To maintain a stable environment inside a bottle of soda, you have to understand microbiology. Our raw materials came from many sources. These ingredients had to be put together and then mass-produced. Mass production can very often alter the original flavor, just as it can alter an original drawing or model construction.

We had to get our formula inside a bottle, get the bottle from the plant to the store, from the store to the buyer, perhaps to a refrigerator, and then from the refrigerator to final consumption. All this had to be accomplished without losing the quality of taste, color, carbonation, and clearness.

I sent for the Federal Food and Drug Administration's Code of Federal Regulations. There are FDA guidelines for making any food product. The most important restriction is that you can use only ingredients on the GRAS (Generally Recognized as Safe) list. Working with these lists, I came up with a flavor concept, which I then took to a flavor extract company.

Once there, I explained my concept verbally, and on speculation their chemists came up with an interpretation of my concept. Once we settled on a flavor, the company made it up for us in a concentrated form.

A bottling plant was our next concern. We needed to investigate various water purification systems since we were not going to add any preservatives. The length of shelf life would depend on the degree of purification. This was particularly important when we approached supermarkets for sales.

Money had become a factor by now. In manufacturing, 95 percent of the people you deal with are on a cash-only basis. Initially, we raised $20,000 through our own savings and a large loan from a friend. Once we had gone into production, we needed another $20,000, which we raised through private investors and a loan from the bank, which was guaranteed by our lawyer. Money is easier to raise once you're in operation and can show an investor both a product and the ongoing nature of the business.

Our original run was about sixteen thousand bottles of soda, the amount one gallon of concentrate would make. We delivered to the bottler the concentrate flavor, the fructose, the labels, the bottles, and the formula (the proportions of ingredients). They put it all in a vat, and pretty soon the product came out bottled, labeled, and capped.

Before Connie joined the company, she had worked on a magazine, and we hired its art director to design our logo on a royalty basis, rather than a flat fee. I tried to work out various options with people to save on the initial outlay of money. We finally found a bottler who would give us a fifteen-day credit, which is very important because we give a ten-day credit to our distributors. Without credit from the bottlers, our cash flow would freeze.

And so we had a product. The next step was to distribute it.

Ideally, we manufacture to order, although we always have a small amount in inventory. Distributors vary. Some are little more than trucking firms; others have good sales departments. But a distributor won't take you on unless it thinks the product will sell, so in the beginning we had to distribute Soho ourselves. This meant going to small retail stores and shops in Manhattan. We felt that positioning Soho in health food stores and gourmet shops would create an identification for the product and lend integrity to it.

We ran ads in the health-food trade papers to promote interest. We also got some publicity—write-ups in "Best Bets" in *New York* Magazine, in *Enterprising Women*, and in newspapers around town. Once we had established customers for the product, we approached the big supermarket chains. There we had to get listed in their authorization book before any store manager could buy our product. This can take months because the authorization committees meet sporadically. We had to make a presentation to them describing how the product would be delivered, its shelf life, and what kind of promotion we were doing. Price is important, too. We priced Soho at slightly more than regular sodas, but less than other natural drinks.

We do not advertise on a national scale as we're not yet prepared to distribute nationally. So far our two markets are the East Coast and the Mountain States. Our main sales effort goes into point-of-sale. This includes in-store promotions, free samples, display, posters, stickers, and a booklet with each six-pack explaining the product.

In any selling situation you have to expect negative responses. Then plan to go back and back again, until the buyer says yes. Each time you reapproach a sale, you must have something new to say about the line. Perhaps it's being sold through a major distributor or competitive outlet; perhaps you have recent publicity, new packaging, or whatever. The point is that any inch of progress gives you a new sales tactic.

On the administrative side the business is kept as simple as possible. We have single-entry books, operate from my apartment, and have not patented the product. Our protection comes through secrecy rather than law. The flavor company has no idea what happens after it gives us the concentrate, and the bottler knows only the combinations of concentrate to water to fructose. No one but us knows how Soho is put together. We carry a $300,000 product insurance policy.

My advice to anyone going into manufacturing is not to limit yourself by trying to do everything by the book. Any field is wide-open for new, innovative thinking. And listen to people; get their advice.

KINDERGRAPHICS

Kindergraphics is a Philadelphia firm manufacturing posters. There are three partners—Diane Stevens, Marlene Kaufman, and artist Michael Chauncey, whose engaging, humorous animal illustrations are the basis for Kindergraphics' distinctive, best-selling wall hangings.

Sold coast to coast in children's stores, bookshops, and department stores, Kindergraphics' posters can be bought individually or in sets of eight which, when hung together, create a giant mural. To date, Chauncey's fanciful animals make up a jungle series, English garden series, barnyard series, and a series entitled *The Snide World of Sports.* Their popularity has inspired a book and, possibly, an animated television special. Look out, Charlie Brown—Kindercharacters may be our next super stars.

In 1974 Marlene and I were partners in a bookstore. We also carried posters and saw a need for more graphics for children. Posters had been popular for years, especially with the college and singles market, but illustrations specifically for the children's market were limited.

About this time we met Michael who was a free-lance illustrator. When we saw his portfolio, we knew instantly that his animal drawings would sell as posters. We found an excellent printer in town who gave us the various costs-per-run figures, and from this we were able to figure how many we would have to sell to make a profit.

Without printing anything, we then rented a small booth at the Stationery Show in New York, where we displayed the original artworks and took orders. The idea was to get a minimum number of orders before launching into production. Our feelings about Michael's art were right; the buyers were very enthusiastic, and we took enough orders to get us started. The show was in May, and the deadline for shipping Christmas goods is August 1, so we had only two months to print, package, and ship.

In the beginning we had to do all the distribution ourselves, by going to trade shows and seeing buyers in department stores. We also had a brochure made and sent out a mailing to buyers all over the country. Buyers register in advance for trade shows, and those names and addresses are printed up and given to each exhibitor, so straightaway you've got a good mailing list. We've always had a good percentage return on our mailings. The brochure is in full color, showing each of the thirty-three illustrations and how they group together to form murals.

Once we had built up a track record in sales we began to develop sales representatives, which is really the key to distribution on a national scale. There are two kinds of representatives. One is a representative firm that has a showroom and covers a territory of three to five states. The showrooms are in Merchandise Marts or buildings leased exclusively by wholesalers, and the buyers come to see goods there. The second kind of rep is an independent who travels within a certain territory and calls on accounts.

The standard commission is 15 percent, but when you're a new line, untried, you start off paying 20 percent. We now distribute solely through representatives in the United States. They display our line and take the orders, but we do all the shipping from our office. We also handle European distribution and have so far opened up markets in Australia, France, the United Kingdom, and Canada.

Display booths at trade shows are essential in opening up markets for your products. It's a concentrated audience and a chance to meet and develop business relationships with people all over the world. We go to all the major shows, such as the Stationery Show, the Gift Show, the China and Glass Show—anything that revolves around retail buyers whose outlets might sell our posters.

Today we sell in all the better stores for children—Childcraft, Creative Playthings, F. A. O. Schwarz—as well as the leading bookstores and department stores. The posters are popular with all ages, and we find our college and adult markets are as strong as the children's market.

Each time we go to a major show we try to have added something new to the line. This is very important because buyers are always on the lookout for something new, and ideas can be introduced or tested for reaction. We are now producing gift enclosure cards and three sizes of napkins, all with the animal illustrations printed on them.

Our original investment in the business was $25,000, which covered printing, packaging, shipping costs, and sales promotions. Packaging was a very important issue with us. The cheaper method for posters is to roll them up and ship them in tubes. But we decided to go for flat, boxed packaging. It lends a more substantial aura to the pieces, and we were going after the upper-income stores.

We also lease Kindergraphics art to other manufacturers, licensing them to reproduce our artworks on other applications—such as games, fabrics, needlepoint, and so on. We're paid an advance royalty based on estimated net sales. They can use the work for a specified run of goods in a specified amount of time.

Once you've got the right visual, there is really no end to how many applications it can be used for. Think of other popular characters, and how many ways they're reproduced— from china to bed sheets to greeting cards to toys. It's endless.

Of course, everything we do is immediately copyrighted. It's an easy and fast process. We just send the illustration to be copyrighted to our lawyer, who specializes in copyright, and he immediately files it in Washington, D.C. Even without copyrighting, there's a new law giving designers and artists protection. However, an official copyright mark stops most people from stealing designs.

I think the basic requirement for anyone getting into manufacturing is that you must be excited about the whole production of getting your product to the public. You must have a total understanding of each vendor, at each stage until the product gets to the individual buyer in the store. That's what makes every day fascinating and fun—the manufacturer is behind it all.

BELTS UNLIMITED

Suzanna Rivera manufactures belts and wholesales them to stores all over the country. She had never designed, nor was she

particularly interested in fashion, when she went into business five years ago. All she knew was that the belt was a proven best-seller and was mainly wholesaled through a large leather goods company the main interest of which was in bags. Knowing already that there was a market for the product, she went after business by offering finer workmanship, a larger selection of colors, and a more efficient and personalized service.

Belts Unlimited has provided her with the income to continue her writing career. She runs the business from a large studio loft in Los Angeles.

I got into this business because I really needed to make money fast, and writing just didn't seem to be the way to do it. I was divorced, and my funds were alarmingly low. The idea that clicked was making belts. There's nothing original about this idea because this belt has been on the market for nine years, but it's a "hotcake" item in all the exclusive specialty shops. This was something I simply knew about from seeing it on friends and shopping in those stores. The belt is a classic, like Pappagallo shoes.

The belt is a leather strip cut to one length. The belt strips can then be attached to different buckles (bought separately), and they're interchangeable, so you can coordinate different colored belt strips with different outfits. The leather comes from the supplier all ready for cutting in big rolls like a giant spool.

My first sales call was on a store in Beverly Hills. I had done my homework and knew where to get my supplies and what my markup should be, but I had never made one of the belts, nor had I bought any materials. I just went into the store with a color chart and asked to see the accessories buyer. I thought that if I were lucky, they might order about fifty. At this point I had invested in one thing: a twelve-dollar pair of scissors, thinking that for fifty belts I could cut them myself. I had no idea what was going to happen but figured I was there with the idea and had nothing to lose by trying.

Well, I sat there for about three hours while they ordered over $4,000 worth of belts. I very calmly pretended I was a well-established businesswoman and in a wild moment promised them a one-week delivery. All the time I knew I didn't have one bit of material or the wherewithal to cut all those belts in one week. Each belt has six cuts; using the scissors, I would have had to do six thousand cuts!

I had taken the order on a Saturday, and they were due the following Friday. Monday morning, I put in an order for the belt strips and a cutting machine, which cost me $400—not a bad investment, considering the first sale paid well over that cost. Both the machine and the materials were ready on Wednesday, and I sat up all Wednesday night and Thursday cutting belts. They were ready and delivered to the store on Friday. It was a frantic week, but definitely a spectacular way to get the business started.

My business is competitive. The only innovative thing I've done has been to have the supplier make a multicolored strip; I sell this exclusively. This also helped buyers to notice me because the belt has been on the market for nine years, and I was the first to offer something new. Otherwise, I compete by offering over a hundred colors, whereas my competitors offer twenty. I also offer immediate delivery, which the competition can't do because they're so big. My price is a little cheaper but not much. Because of my low overhead, I can undercut the competition and still make the same profit. My quality is better, too, because I do the cutting myself. So I offer better delivery, better selection, and better price and quality.

I know where my market is because I talk to people who buy this sort of thing and find out where they shop. I locate stores in these specific areas, send them a flyer, or simply drive there if it's close by. A lot of this business is personality. After all, most of these stores are already buying this belt from someone else, so you really have to be pleasant and fun. I travel with my dog so that everyone remembers me as the girl with the Siberian husky.

I never make appointments ahead of time, just walk in and present the line to the buyer. Buyers are the most frenetic people I've ever run into. If you call for an appointment, maybe they'll see you in three weeks or maybe not at all. But if you just go in, 75 percent of the time she's there and stuck with you.

For me, selling is easy because I know I've got something they want. I'm not pushing a new idea. It's merely a matter of offering all the extra colors and services. I also head for stores that are chains: Lilly Pulitzer has twenty-four stores, and I got the order for all twenty-four. Pappagallo has a hundred stores, and I got their order. Now, when I go to a new store, I can say Pappagallo and Lilly Pulitzer buy from me, which is a further incentive.

It's totally a one-woman operation. I have an accountant, but I do my own shipping. I have an answering service, business cards, and printed description—cost sheets to mail out. For this kind of business you have to be extremely efficient and very dependable. When an order comes in, I get it right out. I keep file cards on each customer with the date I contacted them, the order, billing date, money received or not received, the name of the buyer, whether we're on a first-name basis or not—anything that's relevant to the transaction. When a buyer calls me, I go right to the card and know exactly where we stand. The big companies just can't offer this personalized service.

My strongest advice to anyone starting a business is to start small; don't let a big overhead stare you in the face every month. You need time to grow and develop yourself in the business without the panic of having to meet exorbitant costs. Work within your profit and don't let a good month fool you into thinking every month is going to be better. And be prepared to deliver the service you promise; just one slipup can lose a good customer.

PORTFOLIO—THE ULTIMATE CATALOGUE

In Sugar Loaf, New York, a tiny hamlet sixty miles from the city, Wilma deZanger's mail-order business is flourishing. In 1974, she came up with a five-hundred-year-old idea she thought might be the basis of a business. It was a Dutch *poffertjes* pan for making puffy little pancakes. She arranged to have the pans (which she had adapted for modern ovens) manufactured at a foundry, ran the smallest ad sold in *House and Garden* Magazine, and started selling pans through the mail.

Today, Portfolio's "Ultimate Catalogue" specializes in unusual items imported from all over the world. The products are unique, often one-of-a-kind, like a seventeenth-century Russian icon, which sells for $4,200. Wilma deZanger carries imported art objects, antique jewelry collections, decorative household accessories, gourmet foods and cookwares. Her business is based on elegance in both products and service. As in the best stores, special attention is given to gift wrapping, card enclosures, and prompt mailing.

I feel that anyone who thinks about going into mail-order should first do a great deal of research into what it's all about. The process of building a mail-order business is slow, demanding, and quite risky. As in any retail business, it takes up-front money to get started. Inventory investment, advertising, packaging, and mailing charges run high. Timing is important because ads in major magazines must be placed months in advance, and knowing what will sell, and where the best advertising outlets are, takes experience.

I was a photo stylist before starting Portfolio and was aware of products, how to present them visually, trends in merchandise, and the various magazines and their readership. I have an innate sense of what will sell, and my background gave me the marketing confidence in how to go about reaching the right audience.

The *poffertjes* pan was, and continues to be, a best seller, but because I was manufacturing it myself, I took a prototype around to kitchenware buyers in major New York department stores to test their reactions before investing in my initial run of five thousand pieces. I took orders from the buyers, so before I went into mail order, I had strong wholesale outlets.

Products for mail order are marked up 100 percent over the costs of materials, advertising, packaging, overhead, and shipping. At first I ran the business from my house as we had a large, open work space. You need room for storage, shipping containers, and work tables. And of course, you need office space for the paperwork operations of the business. Organization and excellent record keeping are a must.

I incorporated the business from the start and also carry a lot of product liability insurance. When dealing with the public, especially in food or cooking wares, there are many unknowns. Some people live to sue, so insurance is important for protection.

It is now a law that any mail-order item must be sent to the buyer within three weeks; otherwise, the seller must return the money or notify the person of any delays. To avoid that, you must have enough products on hand before you receive any orders.

The paperwork in this business is tremendous. Each item must be inventoried from the manufacturing or wholesaling end, then recorded as to when it was shipped, how it was shipped, and how much it has been insured for. Each advertisement we run is also coded, so when orders start coming in, I can tell which publication, and which issue, are producing the most business. I also record which part of the country orders come in from. All this becomes vital information in planning future advertising.

Basically, there are two ways to go in mail order. One is with ads in magazines; the other is with a catalog mailed directly to potential customers. There are few cases where it makes sense for beginners to start out with direct mail. It just isn't practical until you can spread that high cost per person over a large number of products by offering a whole product line, rather than just one or two items.

Finding the best publications for ads depends on what you're selling. You'll want to study the various publications and pick the ones which have readers whose interests or income levels will make them better-than-average prospects for your product. Also, look for publications which carry a noticeably large number of mail-order ads. Obviously, these magazines do well for people in mail order.

My first ads were small, with a photograph of the product. A photograph is always the best way to sell products, although sketches can sell fashion items. Expect to run an ad at least three times in a magazine before you can rate its pulling power.

Because the pans sold well, I began building my inventory in cookwares and gourmet foods. After a year I was able to put together my first catalog. A catalog means you have to inventory many items. Portfolio's catalog is very well done, with excellent photographs, printed on good paper in full color. There is a real art to putting together a catalog, and again, my background as a stylist was invaluable. I know how a product should be photographed and how to lay it on the page in an eye-catching way.

With an expanded line, you must get into concrete projections of sales and work out commitments with wholesale vendors. They must guarantee you a fixed price for a certain amount of time. Otherwise, the price may go up after you've run your ads or sent your catalog, cutting into your profit margin. I have the added problem of the import market and fluctuating dollar values in various countries. It's a constant juggling act. You have to pay a lot of attention to details.

My first mailing list was made up from my previous custom-ers—people who had ordered the *poffertjes* pan. You can also rent lists from professional brokers. Here, as in magazine ads, the aim is to get a selected audience: names and addresses of people whose special interest or income levels are tied in with the type of products you deal in.*

Another major area of concern is the various ways of mail-ing. I now employ seven people who work in the office and shipping department. We have a large inventory of boxes and many ways to package goods. Ideally, a mail-order product should be easy to box and unbreakable, but I specialize in such unusual items I must invest in packaging materials that are often costly.

We ship via United Parcel Service whenever possible be-cause its service is far superior to the United States Post Office. But I do all my direct mail through the Post Office. When I started, our local Post Office was about to go out of business because the town is so small. Last fall I mailed 250,000 catalogs, which is more mail than they'd seen since 1890.

The prevailing myth about mail order is that you can start a business from your kitchen table and turn it overnight into a million-dollar enterprise. People rush into mail order, and it's no wonder that at least 75 percent of mail-order businesses fail. On the other hand, every successful catalog house I know of was started on a small scale, like mine, with one or two items, so it certainly can be done. My point is that you must understand the business before you lay out large sums and then find yourself stuck with inventory that won't sell. You have to learn all the aspects—advertising copy and layout, rates, methods for shipping, postal regulations, systems of control, and bookkeeping. On top of this you must have a product not commonly found in regular retail stores, one which will appeal to a good number of people. There's a special merchandising knack. Unfortunately, even if you've laid a sound base, some things that should sell simply don't.

---

* An extensive listing of mailing list brokers can be found in *Direct Mail List Rates and Data*, published by Standard Rate and Data Service, Inc., 5201 Old Orchard Road, Skokie, Illinois 60077. The $65 directory should be available in most larger libraries.

There is a psychology in mail order, just as there is a psychology in retail display.

It's not an easy or fast way to make money, but when it clicks, it can be very profitable. It's fun for me since my products are unique and extensions of my own taste. This makes my business a very personal one, despite the fact that I never see my customers. Many write me long, chatty letters and feel, I think, a kinship with me since my products are so special.

21

SEASONAL BUSINESSES— PART-TIME BUSINESSES

A seasonal business can be anything which thrives during a particular season and then goes into hibernation or low gear for the rest of the year. Seasonal enterprise is indigenous to summer or winter resort and tourist areas, but there are many other nonresort businesses that lend themselves to this concept—Christmas mail order, the school year, and a wide variety of part-time businesses that operate only on weekends or that fit around the hours of another job. Some people are able to live wholly off their seasonal profits; others are content to earn a valuable supplementary income.

Running a part-time or seasonal business means you're going to have to work frantically hard during the time allotted to the business, but seasonal business owners emphasize that the extended vacation time afterward makes the long hours worthwhile.

Starting a seasonal business requires the same amount of preplanning as launching a full-time business. As in any business, ideas, skills, products, and services can become seasonally profitable as long as there is a market for them. The catch is making the business profitable in a shorter amount of working time. Because of this, a detailed business plan is essential, with special focus on operating your business at peak, high-volume capacity.

Any part-time entrepreneur should ask herself these questions:

> What *exactly* will your business do?
>
> When will the business operate? Figure the exact length of your season and the extended hours per day of operation.
>
> Are you filling a demand or creating one?
>
> Who is your target market, and how can it best be reached?
>
> What will it cost to operate for one season?
>
> What (if anything) will it cost you out of season? You may have to carry year-round rent or storage costs for equipment, supplies, and inventory.
>
> How long will it take to set up your business preseason, and close it down postseason? This nonselling time must be figured in your estimate of how much profit you expect to make.
>
> How much do you estimate you can make? Figure three separate sales projections: high, expected, and low.

A seasonal or part-time business has its pros and cons. On the plus side, your time will not be locked up twelve months of the year. The would-be entrepreneur can test her skills in business management without full-time commitment or, in many cases, major investment. When your season is over, you are free to pursue other work or interests. This is especially attractive if you must meet the needs of a family or want to spend the bulk of your time in ventures that may not provide a ready income.

There are minuses, too. In any seasonal type of business, it's a sure bet that competition will run high. In resort areas especially, there will be many business owners vying for the tourist trade. A seasonal business must operate at peak intensity during the entire season. You cannot afford to make mistakes or depend on slow word-of-mouth advertising to bring in your customers. You have only one season to make money, and *that's it.* Outside factors, such as weather, gasoline shortages, a mail strike, or one lost shipment of goods—

things which are completely out of your control—can make or break your business for an entire season.

In the case of a part-time business, remember that most businesses can't operate on a strict time schedule. Any business owner can testify to the unplanned-for hours it takes to keep things rolling. Don't overextend yourself in terms of the time you are capable of working. If your business will operate on weekends, and you work the other five days, then be doubly sure you have the stamina and patience to maintain a nonstop schedule.

Intuition, ambition, and enthusiasm count for a great deal in any business, and they're even more essential when the business isn't full time. Practical know-how must combine with large doses of energy, and you must be prepared to commit yourself totally during the operational span of your business.

THE GOOD SKATES

For health, exercise, and a sense of freedom, join the outdoor roller skating boom. That's the message from Judy Lynn, who has been, for more than a year, developing project ideas which involve roller skating.

Her ultimate goal is to open the Rollerballroom in New York City—the world's first rollerdrome designed especially for roller disco. The first step toward reaching that goal was to launch The Good Skates, an outdoor skate rental concession in Central Park.

The rental business is a popular seasonal enterprise—bicycles, skis, boats, and sports equipment all can turn a tidy profit if your location is a good one. Insurance is important and can be a costly start-up cost; repairing and replacing equipment will be the major operating cost.

But once you're rolling, as in The Good Skates, a rental business is easy to run.

I love to skate! The sensation is fantastic—the speed and movement are so exhilarating that you don't ever want to stop. The roller skating industry has been revolutionized by the development of plastic, urethane wheels which make both indoor and outdoor skating fast and quiet. The latest fad (and one that's here to stay) is roller disco, and once I had started doing that, I knew my future was in roller skating—I just had to get in on this.

My partners and I expect to open a rollerdrome called The Rollerballroom in Manhattan. Poured plastic floors, developed expressly for roller skating, make it possible to design and build indoor contoured paths and courses. The ballroom will have ramps and winding passages, dance floors and viewers' balconies, roller disco and regular disco, natural foods snack bars, and boutiques.

But in the meantime, I wanted to get more and more people interested in roller skating. In California, outdoor skating has caught on in a big way because of a business called The Cheap Skates owned by Jeff Rosenberg. He started a rental business a few years ago on the boardwalks of Venice and Santa Monica with twenty-five pairs of used skates which he bought for $1,200. People lined up for hours waiting to rent a pair so they could skate on the bike paths between the two towns. Now you see people skating in the supermarkets, into restaurants—everywhere. For exercise, it's better than biking and so much more fun than jogging.

When I first saw Jeff's business, I knew it would be a natural for Central Park. Instead of being confined to a rink, skaters could zip along all those paths and drives. But getting the concession was not easy. The parks department dragged its heels, couldn't make up its mind, avoided my calls. So finally, in April, with the warm weather coming on, I just skated into its offices and demanded an answer. I think the man was so shocked to see this speeding form bearing down on his desk that he said yes and gave us an excellent location to set up shop. We're right next to the park snack bar, which is great for business.

Start-up costs are basically your equipment, promotion, insurance, overhead, and staff salaries. This will vary with the area—for us basic costs ran around $30,000, but then New York is more expensive than other places. Skates alone were $10,000, and insurance ran up to $15,000. Our rent was based on 20 percent of our monthly gross sales. We invested a lot in advertising and promotion, but as our rental business was a forerunner of the Rollerballroom, costs reflect a dual promotion campaign.

We almost doubled our investment in gross sales in the five summer months we were open and expect to do as well or better next year because the skating boom has not yet peaked. We invested in four hundred pairs of skates this year but could have used two hundred more. Out of this only seven skates were stolen, and very few were in need of repairs by the end of the season in November. We are open seven days a week, from 10:00 A.M. until 6:00 P.M., and I have a staff of ten people to run the concession.

Operating the business is simple, and we run much the same way a bike rental is run. The skates rent for $2 for the first hour and 75¢ each additional hour. As security, customers must leave a driver's license or other identification, or $50 in cash. Children under twelve must be with an adult.

We've done all sorts of things to publicize and promote the business. On opening day we held a press party with a live salsa band and exhibition skaters. The skaters were fantastic, doing all the disco numbers and speed skating in and around the crowds. We had outdoor pushcarts filled with fresh fruit and got quite a bit of publicity out of it.

Throughout the summer, we sponsored skating marathons, more special exhibitions, and on weekends we offered classes. And we kept getting publicity because it was unique. The only bad thing that happened was that we got a terrific write-up in *The New York Times* and I could hardly wait to get to the stand the next day, expecting hordes of people. Instead, we got torrents of rain and rain and rain. For a solid week! By the time the sun came out again the impact of the article was lost. For the most part, the weather was good, but any outdoor business has got to realize how devastating poor weather can be. Rain is a problem, but it can also be too hot or too cold. Estimate at least a 20 percent weather factor against business.

The Good Skates is only part of the many businesses I've planned around roller skating, but as a seasonal rental business, I think I can safely say it's a good one to get into. It takes less space than a bicycle rental shop and less know-how on repairs and upkeep. Roller skating is certainly no passing fad—New York and California have set the trend, which means the whole country will soon be heavily into roller skates. Indoors or outdoors, skating is contagious.

THE GEORGETOWN FLEA MARKET

During the week, Lisa Berg is a free-lance photographer, but on Sundays she provides the space and management for forty exhib-

You need very little capital to start a flea market; for us it was only two hundred dollars. We were lucky, though, as we have an excellent location in Georgetown for very little rent. Our space is an old parking lot right on the main street, and Sundays in Georgetown are very active.

The key to success is to be within sight of heavy walk-by or drive-by traffic. Location is everything in running a flea market because, for the most part, buyers just happen in.

Once you have the space, you look for exhibitors. We called antique dealers listed in the telephone book, and we watched the for-sale columns in the paper. We don't limit the exhibitors; anyone can show anything—junk, last year's clothes, antiques, plastic buttons, homemade jewelry, whatever.

We average thirty-five or forty dealers every Sunday and charge a flat fee of fifteen dollars per space per day. A parking lot is an ideal location because it's flat and the spaces are already marked off. Usually a parking lot is in plain sight of the street, which is important, and the dealers can drive right up to their space. Other good locations are drive-in movie lots, but there you need to get at least a hundred dealers to make it worthwhile. We provide the exhibitors with publicity and advertising and, most important, the required dealer's licenses and occupancy permits. In Washington, it takes two months to get a secondhand dealer's license, so one-timers and collectors who don't have a shop somewhere else really need our service.

We also provide liability insurance and a food concession. We set up a food wagon because it helps to bring people in, especially on hot days when they want an ice cream or cold drink. The food truck is rented from Pepsi, and it supplies hot dogs, Pepsi, and ice cream. We add lemonade and homemade cookies. The profit we make from it is small, but it's really more of a promotional service than a money-maker. Pepsi delivers the truck and picks it up.

The first year, the space cost $25 per month in the parking lot. Now it's up to fifty. Our hours are from 9:00 A.M. to 6:00 P.M., but the dealers can start setting up at 7:30 A.M. To launch the flea market, we offered the dealers a flat $5 fee to exhibit the first Sunday, on the understanding that the fee would go up if the market was successful.

Either my partner or I are there every Sunday to oversee and manage the market. We set up the spaces, assign each dealer a space, collect the rental fee, and at the end of the day, the sales tax. We are also required by law to keep all the receipts of each day's sales on file for three years. The receipts are also a record of any given Sunday and show if sales are up after a certain advertising or publicity campaign. Each dealer is responsible for keeping track of what he owes in sales tax, and every Sunday night I compare receipts against tax to make sure they tally.

We also bought ten-foot tables, which we rent out for $2 a day to the exhibitors. The exhibitors reserve their space, but we don't require a deposit in advance. The only time I ask for a deposit is from people who made reservations previously and never showed up. If they call again, I get a deposit which is nonrefundable. I'll save spots until about ten-thirty in the morning. Then, if other people are interested, I'll sell the spaces to whoever is in line.

Our total operational expenses are for permits, insurance, the answering service, rent, advertising, and promotion. We have a fairly regular ad budget, about $120 per week for newspaper display ads, and we've just started to survey the crowds to see where they've heard of us so that we can concentrate advertising on the publication that brings in the most people. For promotion we have bright yellow printed flyers and handbills: the larger ones we tack in supermarket and other shop windows, and the small three-by-five cards we stack next to cash registers. Our main concern is to keep a steady stream of people going through the flea market.

Because my partner is a man, people thought, in the beginning, I was his girl friend or assistant, not his partner, and they always wanted to deal with him. But I made sure everyone understood that I had equal responsibility in the business. Now no one has a male-female thing about who's in charge.

PUSHCART VENDING

One of the least expensive and most imaginative ways to get into business is the sidewalk pushcart. Obviously a warm-weather business, street vendors proliferate in high-traffic areas, mainly selling items that are inexpensive and easy to carry away. This is impulse buying in its purest form. Pat Reynolds and her husband, Bob, operate two food carts six months of the year near an entrance to Central Park in New York.

Together they pour fresh lemonade, assemble tacos, chat with the customers, and tune into the street's unpredictable sights and sounds.

Street vending has become a runaway business idea all over the country. And it's not just hot-dog stands anymore. Sidewalk vendors are selling everything from jelly beans to crafts to books. It's fantastic the amount of money you can make on the street if you've got a good corner, but like everything else, there are permits, laws, and restrictions. In some areas, the congestion caused between vendors and buyers makes it difficult to get a license. Even then, new laws banning street vendors crop up from time to time.

People like to buy on the street. It gives everyone a kick, as if you're somehow beating the system because you do business in the open air.

Running a pushcart is not at all difficult. Mostly, it's fun and a constant source of entertainment.

We have two carts, which we line up back to back. One is for hot foods: tacos, egg rolls, hamburgers, and chicken rolls. The other keeps things cold: my homemade sandwiches (tuna and egg salads, cream cheese and raisin, ham) and the drinks (apple cider and fresh lemonade).

Our food supplies come from all over. We go down to Chinatown for the egg rolls and as far away as Connecticut for apple cider. We mark up approximately 50 percent over our cost. And we base that on our monthly expenses, plus the cost of food. We shop once a week for most food; the rest is bought as needed during the week.

I used to be a Playboy Bunny, and Bob was a writer for the Johnny Carson show. The Playboy Club is right around the corner, and I'd stroll over here at lunchtime because it's such a great place. This area is a central point in New York; it's where everyone seems to congregate—tourists because of the hansom cabs and the Plaza Hotel and New Yorkers because of the zoo and biking in the park. In the summer the corner comes alive with Jamaican steel drummers and kids selling their wares. Artists put out their paintings, two book kiosks are open, and people come to catch the sun at lunchtime and lounge near the park.

There were also plenty of pushcarts here, but I thought a cart selling healthful foods like homemade sandwiches and apple cider would be a nice break from hot dogs and pretzels. I was planning to go into partnership with another girl from the Playboy Club, but when the Carson show moved to the West Coast, Bob didn't want to go with them. He has two children by his first marriage, and they live in New Jersey. So he got interested in the idea, too, and pretty soon here we were.

You can buy pushcarts from about five different stores in New York (they're listed in the Yellow Pages). The standard size with a chest for ice and cold drinks below, and a sterno burner up top costs around nine hundred dollars. You can design your own wagon, too, which we did, and specify units for the type of food you're going to sell. We hand-painted ours in bright colors and put large beach umbrellas over each cart. We bought two carts because we wanted to sell a variety of foods.

To get a vendor's license in New York, you first apply for a resale number from the state income tax bureau. With that in hand, you can then apply for a specific vendor's permit at the city licensing bureau. You have to specify on the application form exactly what you will be selling, and if it's food, you then have to notify the board of health for its own special licensing.

Once you're issued your vendor's license, you're entitled to operate anywhere in the city *except* the parks. The real crunch for a food vendor in New York is getting a permit from the parks department. We knew we wanted to operate this corner, which is one of the busiest in the city, but it also falls within the boundaries of Central Park. Getting the permit is about 90 percent who you know, and as we didn't know anyone in city government who could help, we just went ahead and started selling food anyway.

One day, after we'd been in business for a few weeks, the police rolled up with a truck to compound all the carts operating without the park permit. As we were about to be hauled off, a man who had just bought a sandwich stepped up and said he would arrange for our special permit. It was as if he had waved a magic wand because the very next day we had the permit in hand and were finally operating legally. We're still amazed at our luck.

We pay the city $400 per month to operate this corner. The fee is based on 15 percent of our yearly sales. Other than that, our costs include supplies—food, paper cups, napkins, sterno, ice—plus gasoline for our van, which we need to pick up supplies, and our garage space, where we store the carts each night.

The business is fun, and dealing with street life is fascinating. Watching people is really an education, and you come to understand things you never would otherwise. There are normal people (at least they look normal) who are crazy—and crazies who turn out to be nice, sane human beings.

When we first decided to do this our friends thought we were really crazy, especially Bob giving up his job with Johnny Carson. Big deal. He was closed up in a tiny cubicle and never had time to do his own writing. It's interesting what has happened over the years: the worse off the world gets, the more our friends understand why we're doing this and even become envious. Bob's children work with us on weekends, which is great; being able to involve your kids in your work breaks down generation barriers. It lets them see us, and us them, on an equal level.

It's a hassle-free life—something that we can make money at, but it leaves us and we leave it at the end of the day. I go home tired some days but never mentally exhausted. There is nothing upsetting about this job because if someone obnoxious comes up and gives me a hard time, I can deal it right back. Street life lets you act any way you want to act. The other day a photographer arrived to take pictures of models using our carts as a background. He didn't ask our permission, and he blocked people from getting to the carts to buy. He said he would give us $5 for our trouble, and I said, "I'll give you $10 to get lost." You respond to the situation as it happens.

Street vendors can make a lot of money. There's a guy in New York who plays the violin every night down on Broadway with a sign saying, "I'm a student—please help me get through school." Well, he hasn't been near a school in ten years. Rumor has it, he lives in a plush apartment and pulls in more than $100,000 a year. The king of all vendors still sells peanuts down near the library. He's put a son through medical school, another son through law school, and owns a big house on Long Island. You know, the whole rags-to-riches story.

We work six days a week for six months out of the year. My working day is from about 7:00 A.M. to 3:30 P.M. I make the sandwiches and lemonade fresh each day and get here in time for the lunch crowd. If it's really hot, we pack it in early and head for the beach. If it rains, we don't set up. In winter, we travel in the van. Last year, we spent most of the time in the Florida Keys, the year before we went out West, and next year we're planning the whole winter in Europe. Eventually, we hope to write about all of this—the pushcart life.

ROSEMARY ORIGINALS

Elegant, handmade Christmas decorations are the basis of Helena Stevens' seasonal cottage industry. From a farm near Charlottesville, Virginia, the business started twenty-five years ago with hand-decorated miniature Christmas trees mounted on matchbooks. Today the line includes fanciful holiday centerpieces, wreaths, and mistletoe kissing balls.

Wholesaled to leading department stores nationwide, Rosemary Originals averages $15,000 a year in profits.

My business has always provided a steady supplementary income and has helped put my six children through college. It's the perfect business for me because I can design and make the ornaments in between doing all the mother things. I keep a work table set up year round, but my only busy months are in the fall. The business works in and around the family routine, although I think my children get fed up with finding glitter in their cereal.

My original investment was only $700, but supply costs have risen drastically in twenty-five years, not to mention mailing charges. Today I have close to $20,000 invested in raw materials. Profits, of course, are in direct ratio to the amount you have to put into materials and distribution costs.

I sell my decorations to approximately two hundred department stores and specialty shops around the country, including Saks Fifth Avenue, I. Magnin, Garfinkel's, and Bonwit Teller.

In the beginning I'd fill wicker baskets with samples and head for Washington, D.C., and New York to sell direct to the buyers. I hated that part of the business because I'm not the sales type, so I used to drag a friend of mine along who was fantastic. Buyers just couldn't say no to her. In two years, we had built up quite an impressive number of buyers, and I then hired sales representatives to expand my markets.

I still sell directly to many of the original buyers, but most sales are handled by the representatives: one in New York at the Gift Building, one in Dallas at the Merchandise Mart, and one in Los Angeles at the World Trade Building. I found the reps by asking department store buyers whom they would recommend. I pay them 20 percent of the orders they sell, and it's well worth it. I could never cover the territory they represent, and it would be much too costly to position myself in each of those buildings.

In the beginning I made all the decorations myself, but the business is big enough so that now I subcontract the work to a farm family near here. I provide them with the designs and the raw materials. They make the ornaments, and then I buy back the finished pieces. That way I have no payroll hassles.

I work overtime from October 1 until December 15, doing all the packing and shipping myself. The ornaments are so fragile that it takes a long time to package each order so they won't move inside the box. I just tell my friends and family to forget about me until the last order is shipped. Then I get into the Christmas spirit myself.

After Christmas, in January and February, I reorder my raw materials and deliver them to the subcontractors. Ordering is easy now. I just place calls to the people I've been dealing with for years. In the beginning, I found all my suppliers through the New York Yellow Pages and went to New York on buying trips. My ornaments remain traditional, although I keep an eye out for new ideas and materials.

It's a fairly simple business to run, but it took experience to find that out. I used to be oversystematized, but I've eliminated much of the paperwork. I include an invoice with the shipments, and 99 percent of my customers pay me from that.

I keep simple, single-entry books, listing costs—labor, materials, postage, overhead—and sales. Standard markup is 40 percent over labor and materials, and my ornaments wholesale from $5 to $75.

I've kept the business fairly small because of the other commitments in my life. I love what I'm doing, but I warn anybody starting a business to be prepared for plain hard work. The great thing about a seasonal business, though, is that my time is tied up only about four months of the year.

ALICIA WILSON PENINSULA SHOP

Alicia Wilson's Peninsula Shop is a resort boutique in Ephraim, Wisconsin. The shop is open seven days a week from Memorial Day to mid-September and on weekends until the end of October. The shop sells women's and children's clothes and was launched nine years ago. Ephraim is one of the many popular Lake Michigan resorts.

When I was growing up, my family spent vacations in Ephraim, so I knew the town pretty well and knew there was a need for a clothing boutique. Originally, I had planned to do only children's clothes. I added a women's sportswear line because of my own interest in designing. My designs account for about one-half of my inventory line now.

The shop cost $5,000 to open. We rent space in an old building that used to be the town creamery, which is right in the middle of all the commercial activity in town. Of the start-up investment, $2,000 went for renovations, supplies, and interior design, and $3,000 for inventory.

Today my inventory investment is over $10,000. I do two buying trips a year in New York since I carry a summer line and a fall line. Buying is always trial and error in the beginning, and with a short season you can't afford to make mistakes. I know the area well and had a pretty good idea of the kinds of things the women here buy. But a shop is an extension of your own personality, so I buy for my own taste, too.

The first summer I allotted a good portion of my budget for pretty lingerie, which nobody wanted. I cut it out immediately. Now buying is easy. I know the lines and looks we've had luck with, and I know my way around the New York showrooms.

Throughout the spring and summer I work on my own designs and sewing. One room in the shop is set up as a workroom, and we make up our designs. We also do weddings and custom wardrobes.

It's hard to establish credit for a seasonal shop. Now I'm rated in Dun & Bradstreet, but for a long time I had to pay 50 percent when I placed the order and 50 percent on delivery. Most year-round shops can get credit after two deliveries, but it took us longer.

I've set up the shop as a sole proprietorship, which means I pay the taxes on my personal income tax. It works out well because the busy six months are balanced against the rest of the year. I keep overhead to a minimum, do all my own bookkeeping, and am in the shop all the time to save on payroll. This year, there were two others in the shop with me, sewing and minding the store.

On August 1, I put the summer things on sale. I want as little merchandise as possible to carry through the winter. When the shop closes in October, I pack up any unsold merchandise and store it at home. This way, I save on year-round insurance. I have the shop insured only for the time I am in it. The insurance is expensive, but is less than it could be because it's only for six months.

The shop attracts steady walk-by traffic because we are right in the center of town. But I also run ads in the local papers with photographs of my clothes. My total advertising budget is $500. In the spring, right before we open, I send a chatty newsletter to all our regular customers which reminds them of us and opening day. I keep a huge card file on all the customers.

If you're going to have a shop in a resort open only for the season, you have to be prepared to work hard. I usually put in twelve hours a day—and that's seven days a week. It took me two years to make a profit, and now I make enough money to relax and work on my designs the rest of the year. I also travel a great deal, and it's wonderful not to have the pressure to get back to a job. It's the perfect life for me.

22

FRANCHISING

Franchising opportunities come in all sizes and categories. Many are women-owned or -oriented, but there are hundreds and hundreds more to choose from. More and more women pick franchising as the most viable path when they want to get into business for themselves.

The most obvious reason is that the risks involved in a new business are diminished, since a parent company provides guidelines for management, buying, promotion, location, design, and financing. Often a company will help you finance your business (a common stumbling block for many women), and even if not, banks and other investors are easier to convince if you have a national image and product behind you.

Not every woman has the entrepreneurial instinct, but that doesn't mean she should not be in business for herself. Franchising provides the opportunity, the profits, and a large dose of stability, counterbalancing the otherwise precarious undertaking of owning a business.

The following two interviews profile both sides of the coin—how one woman's business became the basis for another's business ownership.

"i" COSMETICS

Lois Muller created "i" Cosmetics in 1970, at a time when health foods were still considered a fad. Her concept was to produce a line of natural cosmetics and skin treatments made from pure, healthful ingredients. The original products included a strawberry cleanser, a grapefruit freshener, a lemon moisturizer, and a beeswax lip gel. Today there are bath oils, shampoos, eyeshadows, lip colors, clay masks, foundations—a complete line, all based on simple natural ingredients.

The packaging is also clean and natural. Clear glass jars and bottles let the colors shine through, and there is no outer packaging, folder, or other extraneous throwaway trash.

The shop opened in the East Sixties in New York, and women loved it. So much so that out-of-towners wanted to know why they couldn't buy the cosmetics in Boston and Atlanta and Denver. The answer has been franchising.

There are sixty "i" Cosmetics shops franchised around the country so far. It's a business that can go into a community of almost any size, and this year the company has developed a new and exciting way to sell the product.

My business started out as an outlet for my need to accomplish something. Today it's a business for other women who also need to express their talents and individuality, be their own boss, and have their own business. Most women who come to us for a franchise have used our product and are fascinated with the concept of "i." But we tell them many times before we finalize the contract that it's fun, it's exciting and very rewarding, but it's *work*. You don't just one day open a door to a shop stocked with products; you open a shop to work. You take inventory, you sell, you see that your salespeople sell, you keep books, you plan promotions; there are a myriad of details to running a business.

The key to sales is location. For our product, location is our number one concern, and sales are directly related to walk-by traffic. Based on that fact, our best locations are in good shopping malls.

Putting together a shop in a mall is very costly, as much as $35,000 just to open. But we've created a new idea that will make it possible for a woman to own a franchise for less than half of that cost. The concept is an "i" kiosk, a prepackaged greenhouse that will be planted right in the middle of the interior walkway of a shopping mall. The effect of the greenhouse will be the same as the shop, situated right in the middle of a good location, and the cost is in line with most women's sources for funding. You can order a greenhouse and be in business six weeks later. All you need do is rent the mall floor space and that's it; the decorations will be the cosmetics themselves.

The package will cost approximately $5,000, complete with fixtures, shelving, lighting, tables, chairs, and greenery. Additional expenses will be the franchise fee, which is $5,000, floor rental, and the initial inventory, which we sell at 40 percent of the retail cost. The space will be about twelve-by-twelve feet, but the best thing about it is that if you don't like the mall, if it doesn't attract the number of people you expect, you can simply pack up your kiosk and move on.

The franchise fee covers an exclusive territory, an eight-day training program, managerial services, and continuing seminars and orientation to new products in the line, sales promotions, and selling techniques. When the shop opens, we go to the location and work with the franchisee on publicity and promotion and advise her on local advertising, but we do no national advertising. The product generates publicity, and articles on the product appear often in the top fashion magazines.

Our prospective franchisees are given the histories of our other franchise shops, and we urge that they visit these operations and talk to the owners. We don't predict what profits will be, but on the basis of the earnings of our shops in similar locations, we can give a very sound idea of profit potential.

We encourage women who have never been in business before to buy a franchise in partnership. It takes away some of the initial fear, but ultimately, the success or failure of a shop or kiosk depends solely on location. If the location is good, the product sells. For further information write to: Mrs. Lois Muller, "i" Cosmetics, Inc., 595 Madison Avenue, New York, New York 10021.

"i" COSMETICS—FRANCHISEE

Vicki Raiffie is one of the "i" Cosmetics franchisees in the United States. She now owns two shops in fashionable shopping malls in suburban towns near St. Louis, Missouri, and reports that business is booming. The parent company fulfilled all its obligations as outlined in the contract, and the relationship continues to satisfy both parties.

The thought of opening a business is scary. But when you buy a franchise, the kinks have already been ironed out. The worries and the unknowns have been handled for you, and you eliminate all the difficult first steps of starting your own business.

For me, it all started when my sister sent me some "i" Cosmetics from Atlanta. I loved them but had no idea of going into business until I went to Chicago and happened to see an "i" Cosmetics shop there. What impressed me most, aside from the quality of the products, was the overall attitude, the friendliness of the shop. It was beautifully designed, and the salespeople were so qualified when it came to helping you put on the makeup. In St. Louis, I had never been offered that kind of service.

I knew it was a franchised business after talking to the shop owner in Chicago and wrote to the company in New York when I got back home. It sent a packet of information, but its main concern was getting the right people for the business. I was on trial as much as it was.

I then went back to Chicago to meet area representatives and to work in the shop there for a weekend, learning the product line and the various sales techniques. By then I was hooked. I knew it could be as big a success in St. Louis as it was everywhere else.

Unfortunately, the shopping mall I wanted to go into did not allow for the kiosk concept. Many malls are simply not designed to incorporate a shop in the middle of the walking area. But I've seen the kiosk in Dallas, and it's really fantastic. My husband and I decided to invest the full amount it took to open a regular shop. Our total investment was $45,000, which included the $5,000 franchise fee, the cost of outfitting the store, inventory, and operating capital.

The parent company did absolutely everything it said it would do. It sent a company representative to St. Louis. She spent ten days with me, helping set up the shop, training the staff, and showing me the administrative systems. In advance, it had sent the prerequisites for space and design, right down to the color scheme and the types of display counters and shelves.

It encourages you to talk to other franchise owners, which I did. I found out that the key to success rests in location. For that reason, it does no national advertising or major promotion. The products sell easily if you're in the right spot.

Some shops will do local advertising, but I don't need to. I do a lot of local PR, which I think is important. We donate gift certificates to various organizations and charity events, and I demonstrate the products and lecture to classes around town. However, the New York office will send sample ad layouts and copy if you think you need them.

It took eighteen months for the shop to show a profit, and at that point, I decided to open a second shop. That's added a great deal of traveling to my day. I employ ten salespeople and have a manager for each shop. Turnover in sales help is my biggest problem. I am now devoting much more time to hiring the right people and creating sales incentives for them.

The New York office is always ready to help you if something goes wrong, but so far I haven't needed any assistance. Obviously, it doesn't want a shop to fail—it's bad for its image and bad for profits. We don't pay back any percentage of sales but, of course, buy all the products wholesale from the company. I have a choice of what I buy as well. Not every product does well in every part of the country. When you first set up the business, they advise you to buy a full line of cosmetics, but I now buy only what I know will sell.

I had never really thought about having a business of my own, but it has had a terrific effect on me personally. I have a tremendous feeling of accomplishment, especially now that I've expanded the operation. I would recommend this to any woman, but caution her that even with the franchisor and all its help, you still have to work very hard. It's very time-consuming. My husband and children help out in the store and love it. I think the support of your family is very important, and I now realize what my husband goes through each day in the business world. Problems arise and moods change, but all in all, it's extremely stimulating.

23

EPILOGUE

Anyone who starts her own business wants to succeed. The question is: what makes a person a success? If there were a simple formula, then all the volumes written about it would be superfluous. Concepts of personal and financial achievement vary individually, but no one can make it without goals and hard work.

Every business owner faces inevitable headaches and hassles in launching her idea, and making it work takes time, money, good health, perseverance, and, above all, a sense of humor. Success in business means financial independence, but the additional rewards of personal freedom, satisfaction of a job well-done, self-discovery, and growth extend into all areas of one's life.

Once a month in Santa Barbara, California, Barbara Hinrichs produces and publishes *The Successful Woman*, a newsletter for and about women going places. The inspirational focus is on motivation, developing one's own special abilities, and increasing self-awareness.

Ms. Hinrichs writes:

I believe that everybody has talent. It's just how you take your basic make-up and shape it into something different, something special that makes you stand apart.

I think probably the biggest single factor that keeps women from undertaking what they want is fear. Fear is simply a roadblock that keeps us from going where we want to go. You have to consider what's the worst thing that could happen? Usually the very worst is nothing you can't deal with. Recognizing that you can handle all possible consequences of a decision makes it easier to get going.

Later, when you're faced with choices, it's an easy matter to ask yourself, What will bring me a step closer to what I want to achieve? If your goals are clearly defined, taking that first step and all the subsequent ones will be easier than you ever imagined.

I have been convinced for a long time that free-lancing or starting your own business offers a viable solution for the woman who wants the best of both worlds—career and independence. Whatever you do, your venture can provide you with a whole new set of people and places and broadened horizons.

The women's movement has helped women develop an overwhelming sense of their own identities and uncover confidence and courage they never suspected they held inside themselves. Freed from traditional concepts of what is and isn't woman's work, women are entering a lot of areas which they never before considered. It's great! I really believe your life is what you make it.

PART THREE

BUSINESS READING AND INFORMATIONAL SOURCES

BIBLIOGRAPHY

The following is a selection of useful books for potential entrepreneurs. Check out your local public library, as well as nearby private, college, and university libraries, which you can join for a membership fee. Libraries offer myriad business and economics books, reference volumes, classified directories, and periodicals. Your librarian can help you find listings for new titles and resources which will apply to your specific business. The more you read, the better off you and your business will be.

Allen, L. L. *Starting and Succeeding in Your Own Small Business.* New York: Grosset & Dunlap.

Anderson, C. B., and G. R. Smith, editors. *A Manual on Bookselling: How to Open and Run Your Own Bookstore.* New York: Harmony Books/Crown.

Auerbach, Sylvia. *A Woman's Book of Money: A Guide to Financial Independence.* New York: Dolphin Books/Doubleday & Co. (Contains chapter on owning a business.)

Baumback, Clifford M., Kenneth Lawyer, and Pearce C. Kelley. *How to Organize and Operate a Small Business.* Englewood Cliffs, N.J.: Prentice-Hall. (Includes extensive bibliography on specific subjects.)

Becker, B. M., and F. A. Tillman. *Family Owned Business.* Chicago: Commerce Clearing House.

Bird, Caroline. *Enterprising Women.* New York: W. W. Norton & Co.

———. *Everything a Woman Needs to Know to Get Paid What She's Worth.* New York: David McKay.

———. *The Two-Paycheck Marriage.* New York: Rawson, Wade.

Bloom, Lynn Z., Karen Coburn, and Joan Pearlman. *The New Assertive Woman.* New York: Dell.

Brightly, D. S., et al. *Complete Guide to Financial Management for Small and Medium-Sized Companies.* Englewood Cliffs, N.J.: Prentice-Hall.

Chesler, Phyllis, and Emily Jane Goodman. *Women, Money and Power.* New York: William Morrow.

Clark, Leta W. *How to Make Money with Your Crafts.* New York: William Morrow.

———. *How to Open Your Own Shop or Gallery.* New York: St. Martin's Press.

Dible, Donald M. *Up Your Own Organization.* New York: Hawthorn Press.

———. *Winning the Money Game: How to Plan and Finance a Growing Business.* New York: Entrepreneur Press/Hawthorn.

Dowd, Merle E. *How to Earn a Fortune and Become Independent in Your Own Business.* Englewood Cliffs, N.J.: Prentice-Hall.

Dyer, Mary Lee. *Practical Bookkeeping for the Small Business.* Chicago: Henry Regnery Co.

Evans, E. Belle, Beth Shub, and Marlene Weinstein. *Day Care: How to Plan, Develop and Operate a Day Care Center.* Boston: Beacon Press. (Write Beacon Press, 25 Beacon Street, Boston, Mass. 02108, for catalog of books, including *Doing Your Own School* by The Great Atlantic and Pacific School Conspiracy.)

Gibson, Mary Bass. *The Family Circle Book of Careers at Home.* New York: Cowles.

Graham, Ellen. *What Do Women Really Want?* New York: Dow Jones. (Contains a section on women as entrepreneurs.)

Grimstead, K., and S. Rennie, editors. *The New Woman's Survival Catalog.* New York: Coward, McCann and Geoghegan.

Gross, Sidney, and Phyllis B. Steckler. *How to Run a Paperback Bookshop.* New York: R. R. Bowker & Co.

Hammer, Marian Behan. *The Complete Handbook of How to Start and Run a Money-Making Business in Your Home.* Englewood Cliffs, N.J.: Prentice-Hall.

Henderson, Bill. *The Publish It Yourself Handbook.* Yonkers, N.Y.: Pushcart Book Press.

Hennig, Margaret, and Anne Jardim. *The Managerial Woman.* New York: Doubleday & Co. (paperback—New York: Pocket Books).

Hilton, Terri. *Small Business Ideas for Women—And How to Get Started.* New York: Pilot Books. (Pilot publishes a number of small-business booklets, including *A Woman's Guide to Her Own Franchised Business*; *Starting a Business After Fifty*; *A Franchising Guide for Blacks*; *How to Buy a Small Business*; *How to Make Money Selling at Flea Markets and Antique Fairs*; *How to Turn Your Ideas into Dollars*; *Directory of State and Federal Funds for Business Development*, and many more. Write to Pilot Books, 347 Fifth Avenue, New York, New York 10016, for a current list of titles.)

Holz, Loretta. *How to Sell Your Arts and Crafts.* New York: Scribner's.

How to Start Your Own Small Business, 4 vols. New York: Drake Publishers. (In-depth information on many types of enterprises.)

Hughes, Marija Matich. *The Sexual Barrier*. Washington, D.C.: Hughes Press. (A complete bibliography of women- and work-related subjects.)

Jessup, Claudia, and Genie Chipps. "Business Begins at Home." *American Home* (September 1977).

————. "Everyone Works." *American Home* (February 1977).

————. "How to Start a Business of Your Own." *Redbook* (July 1977).

————. "Overnight Success Stories." *Harper's Bazaar* (June 1977).

————. "Partners—in Business and Marriage." *Family Circle* (May 31, 1977).

————. "Seasonal Businesses: Work Now, Play Later." *Family Circle* (February 3, 1978).

————. *Supergirls: The Autobiography of an Outrageous Business*. New York: Harper & Row.

————. "Working for Yourself." *Glamour* (March 1977).

Jones, Stacy V. *The Inventor's Patent Handbook*. New York: Dial Press.

Keenan, Elayne J., and Jeanne A. Voltz. *How to Turn a Passion for Food into Profit*. New York: Rawson, Wade.

Klimley, April. *Borrowing Basics for Women* (free from Citibank, Public Affairs Department, Post Office Box 939, Church Street Station, New York, New York 10008).

Kreps, Juanita. *Sex in the Marketplace: American Women at Work*. Baltimore: Johns Hopkins University Press.

Kundsin, Ruth B. *Women and Success: The Anatomy of Achievement*. New York: William Morrow.

Lane, Marc J. *Legal Handbook for Small Business*. New York: Amacom.

Lasser, J. K. *How to Run a Small Business*. New York: McGraw-Hill.

Lynch, Edith M. *The Woman's Guide to Management*. New York: Cornerstone Library.

Melberg, Aaron S., and Henry Shain. *How to Do Your Own Bankruptcy*. New York: McGraw-Hill.

Nelson, Paula. *The Joy of Money*. New York: Bantam Books. (Has sections on becoming an entrepreneur and launching a business.)

Nicholas, Ted. *How to Form Your Own Corporation for Under $50*. Wilmington, Del.: Enterprise Publishing Co.

————. *Where the Money Is and Where to Get It*. Wilmington, Del.: Enterprise Publishing Co.

Paige, Richard E. *Complete Guide to Making Money with Your Ideas and Inventions*. Englewood Cliffs, N.J.: Prentice-Hall.

Paulsen, Kathryn, and Ryan A. Kuhn. *Woman's Almanac*. New

York: J. B. Lippincott Co. (Includes special section on owning a business.)

Phillips, Michael, et al. *The Seven Laws of Money*. New York: Random House.

Pogrebin, Letty Cottin. *Getting Yours: How to Make the System Work for the Working Woman*. New York: David McKay. (Includes an excellent bibliography of feminist business services, training, career counselors, and inspiration, though it is not specifically geared to business owners.)

Portfolio of Accounting Systems for the Small and Medium-Sized Business, 2 vols. Englewood Cliffs, N.J. Prentice-Hall.

Robertson, Laura. *How to Start a Money-Making Business at Home*. New York: Frederick Fell.

Rogers, Mary, and Nancy Joyce. *Women and Money*. New York: McGraw-Hill.

Shaffer, Harold, and Herbert Greenwald. *Independent Retailing*. Englewood Cliffs, N.J.: Prentice-Hall.

Simon, Julian L. *How to Start and Operate a Mail Order Business*. New York: McGraw-Hill.

Smith, Cynthia. *How to Get Big Results from a Small Advertising Budget*. New York: Hawthorn Books.

Solomon, Kenneth I., and Norman Katz. *Profitable Restaurant Management*. Englewood Cliffs, N.J.: Prentice-Hall.

Stern, Ava. *The Self-Made Woman—and the Challenge of Free Enterprise*. New York: Doubleday & Co. (Includes in-depth interviews with female entrepreneurs.)

Stern, Gloria. *How to Start Your Own Food Co-op: A Guide to Wholesale Buying*. New York: Walker Publishers.

Stone, Janet, and Jane Bachner. *Speaking Up: A Book for Every Woman Who Talks*. New York: McGraw-Hill. (How to improve your verbal impact on the phone, in speeches, in selling yourself.)

Szykitka, Walter, editor. *How to Be Your Own Boss: The Complete Handbook for Starting and Running Your Own Business*. New York: Plume/New American Library.

Taetzsch, Lyn, and Herb Genfan. *How to Start Your Own Craft Business*. New York: Watson-Guptill.

Uris, Dorothy. *A Woman's Voice: A Handbook to Successful Private and Public Speaking*. New York: Stein & Day.

White, Richard M., Jr. *The Entrepreneur's Manual: Business Start-Ups, Spin-Offs, and Innovative Management*. Radnor, Pa.: Chilton Book Co. (Special emphasis on manufacturing, retail sales and services, industrial services, franchises.)

Wilbanks, P. M. *How to Start a Typing Service in Your Own Home*. New York: Arco.

PERIODICALS

Currently, most women's magazines run articles on business ideas, professional women, and female entrepreneurs. For back articles of specific interest, consult your librarian and *The Reader's Guide to Periodical Literature*, under "Women Entrepreneurs" and other business-related topics.

Below are periodicals of specific interest. Subscription rates are not included because they fluctuate often.

Briar Patch Review, quarterly, published by Briar Patch Cooperative, 330 Ellis Street, San Francisco, California 94102. (General information for small-business owners.)

Enterprising Women, a national business monthly for women entrepreneurs, 525 West End Avenue, New York, New York 10024. (Of special interest to women business owners around the country. Interviews with women entrepreneurs, in-depth information on all aspects of business—organization, insurance, law, legislature, etc. Back issues available for a fee.)

Entrepreneur Magazine, published monthly by Chase Revel, Inc. 631 Wilshire Boulevard, Santa Monica, California 90401. (The magazine has compiled detailed start-up manuals, available from $5 to $15 apiece, on more than one hundred businesses. Write for list of available titles to Research Department, International Entrepreneurs' Association, at the above address.)

The Executive Woman, newsletter published by Dr. Sandra Brown, 747 Third Avenue, New York, New York 10017.

Dun's Review. For information on rates, write Circulation Department, 666 Fifth Avenue, New York, New York 10019.

Free Enterprise, bimonthly magazine, 1212 Avenue of the Americas, New York, New York 10019.

Joy of Money Newsletter, monthly newsletter published by Joy of Money, Inc., 9301 Wilshire Boulevard, Beverly Hills, California 90210. (A nationwide company offering financial education to women through seminars and the newsletter.)

Mademoiselle. Publishes a series of College and Career Articles. (For catalog of available titles, fifty cents apiece, write *Mademoiselle* Magazine, Box 3389, Grand Central Station, New York, New York 10017.)

Media Report to Women, monthly, published by Dr. Donna Allen, 3306 Ross Place, N.W., Washington, D.C. 20008. (Concerns communications and related media, listings of free-lancers, etc.)

Money, published by Time Inc., 541 North Fairbanks Court, Chicago, Illinois 60611. (Back issues are available for a fee: an index to the previous twelve monthly issues appears in the magazine every January and July.)

Ms. Magazine, 370 Lexington Avenue, New York, New York 10017. (See comprehensive April 1976 issue on starting a business.)

National Business Publications, 1913 I Street, N.W., Washington, D.C. 20006. (Write for specialized information on business periodicals pertaining to your particular industry.)

National Business Women, magazine of the National Federation of Business and Professional Women's Clubs, Inc., 2010 Massachusetts Avenue, N.W., Washington, D.C. 20036.

Prime Time, newsletter for older women, 264 Piermont Avenue, Piermont, New York 10968.

Small Business Reporter, published by the Bank of America, Department 3120, Post Office Box 37000, San Francisco, California 94137. (Current issues are free at any Bank of America community office. Write for a publication index of back issues, available at a dollar per copy. Back issues include profiles on many different types of businesses as well as business operations and management, including "Steps to Starting a Business," vol. 10, no. 10.)

The Spokeswoman, monthly news bulletin, 5464 South Shore Drive, Chicago, Illinois 60615.

The Successful Woman, newsletter published by Barbara Hinrichs, Box 2068, Santa Barbara, California 93120.

Womanpower, published by Betsy Hogan Associates, Post Office Box 360, Brookline, Massachusetts 02146. (Monthly newsletter on equal opportunity for women.)

Women Today, newsletter from Today Publications, National Press Building, Washington, D.C. 20004.

Women's Work, bimonthly, published by Women's Work, 1302 Eighteenth Street, N.W., Suite 203, Washington, D.C. 20036. (Interviews with entrepreneurs, topics of interest to women in the work force.)

Working Woman Magazine, 600 Madison Avenue, New York, New York 10021.

ADDITIONAL INFORMATION SOURCES AND PUBLICATIONS

The larger reference volumes are costly to purchase, but readily available in your library's reference section.

American Crafts Council, National Headquarters, 22 West Fifty-fifth Street, New York, New York 10019. (Myriad services for craftspeople, on a yearly membership basis. Membership includes subscription to its publication, *Craft Horizons*, which includes a section listing crafts shows and fairs around the country. Write for membership information.)

American Women's Economic Development Corporation, Beatrice Fitzpatrick, Executive Director, 1270 Avenue of the Americas, New York, New York 10019. (This counseling program assists women entrepreneurs in solving their business problems. Presently in New York, but expanding nationwide. Write for details.)

Bureau of the Census, Washington, D.C. 20233. (Write the director for a listing of for-sale booklets on business demographics.)

A Business of Your Own in Massachusetts, published by the Women's Bureau, Massachusetts Department of Commerce and Development, 100 Cambridge Street, Boston, Massachusetts 02202. Write for list of its other free booklets. (Not all states have women's bureaus, but all state commerce departments are set up to help new businesses. Contact them to learn what publications and services are available. Larger cities, like New York, have city departments of commerce and industry. In New York City, they sponsor the Executive Volunteer Corps, 41 East Forty-second Street, Room 715, New York, New York 10017.)

Center for Women Policy Studies, 2000 P Street, N.W., Suite 508, Washington, D.C. 20036. (Write for information, including two excellent bibliographies: *Resource Groups for Women in Business* and *Bibliography on Women Entrepreneurs.)*

Chamber of Commerce of the U.S., 1615 H Street, N.W., Washington, D.C. 20006. (Publishes *Sources of State Information* and state industrial directories. Write for list and prices.)

Council of Better Business Bureaus, 1150 Seventeenth Street, N.W., Washington, D.C. 20036.

Directory of Conventions, Successful Meetings, 633 Third Avenue, New York, New York 10017. (Nationwide listing of conventions and trade shows.)

Directory of U.S. Importers, Journal of Commerce, 99 Wall Street, New York, New York 10005.

Dun & Bradstreet Marketing Services, 99 Church Street, New York, New York 10007. (Publishes many booklets and volumes on business management, manufacturers, etc.)

Encyclopedia of Business Information Sources. Gale Research Company, Book Tower, Detroit, Michigan 48226. (When you need any sort of information, look here first.)

Fairchild Publications, 7 East Twelfth Street, New York, New York 10003. (Publishes many books on all aspects of retailing, as well as *Women's Wear Daily* and *Home Furnishings Daily*.)

Federal Trade Commission, Washington, D.C. 20580. (Write for listing of publications. Free publications are available from the Division of Legal and Public Records, Federal Trade Commission, Washington, D.C. 20580. For-sale booklets are available from the Superintendent of Documents, U.S. Government Printing Office, Washington, D.C. 20402.)

The Freelancer's Bible. Kroll Enterprises Inc., Post Office Box 231, West Orange, New Jersey 07052. (See reference section of library. Published by state, it is a guide to creative self-employment, dealing with every aspect of going into business freelance.)

Manufacturer's News, Inc., 3 Huron Street, Chicago, Illinois 60611. (Publishes directories of manufacturers for nearly every state.)

National Association of Accountants, 919 Third Avenue, New York, New York 10022. (Has more than three hundred chapters nationwide, set up to offer free assistance to anyone starting a business.)

National Retail Merchants Association, 100 West Thirty-first Street, New York, New York 10001. (It publishes a catalog of books, films, and periodicals. For a copy, write to the Book Order Department.)

National Trade and Professional Associations of the U.S. and Canada, published by Columbia Books, Inc. Room 601, 734 Fifteenth Street, N.W., Washington, D.C. 20005. (See library reference section.)

Office of Minority Business Enterprise (OMBE), Department of Commerce, Washington, D.C. (It funds several hundred Business Development offices; write for a list. Currently available only to minority women.)

Small Business Administration, 1441 L Street, N.W., Washington, D.C. 20416. (It publishes a catalog of free business information booklets available from any of the regional SBA offices. Check your Yellow Pages for the local listing, or write to the Washington office for Catalog SBA 115A, *Free Management Assistance Publications*, and Catalog SBA 115B, *For-Sale Booklets*. Both free and for-sale booklets are also available from the Superintendent of Documents, Government Printing Office, Washington, D.C. 20402. The SBA also sponsors a number of volunteer management programs and business seminars for small-business owners and helps finance small-business loans. For information, write the national headquarters or contact your regional field office.)

Standard Periodical Directory, Oxbridge Directories, Inc. 150 East Fifty-second Street, New York, New York 10022. (See library reference section: lists more than sixty-three thousand U.S. and Canadian periodicals.)

Standard Rate and Data Service (found in reference section of library, also publishes *Business Publication Rates and Data*, a monthly publication listing all industry periodicals by type of business.)

Thomas' Register of American Manufacturers, 11 vols. Thomas Publishing Company, 1 Pennsylvania Plaza, New York, New York 10001. (Consult reference section of library.)

Trade Directories of the World. Croner Publications, Inc., Queens Village, New York 11428. (A directory of industry trade directories, e.g., the gift/tableware industry, coffee/tea industry, etc.)

Trade Show, Budd Publications Inc., Post Office Box 7, New York, New York 10004. (Lists exhibitions around the country—gifts shows, food shows, etc.)

U.S. Department of Agriculture, Office of Information, Washington, D.C. 20402. (Write for list of services and publications; some handcrafts fall under its aegis.)

U.S. Department of Commerce. For the address of the district office nearest you, write to the District Office, U.S. Department of Commerce, Room 1406, Mid-Continental Plaza Building, 55 East Monroe Street. Chicago, Illinois 60603. (It furnishes a selected publications catalog, which aids business, franchises, and industry. The catalog and publications are available from any of the forty-two district offices. It also publishes *Women-Owned Businesses 1972*, for sale by the Superintendent of Documents, U.S. Government Printing Office, Washington, D.C. 20402.)

The Economic Development Administration of the Department of Commerce (EDA) has research and development centers in twelve major cities, to provide technical assistance to small-business owners. It also helps in finding capital and developing loan packages, and it works with universities to provide free assistance in setting up businesses. For information, and the EDA office nearest you, write to the above address.

The Wharton School of Business, University of Pennsylvania, Thirty-fourth and Spruce, Philadelphia, Pennsylvania 19104. (Periodically runs seminars around the country on "How to Successfully Start Your Own Business," for women and men. Write for details and schedules.)

The Women's Bureau, U.S. Department of Labor, Government Printing Office, Washington, D.C. 20210. (Write for the current catalog of pamphlets.)

WOMEN'S DIRECTORIES

Many women (and associations of women-owned businesses) across the country are forming committees to compile and publish local directories of both women's services and women-owned businesses. Unfortunately many are one-shot projects which go out of date quickly. To keep up to date in your area, check (library, bookstores, local Chamber of Commerce or NOW, etc.) for developments.

Directory of Women Attorneys, Ford Association, 701 South Federal, Butler, Indiana 46701.

Directory of Women-Owned Businesses: Washington/Baltimore Area, edited by Juanita Weaver and Paulette D. Waters. Published by the National Association of Women Business Owners, 2000 P Street, N.W., Washington, D.C. 20036. (The 1979 directory will also include women-owned businesses in Boston and Chicago. Future editions will expand the coverage, eventually resulting in a national directory.)

New York Edition: The Women's Yellow Pages. Edited by Carol Edry in cooperation with Women's Action Alliance, Inc., New York: St. Martin's Press.

Women's Organizations and Leaders Directory, published by Today Publications and News Service, Inc., National Press Building, Washington, D.C. 20004. (Listings are alphabetical, geographical, and by subject.)

WOMEN'S BUSINESS ASSOCIATIONS AND ORGANIZATIONS

The following associations will provide additional source material, business workshops and seminars, or educational programs. Check your area for local organizations, and be aware that banks, your regional Small Business Association, local universities, and so forth, periodically sponsor seminars for women in business.

American Business Women's Association (ABWA), 9100 Ward Parkway, Kansas City, Missouri 64114. (Not specifically for women entrepreneurs, it deals with the needs of women on all levels of business; also publishes a magazine.)

American Society of Women Accountants, 327 South LaSalle Street, Chicago, Illinois 60604.

Business and Professional Women's Foundation, 2012 Massachusetts Avenue, N.W., Washington, D.C. 20036. (Grants loans for women to attend graduate business schools. Also sponsors a project for young women to explore career alternatives, publishes a newsletter, and offers useful bibliographies. Write for information and available pamphlets.)

Catalyst, 14 East Sixtieth Street, New York, New York 10021. (A nationwide organization for women and careers which is beginning to step into the area of entrepreneurship for women. Publishes listings of career counseling centers across the country. Write for additional information and listings of its career opportunities series.)

The Entrepreneurship Institute, 90 East Wilson Bridge Road, Worthington, Ohio 43085. (An international organization, not for women only but for "growth-oriented entrepreneurs." Holds seminars across the country. Write for information.)

Federation of Organizations for Professional Women, 1346 Connecticut Avenue, N.W., Room 1122, Washington, D.C. 20036. (Dedicated to equal rights for women in the professions.)

Feminist Financial Consultants, Reva Calesky, Director, 175 West

Seventy-ninth Street (1A), New York, New York 10024. (FFC offers a complete range of financial services geared to the special needs of women and entrepreneurs and has plans for expanding its services nationwide. Write for information.)

Institute for Independent Businesswomen, Inc., 4101 Nebraska Avenue, N.W., Washington, D.C. 20016.

National Association of Bank Women, 111 East Wacker, Chicago, Illinois 60601.

National Association of Black Women Lawyers, 715 G Street, N.W., Washington, D.C. 20001.

National Association for Female Executives, Inc., 31 Jeremy Way, Annapolis, Maryland 21403. (An organization of executive women and women business owners. Publishes magazine for its members, *The Executive Female Digest.*)

National Association of Insurance Women, 1847 East Fifteenth Street, Tulsa, Oklahoma 74104.

National Association of Minority Women in Business, c/o Inez Kaiser & Associates, Inc., 906 Grand Street, Kansas City, Missouri 64106. (Its members are minority women business owners or managers.)

National Association of Negro Business & Professional Women's Clubs, 2861 Urban Avenue, Columbus, Georgia 31907.

National Association of Women Business Owners, 2000 P Street, N.W., Washington, D.C. 20036. (Publishes a monthly newsletter, available by subscription to nonmembers, free to members. Presently compiling a nationwide directory of women-owned businesses and is a clearinghouse for referrals to connect the talents, products, services, and needs of its members. Eleven chapters in major cities, and growing. Write for membership information and address of chapter nearest you.)

National Association of Women Lawyers, 1155 East Sixtieth Street, Chicago, Illinois 60637.

National Federation of Business & Professional Women's Clubs, 2012 Massachusetts Avenue, N.W., Washington, D.C. 20036.

National Organization of Women, 5 South Wabash Street, Suite 1615, Chicago, Illinois 60603. (Write for list of local chapters.)

New York Association of Women Business Owners, 525 West End Avenue, New York, New York 10024. (Sponsors seminars and is a clearinghouse for women entrepreneurs in the greater metropolitan area.)

Project on the Status & Education of Women, Association of American Colleges, 1818 R Street, N.W., Washington, D.C. 20009. (Lists scholarship programs and women's centers in every state, many with career libraries, counseling services, and child-care information.)

Women Entrepreneurs (WE), Post Office Box 26738, San Francisco, California 94126. (Organization of women business owners for the greater San Francisco-Marin County area.)

Women in Business, 5900 Wilshire Boulevard, Suite 1402, Los Angeles, California 90036. (Association of women entrepreneurs and high-level corporate women in Southern California.)

Women's Action Alliance, Inc., 370 Lexington Avenue, New York, New York 10017. (Write for a catalog of available books and pamphlets.)

Women's Equity Action League, 538 National Press Building, Washington, D.C. 20004. (Write for local WEAL chapters and report on "Money and Credit" and other pertinent subjects.)

Women's Success Teams, Inc., Barbara Sher, Director, 123 West Ninety-third Street, New York, New York 10025. (Seminars teaching women how to define aims and plan action are held nationwide, and WST also publishes a newsletter so participants can keep in touch with each other.)

INDEX